# The
# pre-wrath
# Rapture
# view

RENALD E. SHOWERS

# The
# pre-wrath
# Rapture
# view

## AN EXAMINATION
## AND CRITIQUE

kregel
PUBLICATIONS

Grand Rapids, MI 49501

ISBN 0-8254-3698-2

Printed in the United States of America

1 2 3 / 05 04 03 02 01

# Contents

# Introduction

## A Description of the Pre-Wrath Rapture View

In 1990, a new view concerning the Rapture of the church was introduced publicly through the publication of Marvin J. Rosenthal's book titled *The Pre-Wrath Rapture of the Church.* The view was publicized further in 1992 with the publication of Robert Van Kampen's book *The Sign.* (Van Kampen was the originator and first advocate of the view.)

The Pre-Wrath Rapture view presented in those books teaches that the seven-year seventieth week of Daniel 9 will consist of three divisions (Rosenthal, *Pre-Wrath Rapture*, p. 233; see the diagram near the end of this introduction).

The first division will consist of the beginning of birth pangs (Matt. 24:4–8), or the first four seals (Rev. 6:1–8). It will cover the first half of the seventieth week (first three and one-half years).

The second division will consist of the Great Tribulation (Matt. 24:21). It will begin in the middle of the seventieth week with the breaking of the fifth seal (Rev. 6:9–11) and will be cut short or end with the cosmic disturbances of the sixth seal (Rev. 6:12–14) sometime between the middle and the end of the seventieth week. Thus, the Great Tribulation will not last throughout the entire second half of the seventieth week.

According to the Pre-Wrath view, the sixth seal, with its great cosmic disturbances and major earthquake (Rev. 6:12–17), will be a precursor (forewarning) to the unsaved that the third division (namely, the Day of the Lord) is about to begin with the breaking of the seventh seal.

The church (i.e., the great multitude of Rev. 7:9–17) will be raptured from the earth between the sixth and seventh seals, when Christ will appear from heaven in His glorious Second Coming. Thus, Christ will rapture the church after the Great Tribulation but before the Day of the Lord begins, meaning that the Rapture will not be an event separate from the Second Coming. Rather, it will be the first in a series of events that together will make up the Second Coming.

The third division of the seventieth week will consist of a major part of the Day of the Lord. It will begin with the breaking of the seventh seal (Rev. 8:1) on the same day that the Second Coming begins and the Rapture takes place. Thus, the Day of the Lord will not begin until sometime between the middle and the end of the seventieth week. The Day of the Lord will continue through the end of the seventieth week plus an additional thirty-day reclamation period.

The Day of the Lord will be characterized by the outpouring of God's wrath upon the earth. God's wrath will not begin until the Day of the Lord begins with the breaking of the seventh seal.

The beginning of birth pangs (seals one through four) and the Great Tribulation (seal five) will contain no wrath of God. They will be characterized totally by satanic and human wrath. Thus, there will be no divine wrath throughout the entire first half and a significant part of the second half of the seventieth week.

According to the Pre-Wrath view, the church will be on earth throughout the first half of the seventieth week and the entire Great Tribulation. This means that it will be exposed to satanic and human wrath, including that of the Antichrist, contained in the beginning of birth pangs and the Great Tribulation. But

# PRE-WRATH RAPTURE

|  | 70th Week |  |  |  |  |
|---|---|---|---|---|---|
| 3½ Years | 3½ Years | Reclamation | Restoration | Millennium |
| 1  2  3 | 4  5  6  7 | 30 DAYS | 45 DAYS | 1000 YEARS |
|  | 1 | 2 | 3 | 4 |
| SEALS | TRUMPETS | VIALS |  |  |

RAPTURE

| BEGINNING OF BIRTH PANGS | GREAT TRIBULATION | THE DAY OF THE LORD |
|---|---|---|
| WRATH OF MAN AND SATAN | | WRATH OF GOD |

Antichrist Paralyzed

Armageddon

the church will not be exposed to the wrath of God. It will be raptured from the earth before the Day of the Lord will begin with its outpouring of divine wrath. Thus, the church will experience a pre-wrath rapture.

## The Purpose and Format of this Study

The purpose of this study is to offer a critique of the Pre-Wrath Rapture view. Attention is given primarily to the more significant issues related to the view, not to all that could be critiqued.

The format of the study is as follows. Each section that presents the teaching of the Pre-Wrath view will begin with the paragraph heading "Pre-Wrath View." When the teaching is found in Rosenthal's book *The Pre-Wrath Rapture of the Church,* that fact will be indicated as thus: (Rosenthal, *Pre-Wrath Rapture,* p. #). When the teaching is derived from Van Kampen's book *The Sign,* that fact will be signified thus: (Van Kampen, *The Sign,* p. #).

Each section that critiques the teaching of the Pre-Wrath view will begin with the paragraph heading "Critique." Significant (but not all) parts of the critique sections are taken from the author's book *Maranatha: Our Lord, Come!*

# CHAPTER ONE

# The Word *Tribulation* and Its Concept

## Pre-Wrath View

The Pre-Wrath view teaches the following. The Greek word rendered *tribulation (thlipsis)* in the New Testament is never used for the first half of the seventieth week—the half consisting of the beginning of birth pangs (Matt. 24:4–8), or the first four seals (Rev. 6:1–8; Rosenthal, *Pre-Wrath Rapture*, p. 105). In a prophetic context it is used exclusively for the period of time that begins with the Great Tribulation in the middle of the seventieth week (ibid., p. 105). Thus, it is wrong to use the word *tribulation* for the entire seven-year seventieth week of Daniel 9 (ibid., p. 103).

## Critique

This teaching of the Pre-Wrath view is correct on three points. First, it correctly equates the birth pangs of Matthew 24:4–8 with the first four seals of Revelation 6:1–8. Both passages involve similar descriptions to the approaching end.

Second, this teaching rightly asserts that the Great Tribulation will begin in the middle of the seventieth week. Daniel 9:27 teaches that the abomination of desolation will take place in the middle of the seventieth week, and Jesus indicated that the Great Tribulation will begin when the abomination of desolation takes place (Matt. 24:15–21).

Third, that the beginning of birth pangs, or the first four seals, will be present in the first half of the seventieth week is true. Jesus placed the beginning of birth pangs (Matt. 24:4–8) before the time of the abomination of desolation (v. 15).

Despite these correct points, the Pre-Wrath view has incorrectly concluded that, because the Greek word rendered *tribulation (thlipsis)* in the New Testament is never used for the first half of the seventieth week, it is wrong to use the word *tribulation* for the entire seven-year seventieth week of Daniel 9. This conclusion is incorrect for seven reasons.

First, the presence of a word in the Bible is not the only factor that determines whether it is right or wrong to use that word within a certain biblical context. If the concept being represented by that word is related to a biblical context, then it is right to use that word for that context even when the word itself is not in the biblical text. For example, the words *trinity, incarnation,* and *rapture* are nowhere found in the Bible, but the concepts represented by these words are related to certain biblical contexts; therefore, to use their related words for those contexts is right.

Second, the Bible contains the concept that a woman's birth pangs involve tribulation. That concept appears in the Hebrew Old Testament where one of the major words for *tribulation (tsarah)* is used, for example, as follows: "*tsarah* hath taken hold of us, pain, as of a woman in travail" (Jer. 6:24), and "*tsarah* took hold of him, pangs as of a woman in travail" (50:43).

The same concept appears in the Septuagint (the Greek translation of the Hebrew Old Testament, which Jesus and the apostles quoted). In the Septuagint, the Greek word *thlipsis* is used in place of the Hebrew word *tsarah* as follows: "*thlipsis* hath taken hold of us, pain, as of a woman in travail" (Jer. 6:24), and "*thlipsis* took hold of him, pangs as of a woman in travail" (50:43). The concept appears again in the Greek New Testament where the apostle John stated that, once a woman completes her delivery of a child, she forgets "the *thlipsis*" that was involved in her painful process of giving birth (John 16:21).

These Hebrew and Greek words for *tribulation* refer to the distress of being constricted or hemmed into a trying, painful circumstance of life through which one must go (Swart and Wakely, *"tsarar,"* in *New International Dictionary of Old Testament Theology and Exegesis,* 3:854–55; Schlier, *"thlibo, thlipsis,"* in *Theological Dictionary of the New Testament,* 3:130–40). Thus, the idea behind the biblical concept that a woman's birth pangs involve tribulation is as follows: once a woman's birth pangs begin, those pangs cause her the stress of being hemmed into a trying, painful circumstance of life that she cannot avoid. She has no alternative but to pass through all of the pangs involved in giving birth to a child.

Third, the Old Testament uses the concept of a woman's birth pangs metaphorically to refer to other kinds of trying, painful circumstances of life that must be endured, such as war (Jer. 6:22–24; 50:41–43) and the wrathful judgment of God (Isa. 13:6–9). (A metaphor is a figure of speech that uses a word or phrase to imply an analogy or similarity between two different kinds of things. An example of a metaphor is the statement, "Jesus Christ is the Lamb of God.") In light of the biblical concept that a woman's birth pangs involve tribulation, the Bible's metaphorical use of a woman's birth pangs to refer to other kinds of trying, painful circumstances of life implies that those other kinds of circumstances also involve tribulation. Jeremiah 6:22–24 and 50:41–43 indicate this fact.

Fourth, on the basis of both the metaphorical use of the concept of birth pangs in these and other Old Testament passages and the Daniel 9:27 revelation to the effect that the seventieth week will last for seven years, rabbis of ancient Judaism taught the following beliefs. The current age of history will end with a seven-year period of great suffering and distress. Immediately after this seven-year period, the Messiah will come to begin the new messianic age and to rule the world.

*The Babylonian Talmud* states, "Our Rabbis taught: In the seven-year cycle at the end of which the son of David will come . . . at the conclusion of the septennate, the son of David will come" (*Sanhedrin*, 97a, p. 654). (The word *septennate* refers to a period of seven years.)

Writing about the messianic texts of Judaism, Raphael Patai said, "The idea became entrenched that the coming of the Messiah will be preceded by greatly increased suffering. . . . This will last for seven years. And then, unexpectedly, the Messiah will come" (*The Messiah Texts*, pp. 95–96).

According to *The Babylonian Talmud*, "The advent of the Messiah was pictured as being preceded by years of great distress" (*Shabbath*, 118a, n. on "travails of the Messiah," p. 590).

The Dead Sea Scrolls and ancient rabbinic literature called the severe troubles of this seven-year period "the birth pangs of the Messiah" (Burrows, "More Light on the Dead Sea Scrolls," in *Burrows on the Dead Sea Scrolls*, pp. 343–44). According to *The Babylonian Talmud*, the reason for this designation is because travail precedes birth, and this travail "precedes the birth of a new era"—the messianic age (*Sanhedrin*, 98b, n. on "birth pangs of the Messiah," p. 665). Just as a woman must go through a period of birth pangs before her child is born into the world, so the world must go through seven years of birth pangs before the messianic age is born into the world.

According to the *Apocalypse of Abraham* (ed. G. H. Box, p. 82), the birth pangs of the Messiah will involve such things as the sword (war), famine, pestilence, and wild beasts (the kinds of things involved in the beginning of birth pangs of Matthew 24:4–8 or the first four seals of Revelation 6:1–8). In addition, according to ancient Judaism, heaven will be the source of famine, pestilence, and earthquakes (Patai, *The Messiah Texts*, pp. 95–96).

Obviously, ancient Judaism believed that all seven years of the seventieth week will be characterized by birth pangs.

Fifth, the ancient rabbis were not the only ones who based their teaching upon the Old Testament's metaphorical use of the concept of birth pangs; Jesus Christ did so, too. In Matthew 24:4–8, He taught that birth pangs will be experienced during the first half of the seventieth week. He identified those pangs as "the beginning of birth pangs" (NASB; the word rendered "sorrows" in the expression *the beginning of sorrows* is the Greek term for "birth pangs").

Note two things about Christ's teaching.

1. Because birth pangs will be experienced during the first half of the seventieth week, and because the Bible contains the concept that birth pangs involve tribulation, one can conclude that tribulation will be experienced during the first half of the seventieth week.

Earlier, we noted that the Hebrew and Greek words for *tribulation* refer to the distress of being constricted or hemmed into a trying, painful circumstance of life through which one must go. In light of that fact, we also noted that the idea behind the biblical concept that a woman's birth pangs involve tribulation is as follows. Once a woman's birth pangs begin, those pangs cause her the stress of being hemmed into a trying, painful, and unavoidable circumstance of life. She has no alternative but to pass through all of the pangs involved in giving birth to a child.

In light of this fact, Christ's teaching to the effect that the beginning of birth pangs will be experienced during the first half of the seventieth week indicated the following truths. Once the birth pangs start at the beginning of the seventieth week, those pangs will cause the world the stress of being hemmed into a trying, painful, and unavoidable seven-year circumstance of life. The world will have no alternative but to pass through all of the birth pangs involved in giving birth to the messianic age. Because tribulation will be experienced during the first half of the seventieth week, to apply the word *tribulation* to that three and one-half year period of time is not wrong.

2. The fact that Christ called the birth pangs of the first half of the seventieth week "the *beginning* of birth pangs" (emphasis mine) implies that more birth pangs would follow in the second half of that seven-year period. Obviously, Christ was drawing

an analogy with a woman's birth-pang experience. Just as a woman's initial, less severe birth pangs precede her later, most severe pangs of hard labor, so the initial, less severe birth pangs of the first half of the seventieth week must precede the most severe pangs of hard labor of the second half of the seventieth week. In line with this view, George Bertram wrote that the beginning of birth pangs to which Christ referred "are the woes with which the end-time is ushered in, or the beginning of sorrows which will be followed by others that are even more severe" (*"odin,"* in *Theological Dictionary of the New Testament,* 9:672).

That birth pangs will be experienced during the second half of the seventieth week is substantiated by the fact that "the time of Jacob's trouble" will take place during the second half of the seventieth week and will be characterized by birth pangs and tribulation (Jer. 30:4–7). (The word rendered "trouble" in the expression "the time of Jacob's trouble" is *tsarah,* the same Hebrew word for "tribulation" that we noted earlier.)

The Bible indicates that "the time of Jacob's trouble" will begin in the middle of the seventieth week. Daniel 9:27 reveals that at that point Antichrist will begin to desolate Israel. The Bible also indicates that "the time of Jacob's trouble" will last for three and one-half years (the entire second half of the seventieth week). Revelation 12:6, 12–17 reveals that Israel will be persecuted for 1,260 days or "a time, and times, and half a time." (In the Bible, both of these time designations refer to three and one-half years.) The woman in Revelation 12 represents Israel. Her description in verse 1 is that given to Israel in Genesis 37:9–11. Her giving birth to the Messiah in verse 5 corresponds to the fact that the Messiah was born through Israel. Her flight into the wilderness to escape persecution for 1,260 days, or three and one-half years (vv. 6, 13–17), harmonizes with Christ's command to people in Israel to flee to the mountain wilderness when the abomination of desolation begins in the middle of the seventieth week (Matt. 24:15–21).

Because "the time of Jacob's trouble" will be characterized by birth pangs and tribulation, and because it will last through-

out the entire second half of the seventieth week, one can conclude that birth pangs and tribulation will be experienced
throughout the entire second half of the seventieth week.

Sixth, the Bible indicates that the Day of the Lord will be
characterized by birth pangs and tribulation. Both the prophet
Isaiah (Isa. 13:6-9) and the apostle Paul (1 Thess. 5:2-3; the
term rendered "travail" in v. 3 is the Greek word for birth pang)
signified that the Day of the Lord involves birth pangs. In addition, Zephaniah 1:14-15 states that "the great day of the LORD"
is "a day of trouble." In the Hebrew text of verse 15, the term
rendered "trouble" is *tsarah,* the same word for tribulation noted
earlier. In the Septuagint, the term rendered "trouble" in verse
15 is *thlipsis,* the same Greek word for tribulation noted earlier.

Seventh, the Bible signifies that the sword (war), famine, and
pestilence involve tribulation. For example, in 2 Chronicles 20:9,
"affliction" is associated with all three of these items. In the
Hebrew text, the word translated "affliction" is *tsarah,* and in
the Septuagint, the Greek word translated "affliction" is *thlipsis.*
Once again, these are the same words for tribulation noted
earlier. In addition, in Acts 7:11, "affliction" is associated with
famine. Here, again, the Greek word translated "affliction" is
*thlipsis.*

Because the Bible signifies that the sword (war), famine, and
pestilence involve tribulation, and because the beginning of
birth pangs, or the first four seals, include the sword (war), famine, and pestilence and will take place during the first half of
the seventieth week, one can conclude that tribulation will be
experienced during the first half of the seventieth week.

## Conclusions

In light of all that we have seen in this chapter, we can draw
several conclusions. First, birth pangs will be experienced
throughout the entire seventieth week. Second, the birth pangs
will have two divisions that parallel the two divisions of the seventieth week. The beginning of birth pangs will be in the first
half and the more severe pangs of hard labor will be in the

second half of that seven-year period. (See the following diagram.) Third, because birth pangs involve tribulation, tribulation will be experienced throughout the entire seventieth week. As a result, to use the word *tribulation* for the entire seventieth week is appropriate.

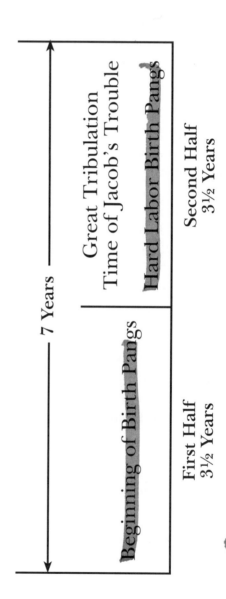

BIRTH PANGS OF THE MESSIAH

70th Week of Daniel 9

7 Years

Great Tribulation
Time of Jacob's Trouble

Hard Labor Birth Pangs

Beginning of Birth Pangs

First Half
3½ Years

Second Half
3½ Years

# CHAPTER TWO

# The Great Tribulation

## The Duration of the Great Tribulation

### Pre-Wrath View

The Pre-Wrath view teaches the following. The Great Tribulation will begin in the middle of the seven-year seventieth week when the fifth seal is opened (Rev. 6:9–11) and the abomination of desolation begins (Dan. 9:27; Matt. 24:15–21; Rosenthal, *Pre-Wrath Rapture,* pp. 179, 183). The Great Tribulation will be the time of Jacob's trouble (ibid., p. 74). It will be contained totally within the fifth seal (ibid., p. 152), or within a combination of the fifth seal plus some aspects of the sixth seal (ibid., p. 150), and, therefore, will end sometime between the middle and the end of the seventieth week. Thus, the Great Tribulation will not last throughout the entire second half of the seventieth week. The seventieth week will not be cut short, but Christ taught that the Great Tribulation will be cut short to fewer than three and one-half years duration (Matt. 24:22; ibid., pp. 51, 108–10, 112).

## Critique

This teaching of the Pre-Wrath view is correct on two points. First, it is correct that the Great Tribulation will begin in the middle of the seventieth week when the abomination of desolation begins. Second, this teaching rightly equates the Great Tribulation with the time of Jacob's trouble. Christ's statements in Matthew 24:15–21 clearly indicate that the Great Tribulation will involve great persecution of the people of Israel.

The Pre-Wrath view is incorrect, however, in concluding that the Great Tribulation will be cut short to fewer than three and one-half years and, therefore, will not last throughout the entire second half of the seventieth week. This conclusion is wrong for six reasons.

First, Daniel was told that in the future there would be a "time of trouble, such as never was since there was a nation even to that same time" (Dan. 12:1). Christ referred to this time of trouble in Matthew 24:21–22 and called it "great tribulation." His teaching in that passage indicated that the Great Tribulation will begin with the abomination of desolation in the middle of the seventieth week (Matt. 24:15–21). Thus, Daniel 12:1 refers to the Great Tribulation. Both it and Christ's statements about it indicate that the Great Tribulation will be the unparalleled time of trouble.

In Daniel 12:6, an angel asked a heavenly being, "How long shall it be to the end of these wonders?" The word translated "wonders" refers to something extraordinary that surpasses what people are used to (Kruger, *"pele,"* in *New International Dictionary of Old Testament Theology and Exegesis,* 3:615). Because this question was asked in the context of Daniel 12:1, the word *wonders* apparently was a reference to the extraordinary events that will characterize the Great Tribulation. Being unparalleled, that time of trouble will certainly surpass what people are used to. The angel, therefore, was asking how long the Great Tribulation will last.

The heavenly being gave two answers to the angel's question in Daniel 12:7. In his first answer, he declared that the Great

Tribulation will last for "a time, times, and an half." In the Bible, this phrase refers to three and one-half years. Because the Great Tribulation will begin in the middle of the seventieth week, this statement means that it will last throughout the entire second half of the seven-year seventieth week.

Second, another reason why the conclusion of the Pre-Wrath view concerning the length of the Great Tribulation is wrong is found in the heavenly being's second answer to the angel's question. The heavenly being indicated that all of the events of the Great Tribulation will be finished "when he shall have accomplished to scatter the power of the holy people." The primary meaning of the word translated "to scatter" is "to beat to pieces, to shatter" (Keil, *Biblical Commentary on the Book of Daniel,* pp. 490–91).

The word translated "power" is literally the word for "hand." "The primary meaning of this noun is 'the terminal part of the arm used to perform functions of man's will'" (Alexander, *"yad,"* in *Theological Wordbook of the Old Testament,* 1:362). Because this word is related to the function of the human will, it is sometimes used to express "obstinate rebellion" (ibid., p. 363).

The expression "the holy people" refers to the people of Israel. In Deuteronomy 7:6, Moses said to Israel, "For thou art an holy people unto the Lord thy God: the Lord thy God hath chosen thee to be a special people unto himself, above all people that are upon the face of the earth."

In light of the meanings of these words, the second answer to the angel's question indicates that the Great Tribulation will be finished when God has completely shattered the obstinate rebellion of the nation of Israel against Him. In other words, the Great Tribulation will end when Israel's rebellion against God's rule ends.

In light of Israel's persistent rebellion, God revealed in Daniel 9:24–27 an extended future program that He has determined specifically for Israel and its holy city, Jerusalem. God indicated that this program would involve seventy weeks (literally seventy "sevens") of time (v. 24).

God revealed that He would use the seventy weeks of this program "to finish the transgression" (v. 24). The word rendered "transgression" has the root meaning "to rebel" (Leupold, *Exposition of Daniel,* p. 412). Since it is preceded by the article *the,* this word refers to Israel's specific sin of rebellion against God's rule. God was revealing that Israel will not stop its rebellion until all seventy weeks of His extended program for that nation have run their course. Thus, Israel's rebellion will be shattered, or end, when the seventieth week of Daniel ends.

In line with this view, Zechariah 12 signifies that Israel will repent of its rebellion and receive Jesus Christ as its Messiah-Savior when it sees Him at His Second Coming (vv. 10–14), when the armies of all nations are gathered in its land and are warring against it (vv. 1–9; cp. Joel 3:9–17; Zech. 14:1–5; Rom. 11:25–27; Rev. 19:11–21).

Revelation 16:12–16 indicates that the armies of all nations will not begin to gather in Israel until the sixth bowl is poured out—after the seven seals, seven trumpets, and first five bowls of the seventieth week have taken place (Rev. 6:1–16:11), and when only one more judgment remains (the seventh bowl; Rev. 16:17–18:24) before the end of the seventieth week and the Second Coming of Christ (Rev. 19:11–21). This indication means that the armies of the nations will not gather in Israel until nearly the end of the seventieth week.

Because Israel will repent of its rebellion and receive Jesus Christ as its Messiah-Savior (when it sees Him at His Second Coming, when the armies of all nations are gathered in its land and are warring against it), and because those armies will not begin to gather in Israel until nearly the end of the seventieth week, one can conclude that Israel's rebellion will be shattered, or end, when the seventieth week ends.

As we noted earlier, because the Great Tribulation will end when Israel's rebellion ends, one can conclude that the Great Tribulation will end when the seventieth week ends. Thus, the Great Tribulation will last throughout the entire second half of the seventieth week.

When the heavenly being gave his two answers to the angel's question, he raised both hands toward heaven and swore an oath by God (Dan. 12:7). Usually only one hand is raised when swearing an oath. The fact that this heavenly being raised both hands emphasized the solemnity and importance of the oath (Wood, *A Commentary on Daniel,* p. 323). Because the heavenly being put his answer in the form of an oath, and because he based that oath on the eternal God, who is sovereign and truthful, he thereby asserted the truthfulness and reliability of his answer in the strongest possible way. He affirmed the absolute certainty of the Great Tribulation lasting for three and one-half years, until Israel's rebellion against God ends at the end of the seventieth week.

Third, Jesus' statements in Matthew 24:15–21 indicate that the Great Tribulation will begin when the abomination of desolation of Daniel 9:27 takes place in the middle of the seventieth week. His statements signify that a definite connection will exist between the Great Tribulation and the abomination of desolation and the activities that the abomination will initiate.

The abomination will involve the setting up of a detestable thing (probably an image of the Antichrist) in Israel's future temple (Matt. 24:15). This activity in the middle of the seventieth week will be the starting point of Antichrist's program of magnifying himself to the level of deity, taking his seat in the new temple, announcing that he is God, demanding worship of himself, and waging war against the saints (Dan. 7:21, 25; 11:36–37; 2 Thess. 2:3–4; Rev. 13:4–7).

All of this information indicates that worship of the Antichrist and his warring against the saints will be two characteristics of the Great Tribulation. Consequently, any biblical revelation concerning the length of time that Antichrist will be worshiped and will war against the saints will indicate how long the Great Tribulation will last. Several passages reveal that length of time.

Daniel 7:25 states that Antichrist will "wear out the saints of the most High . . . and they shall be given into his hand until a time and times and the dividing of time." In the Bible, this phrase means three and one-half years.

Revelation 13:4–8 indicates that once Antichrist begins to blaspheme God by claiming deity for himself, to be worshiped, and to war against the saints, he will be given power to continue these activities for forty-two months (v. 5), which equals three and one-half years.

Daniel 7:21–22 signifies that Antichrist will make war with the saints and prevail against them until the time comes that the saints possess the kingdom. This fact means that Antichrist will be able to continue this Great Tribulation activity until the time comes for the millennial kingdom to begin. Matthew 25:31–34 indicates that the millennial kingdom will begin, and the saints will inherit it, when Christ, the Son of Man, "shall come in his glory, and all the holy angels with him." This fact means, then, that Antichrist will be able to continue his Great Tribulation activity until the Matthew 25 coming of Christ.

Contrary to this position, the Pre-Wrath view teaches that Antichrist will be "rendered useless," "helpless, idle, or paralyzed," or handcuffed at the coming of Christ shortly after the cosmic disturbances of the sixth seal (Rev. 6:12–16) part way through the second half of the seventieth week (Van Kampen, *The Sign*, pp. 315–16, 318, 347; see also the chart at the end of *The Sign*). Then Antichrist will be totally destroyed at the Battle of Armageddon thirty days after the end of the seventieth week (ibid., pp. 316, 360–65; see also the chart at the end of *The Sign*). But the Matthew 25 coming of Christ and the beginning of the Millennium will not take place until forty-five days after Antichrist is destroyed at Armageddon (ibid., pp. 273, 383, 387–90). How can these concepts be true in light of the teaching of Daniel 7:21–22 that Antichrist will make war with the saints and prevail against them until they possess the kingdom?

Because Antichrist will begin his Great Tribulation activities in the middle of the seventieth week, one can conclude that Daniel 7:21–22, 25 and Revelation 13:4–8 reveal that he will be worshiped and will war against the saints throughout the three and one-half years of the second half of the seventieth week. In other words, he will continue these activities through the end of the seventieth week until Christ returns in His Second Coming, when it is time for the Millennium to begin. Because these activities will characterize the Great Tribulation, the Great Tribulation must last throughout the entire second half of the seventieth week.

In light of the time factors revealed in Daniel 7:21–22, 25 and Revelation 13:4–8, we should note the following comments by Irenaeus, a prominent church leader during the last quarter of the second century:

> But when this Antichrist shall have devastated all things in this world, he will reign for three years and six months, and sit in the temple at Jerusalem; and then the Lord will come from heaven in the clouds, in the glory of the Father, sending this man and those who follow him into the lake of fire; but bringing in for the righteous the times of the kingdom. (Irenaeus, *Against Heresies*, vol. 1, bk. 5, chap. 30, sec. 4)

These comments are especially significant in light of the fact that Irenaeus was discipled by Polycarp, a prominent church leader who had been taught by the apostle John.

Fourth, Daniel 11:36 declares that Antichrist will "prosper till the indignation be accomplished." The Hebrew word translated "be accomplished" means to be brought to a "full end. . . . The basic idea of this root is 'to bring a process to completion'" (Oswalt, *"kala,"* in *Theological Wordbook of the Old Testament,* 1:439).

A study of the term *indignation* throughout Scripture reveals that "the indignation" refers to the period of history during which God is indignant or angry with Israel because of its rebellion against Him. It is the time when God judges Israel, usually at the hands of the Gentiles. For example, the indignation included Israel's conquest and cruel treatment by Assyria (Isa.

10:5, 24) and its conquest and captivity by Babylon (Lam. 2:5–6; Zech. 1:12). Daniel 11:36 indicates that the indignation will also include the time when Antichrist will exercise great authority in the world and be worshiped as God.

As a result of putting together the meanings of the terms *be accomplished* and *the indignation,* one can conclude that Daniel 11:36 is teaching that Antichrist will exercise great authority in the world and be worshiped as God until the period of time during which God's indignation or anger with Israel (because of its rebellion against Him) is brought to its full end.

Obviously that period will end when Israel's rebellion against God ends. In our earlier study of Daniel 9:24 and 12:7, we demonstrated that Israel's rebellion will terminate at the end of the seventieth week. One can conclude, then, that the indignation will terminate at the end of the seventieth week. Because the indignation will include the time when Antichrist will be worshiped as God, and because, as was noted earlier, the Great Tribulation will be characterized by the worship of Antichrist, then the Great Tribulation must end when the indignation ends—at the termination of the seventieth week.

Fifth, as is noted in chapter one of this critique, the time of Jacob's trouble will last for 1,260 days, or three and one-half years, the entire second half of the seventieth week (Rev. 12:6, 12–17). It is important to observe two points concerning this fact.

First, Christ revealed these Revelation 12 time designations to the apostle John several decades after His statement in Matthew 24:22 to the effect that the days of the Great Tribulation "shall be shortened." Thus, years after this statement about the duration of the Great Tribulation Christ revealed that the time of Jacob's trouble will last for the entire second half of the seventieth week.

The second important point to observe is that Christ told John that the future things He would reveal to the apostle in Revelation 4–22 are "things which must be hereafter" (Rev. 4:1). The Greek word translated "must" in this expression "denotes that God is in Himself committed to these plans. It thus expresses a necessity which lies in the very nature of God and which issues in the execution of His plans" (Grundmann, *"dei,"* in *Theological Dictionary of the New Testament,* 2:23).

In light of this meaning of the Greek word translated "must," Robert Thomas indicated that Christ's statement to John had the following implication: "The time has arrived to deal with what God has destined for the future. The events to be predicted are not just probable. They are fixed and certain because they are the outworking of God's will" (*Revelation 1–7,* p. 337). Because this revelation of future "things which must be hereafter" included the Revelation 12 time designations for the duration of the time of Jacob's trouble, one can conclude that the amount of time in those designations was destined by God and, therefore, is fixed and certain. That this is so is made even more significant by the fact that it was God Himself who gave all of this revelation to Christ to pass on to others (Rev. 1:1). This means, then, that the time of Jacob's trouble certainly will last throughout all three and one-half years of the second half of the seventieth week.

This certainty prompts two conclusions. First, because the Great Tribulation is the time of Jacob's trouble, the Great Tribulation certainly will last throughout all three and one-half years of the second half of the seventieth week. Second, the fact that Christ delivered the revelation that presented this certainty several decades after His Matthew 24:22 statement prompts the following conclusion: in His Matthew 24:22 statement, Christ was not saying that the days of the Great Tribulation will be cut shorter than the 1,260 days, or three and one-half years, of the second half of the seventieth week.

Sixth, what is to be done, then, with the Matthew 24:22 statement of Christ concerning the Great Tribulation: "And except those days should be shortened, there should no flesh be saved: but for the elect's sake those days shall be shortened"?

Mark's record of Jesus' same statement sheds light on its meaning: "And except that the Lord had shortened those days, no flesh should be saved: but for the elect's sake, whom he hath chosen, he hath shortened the days" (Mark 13:20). We should note the following two points about Jesus' statement.

1. In the ancient world, the Greek verb translated "shortened" in the Matthew and Mark passages primarily meant "to cut off" (Thayer, *"koloboo,"* in *A Greek-English Lexicon of the New Testament,* p. 353).

2. The Greek verbs translated "had shortened" and "hath shortened" in the Mark passage and the verb translated "should be shortened" in the Matthew passage are all in the aorist tense and the indicative mood with the augment. Unless the context indicates otherwise, that form is used to express past time (Dana and Mantey, *A Manual Grammar of the Greek New Testament,* p. 193).

A number of scholars have concluded that because the two Greek verbs in Mark 13:20 are in that form, they express action in the past and, therefore, have significant bearing on the meaning of Jesus' statement. For example, Ezra P. Gould stated, "The [aorist] tenses put this action in the past—*if the Lord had not shortened the time, no flesh would have been saved.* The language is proleptic, stating the event as it already existed in the Divine decree" (*A Critical and Exegetical Commentary on the Gospel According to St. Mark,* p. 247).

Gerhard Delling wrote,

> God has already (Mk. 13:20 . . .) "cut short" the time of the tribulation in Judaea. That is, He has made it shorter than it would normally have been in terms of the purpose and power of the oppressors. If He had not done so, even those who prove themselves to be the elect by their faithfulness, and who have been wonderfully kept thus far, would be brought to physical destruction. (*"koloboo,"* in *Theological Dictionary of the New Testament,* 3:823–24)

Through these statements, these scholars were indicating that Jesus was teaching that God in the past had already shortened the Great Tribulation. He did so in the sense that He determined to cut it off at a specific time rather than let it continue indefinitely. God knew that if the Great Tribulation were to continue indefinitely, all flesh would perish from the earth. To prevent that from happening, in the past God sovereignly set a specific time for the Great Tribulation to end.

The Bible reveals that it was in eternity past that God decreed or determined what would happen during history. It refers to His "eternal purpose" (Eph. 3:11) and His "own purpose . . . before the world began" (2 Tim. 1:9). In Isaiah 46:9–11 God said, "I am God . . . and there is none like me, Declaring the end from the beginning, and from ancient times the things that are not yet done, saying, My counsel shall stand, and I will do all my pleasure: . . . I have spoken it, I will also bring it to pass; I have purposed it, I will also do it."

The apostle Paul declared that God, who made the world and all things in it, "hath determined the times before appointed" (Acts 17:26). The Greek word translated "determined" sometimes refers to what God decreed (Thayer, *"horidzo,"* in *A Greek-English Lexicon of the New Testament,* p. 453). The words translated "the times before appointed" refer to "fixed times" (Arndt and Gingrich, *"prostasso,"* in *A Greek-English Lexicon of the New Testament,* p. 725). James Hope Moulton wrote that the tenses of the verbal forms in Acts 17:26 indicate that this determination took place "in the Divine plan" before the creation of man (*A Grammar of New Testament Greek,* p. 133). Thus, in this context Paul taught that in eternity past, as part of God's eternal plan for history, He determined or decreed fixed times by which to govern man.

Note that just as the Greek verb that is consistently translated "shortened" in Jesus' statement concerning the shortening of the Great Tribulation primarily means "to cut off," so the Old Testament Hebrew verbs that refer to God's decree or determination have the basic meaning of "to cut." For example, that is the basic meaning of the Hebrew verb translated "determined" in the statement "Seventy weeks are determined upon thy people and upon thy holy city" (Dan. 9:24; Alden, "hatak," in *Theological Wordbook of the Old Testament,* 1:334). God cut a fixed time of seventy weeks (sevens) of years to chasten Israel and end its rebellion against Him.

The Hebrew verb translated "determined" in the declaration that Antichrist "shall prosper till the indignation be accomplished: for that that is determined shall be done" (Dan. 11:36) also has the basic meaning of "to cut." "The word connotes the concept of 'determined' and refers to something which cannot be changed. Perhaps the basic idea of 'cut' is evident here in that that which is incised cannot be altered" (Coppes, "haras," in *Theological Wordbook of the Old Testament,* 1:326). God cut a fixed time for Antichrist to prosper and for the indignation to be brought to a full end. This fixed time cannot be changed.

In light of what has been seen, one can conclude that in eternity past God shortened the Great Tribulation in the sense that He decreed or determined to cut it off at a specific time rather than let it continue indefinitely. He sovereignly fixed a specific time for the Great Tribulation to end—when it had run its course for three and one-half years, or forty-two months or 1,260 days. That fixed time cannot be changed.

Isaiah 46:9–11 (which we noted earlier) reveals that from the beginning of time God could declare in advance what would happen during history. He could do so because in eternity past He determined what would happen, and everything He determined He causes to happen. In many instances, God has declared in advance events that He determined in eternity past. Those declarations are the prophecies of future happenings contained in the Bible. Thus, the prophecies already noted (to the effect that the Great Tribulation will last for three and one-half years and until Israel's rebellion against God ends at the end of the seventieth week) are divine declarations of what God determined in eternity past.

When Christ spoke of the Great Tribulation being shortened,

He did not mean that it will be cut shorter than the three and one-half years already prophesied before His statement. The tense of the Greek verbs translated "shortened" in the Mark 13:20 record of Christ's statement indicates that He meant that God cut the Great Tribulation short in eternity past when He determined that it will last for the fixed time of three and one-half years.

As we noted earlier, because the tense of the first Greek verb translated "shortened" in the Matthew 24:22 record of Christ's statement is the same as the tense of the Mark 13:20 verbs, one can conclude that the Matthew and Mark passages have the same meaning. The second Greek verb translated "shortened" in Matthew 24:22 is in a different tense (future) from the others, but that fact does not nullify this conclusion. That verb simply indicates that in the future God will actually cause to happen what He determined in eternity past and prophesied in the Old Testament.

John D. Grassmick wrote the following concerning Mark 13:20:

> *If the Lord* (Yahweh God; cf. 12:29), *had not* already decided in His sovereign plan to *cut short* (terminate, not reduce the number of) *those days* (lit., "the days"; cf. 13:19), *no one would survive* (esothe, "would be saved"; cf. 15:30–31), that is, be delivered from physical death; . But God set limits on the duration of the end-time Tribulation, because of *the elect.* ("Mark," in *The Bible Knowledge Commentary, New Testament,* p. 170)

## The Proposed Distinction of the Great Tribulation

### Pre-Wrath View

The Pre-Wrath view insists that a complete distinction exists between the Great Tribulation and the Day of the Lord. In fact, the view is dependent upon and therefore requires that distinction. The view teaches both a time and a nature distinction between the Great Tribulation and the Day of the Lord.

Concerning the time distinction, the Pre-Wrath view claims the following. The Great Tribulation will begin when the fifth seal is opened (Rev. 6:9–11; Rosenthal, *Pre-Wrath Rapture,* pp. 179, 183) and will end sometime before the seventh seal (ibid., pp. 150, 152). The Day of the Lord will not begin until the seventh seal is opened (ibid., p. 137).

Concerning the nature distinction, the Pre-Wrath view asserts the following: The Great Tribulation will be characterized entirely by the persecution of God's elect by wicked people (in other words, the wrath of man against man). No wrath of God will be administered during the Great Tribulation (ibid., p. 105). The fact that the word *wrath* does not appear in the book of Revelation until after the sixth seal has been opened (Rev. 6:12–17) and the Great Tribulation has ended indicates that this point is so (ibid., p. 171). By contrast, the Day of the Lord will be characterized entirely by God's wrath against man (ibid., p. 105). God's wrath will not begin until the Day of the Lord begins with the opening of the seventh seal (ibid., pp. 153, 173).

On the basis of these proposed time and nature distinctions, the Pre-Wrath view concludes that no overlapping or involvement of the Great Tribulation with the Day of the Lord will occur. It offers as substantiation of this conclusion the following claim: the Old Testament never identifies the Day of the Lord as the Great Tribulation (ibid., p. 115).

## Critique

This distinction between the Great Tribulation and the Day of the Lord has seven problems.

First, according to the Pre-Wrath view, the Day of the Lord will begin with the opening of the seventh seal somewhere between the middle and the end of the seventieth week, and it will continue beyond the end of the seventieth week (Rosenthal, *Pre-Wrath Rapture,* p. 146). Earlier, this chapter presented biblical evidence that the Great Tribulation will continue until the end of the seventieth week. Because both the Great Tribulation and the Day of the Lord will continue to the end of the seventieth week, they cannot be totally distinct from each other in time. Some overlapping and involvement between them must occur.

Second, that the Great Tribulation will be characterized by tribulation is obvious. In light of this fact and because the Pre-Wrath view insists on a complete distinction of nature between the Great Tribulation and the Day of the Lord, to be consistent, it must also insist that the Day of the Lord will not be characterized by tribulation. But, Zephaniah 1:14–15 reveals that "the great day of the LORD" is not only "a day of wrath" but also "a day of trouble" *(yom tsarah)*. As noted in the first chapter, the Hebrew word *tsarah* was a major word for "tribulation." In addition, in the Septuagint the word translated "trouble" in verse 15 is *thlipsis,* the Greek word for "tribulation." Thus, this biblical passage characterized "the great day of the LORD" as a day of wrath and tribulation.

The apostle Paul indicated that "the day of wrath and revelation of the righteous judgment of God" will be characterized by "tribulation" (*thlipsis;* Rom. 2:5, 9). In addition, Paul signified that God recompenses "tribulation" *(thlipsis)* to those who "trouble" (the verb form of *thlipsis,* "tribulate") believers (2 Thess. 1:6), and he made clear that this fact certainly will be true at the Second Coming of Christ (2 Thess. 1:7). These biblical expressions indicate that "tribulation" is not caused exclusively by the wrath of man against God's people. It is also caused by the wrath of God against the ungodly.

Third, the Pre-Wrath argument that because the word *wrath* does not appear in the book of Revelation until after the sixth seal has been opened that no wrath of God will be administered during the Great Tribulation is a two-edged sword. If the absence of the word prompts the conclusion that no wrath of God will be administered during the Great Tribulation, then it could also prompt the conclusion that no wrath of man will be administered during the Great Tribulation.

Fourth, the absence of the word *wrath* does not automatically mean that the concept of wrath is absent. For example,

Genesis contains no word for the wrath of God (Fichtner, *"orge,"* in *Theological Dictionary of the New Testament,* 5:396 n. 101). But surely no one could deny that God's wrath was poured out in the destructions of the world through the Flood (Gen. 6–8) and the destruction of Sodom and Gomorrah (Gen. 19).

As we noted in the first chapter, the presence of a word in the Bible is not the only thing that determines whether it is right or wrong to use that word for a certain biblical context. If the concept that is represented by that word is related to a biblical context, then it is right to use that word for that context. In chapters three and four, which deal with the seals of Revelation, evidence will be offered that the wrath of God will be related to the first six seals and, therefore, that it is right to use the word *wrath* for the entire context of the first six seals, including the part that the Pre-Wrath view claims includes the Great Tribulation.

Fifth, Christ's statement in Matthew 24:22 indicated that, if the Great Tribulation were to continue beyond the cutoff time determined by God, all flesh would perish from the earth. The only way that situation could be true is if the Great Tribulation involved both the ungodly being killed by God's wrath and the godly being killed by man's wrath. If the Great Tribulation were to involve only the wrath of man against the godly, then it would threaten only the existence of the godly. If God's wrath is not poured out during the Great Tribulation, then the existence of the ungodly would not be threatened.

Sixth, Christ's statement in Matthew 24:21 indicated that the Great Tribulation will be the unparalleled time of trouble in all of world history. Because God's wrath is far greater than man's wrath, if the Great Tribulation ends before God's wrath begins, then it will not involve the greatest outpouring of wrath in all of world history. If the Great Tribulation does not involve both God's wrath and man's wrath, then it cannot be the unparalleled time of trouble.

Seventh, the Bible indicates that the Great Tribulation and the Day of the Lord have several characteristics in common, including the following.

- The concept of trouble or tribulation is associated with both time periods (the Great Tribulation in Dan. 12:1 and the Day of the Lord in Zeph. 1:14–17). Both of these Old Testament passages use the same Hebrew word for trouble or tribulation *(tsarah)*. In addition, the Hebrew scholars who produced the Septuagint used in these passages the Greek word for tribulation *(thlipsis)* to translate this Hebrew word. They thereby revealed that they understood that both the Great Tribulation and the Day of the Lord will be characterized by tribulation.
- The concept of an unparalleled time of trouble is associated with both time periods (the Great Tribulation in Dan. 12:1 and Matt. 24:12, and the Day of the Lord in Joel 2:1–2). Because only one unparalleled time of trouble can occur, one can conclude that the Great Tribulation will be included within the Day of the Lord.
- The term *great* is used for both time periods (the Great Tribulation in Matt. 24:21 and Rev. 7:14 and the Day of the Lord in Zeph. 1:14).
- Israel's future repentance or spiritual restoration to God is associated with both (the Great Tribulation in Deut. 4:27–30; 30:1–3 and the Day of the Lord in Zech. 12:2–3, 9–14; 13:1–2; 14:1–3).

These common associations indicate that the Great Tribulation and the Day of the Lord will not be totally separate or distinct from each other.

## Conclusion

This chapter has examined evidences that the Great Tribulation will last to the end of the seventieth week and will not be totally distinct from the Day of the Lord in time and nature. Rather, it will be included within the Day of the Lord.

# CHAPTER THREE

# The Significance of the Seals and the Sealed Scroll

## The Significance of the Seals

In Revelation 4 and 5, where John began to be introduced to things that must take place in the future (4:1), the apostle saw Christ take a scroll from the hand of God the Father. The scroll was sealed with seven seals. Christ took the scroll so that, as a result of breaking its seals, He could open it and read what was written inside (5:1–7). What is the significance of the seals and of Christ's breaking them?

### Pre-Wrath View

The Pre-Wrath view teaches the following. Seals in the Bible signify security or protection. Thus, Christ breaks the seals of the scroll to signify the eternal security of those believers who will be martyred for their faith by Antichrist and his forces. The wrath of man will be able to harm their bodies, but not their eternal souls. Thus, the seals do not involve God's wrath. Instead, they are God's commitment of eternal protection for His saints while they are under man's wrath (Rosenthal, *Pre-Wrath Rapture*, pp. 143, 145).

**Critique**

Truly, seals in the Bible often signified security or protection. A major function of some seals was to make objects secure from tampering or change by unscrupulous people. Sealed objects could be opened legitimately only by authorized persons. But we must note two important facts concerning this function of seals.

First, seals were intended to secure the object to which they were applied, not some other object. In light of this fact, one should observe that the seven seals of Revelation were applied to the scroll of Revelation 5, not to people. Thus, the seven seals had the significance of making the scroll secure from tampering or change; they did not have the purpose of signifying the eternal security of believers.

Second, seals made an object secure when they were applied and as long as they remained intact. That security was removed when the seals were broken. In light of this fact, one should note that in Revelation 6–8 Christ neither applied the seven seals to the scroll of Revelation 5 nor kept those seals intact. Instead, He broke the seven seals and thereby removed the security they were designed to provide. Thus, His breaking of the seven seals has nothing to do with making people secure. Because the breaking of seals removes security, if the Pre-Wrath view were correct, then Christ's breaking of the seven seals would signify the removal of eternal security from believers—the opposite of what the Pre-Wrath view claims.

## The Identification of the Sealed Scroll

The identification of the sealed scroll of Revelation 5 is critical to an understanding of the significance of the seals and their being broken by Christ in the future.

### Truths Emphasized in Revelation 4 and 5

To determine the identification of the sealed scroll, we must observe four truths emphasized in Revelation 4 and 5.

First, Revelation 4:11 emphasizes that God created "all things" that have been created, and that He created these things for His own benefit or purpose.

Second, God's power or authority to rule all of creation is emphasized in chapters 4 and 5. God's throne is mentioned seventeen times. The Greek word for *throne,* when used figuratively, indicates dominion or sovereignty (Arndt and Gingrich, *"thronos,"* in *A Greek-English Lexicon of the New Testament,* p. 365).

Additionally, the doxologies in 4:11 and 5:13 use two Greek words to ascribe great power to God. One of these words (*kratos;* 5:13) sometimes "is designed to stress the power of God which none can withstand and which is sovereign over all" (Michaelis, *"kratos,"* in *Theological Dictionary of the New Testament,* 3:907). "It denotes the superior power of God to which the final victory will belong" (ibid., p. 908).

The other word (*dunamis;* 4:11) was used in statements that express "the hope and longing that God will demonstrate His power in a last great conflict, destroying His opponents and saving those who belong to Him. Thus, the righteous wait for God to reveal Himself in His power and definitively to establish His dominion" (Grundmann, *"dunamis,"* in *Theological Dictionary of the New Testament,* 2:295).

These Greek words portray a divine power that is active in history, a power that shapes and sets a goal for history in accordance with God's own sovereign will and purpose (ibid., pp. 292, 306).

In light of the usage of these power words, Grundmann explains the significance of the Revelation 4 and 5 doxologies as follows: "These doxologies in Rev. imply acknowledgment and acceptance of the power of God which has an eschatological character, which destroys hostile powers and which brings the world to perfection" (ibid., p. 307).

Third, Revelation 5 portrays Christ as the Redeemer. It emphasizes His work of redemption through His death and shed blood and that He alone is worthy to take the scroll from God's hand, break its seals, and open and read it because of His work of redemption.

Fourth, Revelation 5:12–13 points out Christ's worthiness as the Redeemer to exercise God's ruling power. In this passage, the same power words for God's rule that we noted earlier are ascribed to Him. In fact, in 5:13 one of those words is used jointly for God and Christ.

In light of these four truths emphasized in the part of Revelation that introduces the sealed scroll, we can draw the following conclusion: the identification of the sealed scroll must relate to the facts that God created all of creation for His own benefit and purpose; that He has the power or authority to rule all of creation; and that, as the Redeemer, Christ alone is worthy to take the scroll from God's hand, break its seals, open and read it, and exercise God's ruling power.

## The Background of the Sealed Scroll

The Scriptures teach that because God created the earth and everything in it, He is its owner and sovereign King (Exod. 19:5; 1 Chron. 29:11; Pss. 24:1–2; 47:2–3, 7–9).

God gave His earth to mankind to possess as an inheritance forever (Gen. 1:26–28; Ps. 115:16; Isa. 24:5 ["the everlasting covenant"]). Mankind, however, was not to regard themselves as the sole owner and authority of the earth. Because God was the ultimate owner of the earth, mankind was responsible to serve as His representative, administering His rule over the earth for His benefit in accord with His sovereign purpose and in obedience to His commands (Gen. 2:15–17). God was the landlord; mankind was the tenant possessor. This fact indicates that God established a theocracy with mankind at the time of creation.

Because God was the ultimate owner of the earth and mankind was only God's tenant administrator, mankind did not have the right or authority to forfeit forever tenant possession or administration of God's earth to anyone else (i.e., to a nonkinsman). Tragically mankind forfeited tenant possession or administration of their earth inheritance to Satan (a nonkinsman of mankind) by following his lead to rebel against

God (Gen. 3). As a result of getting the first man, Adam, to join his revolt, Satan usurped tenant possession of the earth from its original tenant (mankind) and has been exercising administrative control of the world system against God ever since. In other words, the theocracy was lost and replaced by a satanocracy. Several facts indicate that this is so. Satan had the authority to offer Christ all of the power and glory of the kingdoms of the world (Luke 4:5–6), Satan declared that it had been delivered to him by someone else (Adam; Luke 4:6), Christ called Satan "the prince of this world" (John 12:31; 14:30; 16:11), and Paul called Satan "the god of this age" (2 Cor. 4:4 NIV).

Because mankind forfeited their God-given tenant possession of the earth to Satan, God placed nature under a curse (Gen. 3:17–19). As a result, the earth was made subject to defilement, vanity, corruption, groaning, and pain, and it can hardly wait until the day when, in conjunction with redemption, it will be released from this curse (Isa. 24:5–6; Rom. 8:19–23).

Mankind's loss of their tenant possession inheritance of the earth to Satan is temporary because God has established a program of redemption to prevent this loss from being permanent. This program is based upon the work of a kinsman-redeemer (a relative of the same human nature as mankind).

Several truths indicate that God has provided a qualified kinsman-redeemer for mankind. First, immediately after mankind forfeited their tenant possession inheritance of the earth to Satan (Gen. 3:1–7), God promised that the woman's "seed" (a human born of woman during the course of history) would "bruise" Satan (crush the usurper of mankind's inheritance; Gen. 3:15). Second, Paul declared that this promised one was sent by God and was "made of a woman" to do the work of redemption (Gal. 4:4–5). Third, Hebrews indicates that Christ is the one who does the work of redemption (Heb. 9:12–15) and that He partook of mankind's flesh and blood so that He might "destroy" Satan (2:14–16). Fourth, John asserted that Christ, the Son of God (1 John 2:22), came into the world in human flesh (4:2) with a literal, physical, human body that could be seen and touched (1:1) "that he might destroy the works of the devil" (3:8).

Fifth, Christ foretold "the regeneration" that will take place in the future (Matt. 19:28). The word translated "regeneration" consists of two Greek words that together mean "back to genesis," or "genesis again." Thus, the word refers to a situation in which "a state of being recurs in the same (or nearly the same) way as at first" (Arndt and Gingrich, *"palin"* and *"genesis,"* in *A Greek-English Lexicon of the New Testament,* pp. 611, 154). Christ thereby foretold that in the future nature will be restored to its original condition that existed from creation until the fall of man, as recorded in Genesis 1–2. In other words, it will be redeemed from the curse that came because mankind forfeited their tenant possession inheritance to Satan.

In Matthew 19:28, Christ declared that "the regeneration" will take place "when the Son of man shall sit in the throne of his glory." His terminology is significant. It indicates that when Christ, as the Son of Man (as an offspring of mankind, a kinsman), will rule the earth in the future, nature will be restored to its original condition that existed when mankind held tenant possession or administration of the earth as God's representatives. Christ taught that He will begin to exercise that rule when He returns in glory with His holy angels after the Great Tribulation (Matt. 24:29–31; 25:31). As He takes over the rule of the earth as the Kinsman-Redeemer, He will restore mankind's forfeited inheritance. The First Adam lost that inheritance for mankind; Christ, as "the last Adam" (1 Cor. 15:45), will restore it.

Sixth, in Acts 3:19–21 Peter declared that "the times of refreshing" and "the times of restitution of all things" will come when God sends Christ back to be present personally on earth. Earlier in his declaration (vv. 13–15) Peter made clear that Christ was crucified and resurrected, thereby indicating that He was human (a kinsman of mankind), having a physical body.

Arndt and Gingrich stated that the word for "times" in the expression "the times of refreshing" is "one of the chief eschatological terms" and that the entire expression is a reference to "the messianic age" (*"kairos"* and *"anapsuxis,"* ibid., pp. 396, 63). Eduard Schweizer wrote that the entire expression refers to "eschatological redemption" (*"anapsuxis,"* in *Theological Dictionary of the New Testament,* 9:664). Albrecht Oepke signified that both "the times of refreshing" and "the times of restitution of all things" refer to the same restoration of the original order of things (*"apokatastasis,"* in *Theological Dictionary of the New Testament,* 1:391). F. F. Bruce asserted that "the restitution" to which Peter referred in Acts 3:21 "appears to be identical with" "the regeneration" to which Christ referred in Matthew 19:28 and that the restoration involved will include "a renovation of all nature" (*Commentary on the Book of the Acts,* p. 91 n. 36).

In light of what we have seen, one can conclude that in Acts 3:19–21 Peter was referring to the future messianic age (the Millennium) when, in conjunction with His return to earth as the Kinsman of mankind after the Great Tribulation, Christ will redeem the earth by restoring the original order that God established at creation. That act will include both the restoration of mankind's tenant possession or administration of the earth as God's representatives and the removal of the curse from nature.

As the Kinsman-Redeemer, Christ had to pay a redemption price to redeem mankind and their forfeited inheritance. The redemption price He paid was the shedding of His blood (Eph. 1:7; Col. 1:14; 1 Peter 1:18–19; Rev. 5:9).

Although Christ paid the redemption price to redeem mankind's forfeited tenant possession inheritance of the earth, He will not return the administration of the whole earth to Adam, the man who forfeited it for mankind. As the Kinsman-Redeemer and the last Adam, Christ will keep the earth to administer it for God's purposes (Rev. 11:15). Christ "shall be king over all the earth: in that day shall there be one Lord, and his name one" (Zech. 14:9).

## Conclusion Concerning Identification

In light of what we have observed regarding the things emphasized in Revelation 4 and 5 and the background of the sealed scroll, one can draw the following conclusion concerning the identification of the sealed scroll of Revelation 5: the sealed scroll is the deed of purchase for mankind's tenant possession inheritance or administration of the earth that was forfeited when mankind fell away from God. Just as scroll deeds of purchase were made when Jeremiah paid the redemption price to redeem his cousin's tenant possession of land (Jer. 32:6–12), so a scroll deed of purchase was made when Christ paid the redemption price to redeem mankind's tenant possession of the earth by shedding His blood on the cross.

The fact that the sealed scroll of Revelation 5 had writing on both the inside and the outside (v. 1), in the same manner as Jeremiah's (Jer. 32:10–12) and other deeds of purchase in Israel's land-redemption system, indicates that it is a deed of purchase. Concerning this twofold writing on the Revelation 5 scroll, Joseph A. Seiss wrote, "This again tends to identify it with these books of forfeited inheritances. Within were the specifications of the forfeiture; without were the names and attestations of the witnesses; for this is the manner in which these documents were attested" (*The Apocalypse*, p. 273).

When writing about the Revelation 5 scroll, Alfred Jenour stated, "We regard it as a COVENANT DEED, the book in which were registered the terms of man's redemption, and his restoration to the dominion of the earth and all those privileges which he had forfeited by transgression" (*Rationale Apocalypticum*, 1:202).

Jeremiah's scrolls were legal evidence of his payment of the redemption price and, therefore, of his right of tenant possession of the land. The Hebrew word translated "evidence" and "book" in Jeremiah 32:12 was used for important legal documents (Deut. 24:1, 3; Isa. 50:1; Jer. 3:8) that were usually in scroll form (Patterson, *"seper,"* in *Theological Wordbook of the Old Testament*, 2:633). In the same manner, Christ's scroll deed is legal

evidence of His payment of the redemption price and, therefore, of His right of tenant possession of the earth.

## The Need for the Sealed Scroll Deed

One of Jeremiah's scroll deeds was sealed to prevent anyone
from changing its contents. Thus, that scroll had the nature of
irrefutable evidence. Parallel to this, the scroll deed of Revelation 5 is sealed with seven seals (vv. 1, 5). Because in the Bible
the number seven signifies "what is total or complete" (Rengstorf,
*"hepta,"* in *Theological Dictionary of the New Testament,* 2:628), the
seven seals on Christ's scroll make it totally secure from tampering or change. Thus, they are the guarantee that the Revelation 5 scroll deed is absolutely irrefutable evidence that Christ
is the Kinsman-Redeemer who has the right to take tenant possession of the earth. Gottfried Fitzer wrote that "the seal served
as a legal protection and guarantee in many ways, esp. in relation to property" (*"sphragis,"* in *Theological Dictionary of the New
Testament,* 7:940).

Jeremiah's scroll deeds were placed in a secure place where
they could be preserved for a long period of time because he
did not take actual possession of the land immediately after
paying the redemption price for it. Circumstances removed him
for many years to a location far from the land. In like manner,
Christ's scroll deed was placed in a secure place (God's right
hand in heaven, Rev. 5:1, 7) for a long period of time because
He did not take actual possession of the earth immediately after paying the redemption price for it at the cross. He removed
for many years to a location far from the earth (heaven; Acts
1:9–11).

Just as foreign squatters controlled the land of Israel (including the land that Jeremiah had purchased) for many years while
the Jews and Jeremiah were removed from it, so foreign squatters (Satan and the human members of his kingdom) are controlling the world system during the years that Christ is removed
from the earth.

## The Two Responsibilities of the Kinsman-Redeemer

Land redemption in Israel involved two responsibilities for the kinsman-redeemer. First, he had to pay the redemption price for the forfeited land and thereby obtain the right of tenant possession. Second, he then had to take actual possession of the land and exercise administrative rule over it. Sometimes this task required him to evict usurpers who had begun to exercise tenant possession of the land illegally.

In like manner, the redemption of the earth involves the same two responsibilities for Christ, mankind's Kinsman-Redeemer. First, He had to pay the redemption price for the earth and thereby obtain the right of tenant possession. Second, now that Christ has obtained that right, He must take actual possession of the earth and exercise administrative rule over it as the last Adam, God's representative. This task will require Him to evict usurpers, Satan and his forces, who have exercised illegal tenant possession of the earth since the fall of mankind.

Several truths in Revelation 5 relate directly to Christ's two responsibilities as mankind's Kinsman-Redeemer.

### The First Truth

The first truth concerns the three titles applied to Christ (Rev. 5:5–6). Those titles portray Him as both the one who has paid the redemption price and the one who will take possession of the earth to rule it.

The first title is "the Lion of the tribe of Judah." Historically, the lion has been regarded as the king of the animal realm. Thus, Christ as "the Lion" has power to rule. This idea is emphasized further by the designation of Christ as the Lion "of the tribe of Judah." This title is based on Jacob's prophecy (Gen. 49:8–10) that Judah would be the ruling tribe of Israel, would have the power to defeat its enemies, would be characterized by the action of a lion, would always have the right to rule, and would have all of this power and right to rule in its ultimate descendant, the Messiah, to whom the people will gather for leadership and instruction. In the context of Revelation 5, this title is applied to Christ to indicate that He is the one who has the power and right to defeat Satan and his followers by evicting them and their rule from the earth and to take possession of the earth, ruling it as the last Adam.

The second title applied to Christ is "the Root of David." This title is based on Isaiah 11:10, where the Messiah is called "a root of Jesse" (a root out of David's father; Maurer, "*rhiza,*" in *Theological Dictionary of the New Testament,* 6:986). It relates Christ to the royal family of Judah, the family of David, and thereby indicates that He has the right and authority to rule.

The Hebrew word translated "root" in the expression *root of Jesse* "denotes both the relic of past glory and also the hopeful starting-point for a better future" (ibid.). It involves the idea that "From the root a fallen tree can renew itself and put forth fresh shoots, Job 14:7–9. The root, then, is the hope of a new beginning after catastrophe" (ibid.). This idea applies to the expression *root of Jesse* in Isaiah 11:10 and sheds light on the significance of the title *the root of David* assigned to Christ in Revelation 5:5. As a result of ungodly kings and rebellious people, the royal family of David was cut down like a tree from exercising rule, and the nation fell on very hard times through foreign captivity and scattering. Since that captivity, the royal family of David has not exercised rule but has remained dormant, just as a stump gives no evidence of life. But in the future, the stump of this royal family will spring suddenly to life again when its ultimate King (the Messiah, Christ) springs forth from it to rule (ibid.).

Concerning the Messiah, Isaiah 11:10 says, "his rest shall be glorious." This verse indicates that the Messiah will impress the world by defeating His enemies and giving the earth rest (Coppes, "*nuah,*" in *Theological Wordbook of the Old Testament,* 2:562). Thus, Isaiah 11:10 (and, therefore, the title "the root of David" in Revelation 5:5) indicates that, as a descendant of the royal family of Judah, Christ will defeat His enemies (Satan and his followers), give the earth rest from their rebellious rule and the curse on nature, and rule the entire world with peace and righteousness.

The third title applied to Christ in Revelation 5 is "the Lamb that was slain." The song recorded in Revelation 5:9–10, which emphasizes Christ's crucifixion and the shedding of His blood, indicates that this title refers to the redemptive work of Christ. As the Lamb that was slain, Christ fulfilled the first responsibility of a kinsman-redeemer—He paid the redemption price and thereby obtained the right of tenant possession. In line with this achievement, the song of Revelation 5:9–10 declares that Christ is worthy to take the scroll and open its seals because He was slain and accomplished His redemptive work.

Note, however, that the Lamb that was slain had seven horns (5:6). Werner Foerster stated that in the Old Testament the horn "is a direct term for power" (*"keras,"* in *Theological Dictionary of the New Testament,* 3:669; see Deut. 33:17; 1 Kings 22:11; Zech. 1:18–21). In light of this fact, Foerster explained the implication of the seven horns on the Lamb in Revelation 5 as follows: "In accordance with the symbolical meaning of the number seven and the figure of the horn, the seven horns of the Lamb express the divine plenitude of power" (ibid., p. 670). As the slain Lamb of God who paid the price of redemption, Christ has the fullness of divine power necessary to crush His enemies and take over the rule of the earth.

In line with this understanding, William Barclay wrote, "Here is the great paradox: the Lamb bears the sacrificial wounds upon it; but at the same time it is clothed with the very might of God which can now shatter and break its enemies. The Lamb has *seven* horns; . . . the power of the Lamb is perfect, full, complete, beyond understanding" (*The Revelation of John,* 1:217).

In addition, Joachim Jeremias asserted that "the statements of Revelation concerning Christ as" Lamb "depict Him as Redeemer and Ruler" (*"arnion,"* in *Theological Dictionary of the New Testament,* 1:341). Jeremias stated further that, as the Lamb, Christ "takes over the government of the world by opening the book of destiny in the heavenly council (4:2ff.; 5:7ff.)" (ibid.). In line with this, according to Revelation, as the Lamb that was slain, Christ is worthy to take the scroll and open its seals (5:9); as the Lamb, He will in reality break the seals (6:1); as the Lamb, Christ will be feared by the ungodly as a source of divine wrath (vv. 15–16); as the Lamb, He will be warred against jointly by the rulers of the future kingdom of Antichrist (17:14); and, as the Lamb, Christ will defeat these enemies, "for he is Lord of lords, and King of kings" (v. 14).

## The Second Truth

The second truth in Revelation 5 that is directly related to Christ's two responsibilities as mankind's Kinsman-Redeemer is the statement that Christ "hath prevailed to open" the scroll, and to break its seven seals (v. 5). Concerning the Greek word translated "hath prevailed" and the word group to which it belongs, Otto Bauernfiend stated, "The word group denotes 'victory' or 'superiority,' . . . the basic sense of genuine superiority and overwhelming success generally remains" ("*nikao,*" in *Theological Dictionary of the New Testament,* 4:942). He further declared that it is generally assumed that such victory "is demonstrated by an action, by the overthrow of an opposing force" (ibid.). Thus, Revelation seems to indicate that Christ has authority to break the seals and open the scroll because of a previous victory He gained over Satan and his forces.

Because Revelation 5:9 asserts that Christ is worthy to take the scroll and open its seals because He was slain and has redeemed mankind by His blood, one can conclude that the previous victory that Christ gained over Satan and his forces was His redemptive work on the Cross. By paying the redemption price, Christ defeated Satan and his forces in the sense that He gained the right to take from them tenant possession of the earth and to rule the earth as the last Adam. This truth sheds light on the meaning of Christ's statement when, just before He went to the cross, He said, "the prince of this world is judged" (John 16:11). Christ's death sealed Satan's doom. At the proper time, determined sovereignly by God, Christ will exercise the right that He gained at the Cross to throw out the usurper.

Concerning this fact, Gottlob Schrenk wrote, "Triumphant in His sacrificial death, Christ can exercise the divine will up to the final consummation. Thus the cross is the basis of His ruling power, which can bring the divine lordship to its goal" (*"biblion,"* in *Theological Dictionary of the New Testament,* 1:619).

## The Third Truth

The third truth in Revelation 5 that relates to Christ's two Kinsman-Redeemer responsibilities is the declaration that those people who have been redeemed by Christ's blood "shall reign on the earth" (vv. 9–10). Note that the verb translated "shall reign" is in the future tense in the Greek text and that this declaration will be made when Christ takes the scroll from God's hand. Thus, the redeemed will reign on the earth after Christ takes the sealed scroll.

The significance of this declaration and the future tense of its verb is stated by Alfred Jenour:

> Now, why does the ransomed Church in celebrating the praises of its Redeemer, and declaring his worthiness to open the book, add, at the close of its doxology, "and we shall reign upon the earth," but because the redemption wrought out has reference to the earth, and its restoration to its original possessor? And what makes this the more striking is, the use of the future tense in regard to this anticipated dominion over the earth. It is not said, *we reign,* but *we shall reign;* i.e., when thou hast opened the sealed covenant deed, and fully established thy right to the purchased possession, and hast put all opposing enemies under thy feet, *then* shall we reign with thee upon the earth. (*Rationale Apocalypticum,* 1:211–12)

Thus, once again, Revelation 5 associates Christ's redemptive work with the future rule of the earth. Interestingly, Paul also declared that church saints "shall also reign" (future tense) with Christ (2 Tim. 2:12).

## The Fourth Truth

The fourth truth in Revelation 5 that relates to Christ's two responsibilities as the Kinsman-Redeemer concerns the doxologies found in verses 9–13, which were expressed when Christ took the scroll from God's hand (vv. 7–8). The first doxology (vv. 9–10) emphasizes Christ's payment of the redemption price through the shedding of His blood; but, as we noted earlier, it includes the rule of the earth by the redeemed.

The second doxology (vv. 12–13) declares that, as the redemptive Lamb that was slain, Christ is worthy to receive many significant things, including power. In the Greek text, that power is expressed with different words. Earlier in this chapter, we noted that these words refer to God's power to crush His enemies and establish and exercise His sovereign rule over His creation. Thus, the second doxology of Revelation 5 declares that, because Christ has already paid the redemption price, He is worthy to have and exercise God's power to crush Satan and his forces and to rule the earth as God's representative.

## Conclusion

Taken together, these four truths in Revelation 5 indicate three facts concerning Christ's two Kinsman-Redeemer responsibilities. First, Christ fulfilled the first responsibility when He paid the redemption price by shedding His blood on the Cross. He thereby obtained the right to take tenant possession of the earth. Second, because He fulfilled the first responsibility, Christ is worthy to take the scroll, break its seals, open it, have and exercise God's power to crush Satan and his forces, and rule the earth. Third, Christ will do these things, thus fulfilling His second Kinsman-Redeemer responsibility.

## The Significance of Christ's Action with the Scroll

John wept much when seemingly no one was able to take the scroll from God's hand, break its seals, open it, and read its contents (Rev. 5:2–4). When Christ took the scroll from God's hand, however, God's creatures expressed tremendous praise

(vv. 7–14). These responses indicate that Christ's action of taking the scroll, breaking its seals, opening it, and reading its contents will have great significance.

### The Need for Evidence

Earlier, we noted that Christ's deed of purchase was sealed and placed in a secure place so that it could serve as irrefutable evidence that He is the Kinsman-Redeemer who has the right to take tenant possession of the earth. This legal evidence would be critical if Christ's right to take tenant possession of the earth was challenged. The possibility of such a challenge is especially strong in light of the following facts. Christ did not take actual possession of the earth immediately after paying the redemption price. Instead, He ascended to heaven, far from the earth, and has remained there ever since. During Christ's absence, Satan and his forces, who usurped tenant possession of the earth when mankind fell, have continued to exercise that tenant possession.

The Scriptures indicate that Satan and his forces will challenge Christ's right to take tenant possession of the earth as the time of His return draws near. Because Christ will take actual possession of the earth in conjunction with His Second Coming after the end of the seventieth week and the Great Tribulation, Satan and his forces will issue their challenge during the seventieth week (the last seven years before Christ returns). This challenge will involve strong, deceptive, violent action. For example, Satan and his forces will wage war against those who testify for Christ and the Word of God during the seventieth week (Dan. 7:21–22, 25–27; Rev. 6:9–11; 11:3–10; 13:7). They will put many of these witnesses to death, trying to deny Christ a following on earth when He comes.

Because Christ will not crush Satan and his forces and take possession of the earth until the nation of Israel repents (Zech. 12–14; Acts 3:12, 19–21), during the seventieth week Satan and his forces will exert great effort to annihilate Israel before it can repent (Dan. 9:27; Matt. 24:15–16; Rev. 12:7–17), thereby trying to rob Christ of a major key to His defeating His enemy and taking possession of the earth.

By the end of the seventieth week, Satan and his forces will have drawn all of the rulers and armies of the world into the land of Israel for the Battle of Armageddon (Rev. 16:12–16). That battle will take place at Christ's Second Coming and will pit Satan and his ungodly allies against Christ and His forces (Rev. 19:11–20:3). This battle will be Satan's ultimate challenge to Christ's right to take tenant possession of the earth and to rule it. The combined military might of rebellious mankind will be gathered to the precise location to which Christ will return to take possession of the earth because Satan will want all of the help he can get to try to prevent Christ from exercising His right (Ps. 2:1–3).

Satan's challenge to Christ's Kinsman-Redeemer right of tenant possession of the earth will require Christ to provide irrefutable evidence of His right of tenant possession before He takes actual possession of the earth at His Second Coming. The Lord's irrefutable evidence will consist of His taking the sealed deed of purchase of the earth from its secure place (God's right hand), breaking its seven seals, opening it, and reading its contents publicly. Thus, the significance of Christ's action with the sealed scroll of Revelation 5 is the evidence it provides—that He is the true Kinsman-Redeemer, the one who paid the redemption price in the past and, therefore, has the right to take tenant possession of the earth.

### The Breaking of the Seals

Note that Christ—not Satan, the Antichrist, or rebellious mankind—will break the seals of the scroll deed of purchase. Revelation 5 makes clear that He alone is worthy to break them because only the kinsman-redeemer could legitimately break the seals of a deed of purchase, and Christ is the only Kinsman-Redeemer of mankind's forfeited inheritance. Only He has paid the redemption price.

Therefore, Christ—not Satan, the Antichrist, or rebellious

mankind—will instigate the events that will transpire when the seven seals are broken. In conjunction with this fact, Martin Kiddle wrote:

> The strong angel's challenge to find some one worthy to open the scroll and to break its seals was much more than to ask for some one capable of *revealing* the world's fate. The demand was for one able not only to disclose God's plan, but to set it in motion, accomplish it, bring it to pass. . . . This is clearly implied in the song of praise, when at last the Lamb accepts the challenge and takes the scroll. . . . That is why John is careful to note in chaps. vi.–viii. that the enactment of the last things is performed through the Lamb. One by one, He opens the seals, and as each is broken, so God's plan is wrought. (*The Revelation of St. John*, p. 96)

Note that Christ's breaking of the seven seals is one aspect of His process of providing irrefutable evidence through His action with the scroll. Thus, the events that transpire when Christ breaks the seals will be part of the irrefutable evidence that He is the true Kinsman-Redeemer with the right, authority, and power to evict Satan and his forces and take tenant possession of the earth.

Some of the events that will transpire when Christ breaks the seals will devastate significant areas of Satan's domain. They will be expressions of God's Day-of-the-Lord wrath or judgment on that domain. Gottlob Schrenk wrote, "The book of seven seals declares the ways of God in judgment as ordained by His ruling power" (*"biblion,"* in *Theological Dictionary of the New Testament,* 1:619). Just as an armed force will attack an alien occupying army with a tremendous bombardment before it launches the invasion that will evict that alien army, so Christ, through the breaking of the seals, will attack the domain of Satan and his forces (the alien forces occupying the earth since the fall of mankind) with a tremendous bombardment of divine wrath or

judgment before He launches the invasion (His great and terrible Day-of-the-Lord invasion of the earth when He comes with
His angels in His Second Coming), which will evict Satan and
his forces from the earth.

The fact that Satan and his forces will be incapable of stopping this bombardment of their domain will demonstrate that
they are not the ultimate authority over the earth. In addition,
this bombardment, instigated by Christ through the breaking
of the seals, will demonstrate not only that He has power and
authority to fulfill the second responsibility of the Kinsman-
Redeemer (the taking of tenant possession by eviction of the
usurpers) but also that He is preparing to do so. Thus, the breaking of the seals will produce part of the evidence that Christ is
the true Kinsman-Redeemer.

In line with this fact, James Kelly signified that when Christ
takes the scroll and breaks its seals, He will thereby assert His
right to recover mankind's forfeited inheritance (*The Apocalypse
Interpreted in the Light of "The Day of the Lord,"* 1:289). Kelly declared that Christ will do this "amidst demonstrations of judgment, affecting every department of nature, as though to shake
it from the enemy's grasp" (ibid.). Kelly further stated:

> Here, in Revelation, the inheritance of the earth, is con-
> veyed to Christ from the Father, by the formal instru-
> ment of the sealed book, the opening of the seals of
> which, is as it were so many judicial stages towards the
> establishment of His righteous empire. (Ibid., p. 295)

Similarly, Jenour wrote, "For the opening of the seals is the
preliminary act whereby the GOEL, or Redeemer, begins to take
possession" (*Rationale Apocalypticum,* 1:213).

### The Reading of the Scroll Deed

A study of Revelation 8 through 18 indicates that the seventh seal will contain the seven trumpets and the seven bowl
judgments. Thus, when Christ breaks all seven seals of the Rev-

elation 5 scroll, He will thereby instigate the total bombardment of divine wrath or judgment against the domain of Satan and his forces. This total bombardment will cover the seventieth week of Daniel 9 up to Christ's Second Coming after the seventieth week and the Great Tribulation.

Thus, by the time Christ will come from heaven to confront Satan and his forces as they are gathered together against Him to deliver their ultimate challenge to His right to take tenant possession of the earth (Ps. 2:1–3; Rev. 19:11–19), all seven seals of the scroll deed of purchase will have been broken. As a result, the scroll deed will be totally open for Christ to read its contents. Christ will read it publicly as the final, conclusive part of the irrefutable evidence that He is the true Kinsman-Redeemer of mankind's forfeited inheritance and, therefore, has the right to evict Satan and his forces and to take tenant possession of the earth. After presenting this evidence and thereby declaring His right, Christ will proceed to rid the earth of Satan and his forces and to take rule of the earth (Rev. 19:19–20:6).

Psalm 2 presents the same scenario. Verses 1–3 describe the rebellious world forces gathered together to try to prevent God's Messiah from taking tenant possession or administration of the earth. According to verse 7, when the Messiah confronts this challenge, He will declare what God has already decreed concerning Him: "Thou art my Son."

The biblical term *son* involves the concept of "heir" (Gal. 4:7). Thus, as God's Son, the Messiah is the heir of an inheritance given to Him by God. Psalm 2:8 presents God's description of that inheritance: "I shall give thee the heathen for thine inheritance, and the uttermost parts of the earth for thy possession." In verse 9, God stated what the Messiah will do when the rebel forces gather against Him: "Thou shalt break them with a rod of iron; thou shalt dash them in pieces like a potter's vessel."

In light of what we have seen, we can conclude that Psalm 2 is saying that on the day when the Messiah comes to confront the rebel forces gathered to challenge His right to take tenant possession of the earth, He will declare what God has already decreed concerning Him (in other words, that, as God's Son, the Messiah has the right to inherit the people and the uttermost parts of the earth as His possession). Once Christ, the Messiah, has delivered that declaration through the reading of the scroll and thereby given irrefutable evidence of His right, He will proceed to crush the rebel forces.

# Observations Related to the Seals

## Observations Related to All of the Seals

### Pre-Wrath View

The Pre-Wrath view teaches the following. The wrath of God will not begin until the seventh seal is broken (Rosenthal, *Pre-Wrath Rapture,* pp. 153, 173). Thus, no wrath of God will be poured out within the first six seals. The first five seals will consist of the wrath of man—the ultimate rebellion of mankind under Antichrist (ibid., p. 181). The sixth seal will indicate that the wrath of God is about to come (when the seventh seal will be broken; ibid., pp. 164–66, 180).

### Critique

We should note several facts concerning all of the seals.

First, all seven seals are part of the same sealed scroll (Rev. 5:1–2, 5, 9).

Second, as we noted earlier, before Christ breaks them, all the seals have the same purpose—to make the scroll secure from

57

tampering or change, thereby providing a sevenfold guarantee of the scroll's integrity so that the scroll can serve as irrefutable evidence that Christ is the true Kinsman-Redeemer.

Third, as we also noted earlier, when Christ breaks the seven seals, the resultant events will be part of that irrefutable evidence and will demonstrate that He has the power and authority to fulfill the second responsibility of the Kinsman-Redeemer.

Fourth, Revelation 5 clearly indicates that only Christ is worthy to take the scroll and break its seals, and in Revelation 6–8 Christ alone breaks all seven seals. Not one seal is broken by Satan, the Antichrist, or rebellious mankind.

Taken together, these four items prompt the following three conclusions.

- All seven seals are part of Christ's Kinsman-Redeemer program of taking tenant possession of the earth by bombarding Satan's domain and then evicting Satan and his forces. Although Satan and his forces will carry on activity during the execution of that program, the seven seals are not part of their program.
- Because Christ alone breaks all of the seals, He alone instigates the events that will transpire when all seven seals are broken.
- Because all seven seals are part of Christ's Kinsman-Redeemer program, and because Christ alone instigates the events that will transpire when all seven seals are broken, we can conclude that the events that will transpire when all seven seals are broken will be expressions of divine wrath poured out upon Satan's domain.

### Observations Related to the First Seal

#### Description of the First Seal
When Christ breaks the first seal, a rider on a white horse goes "forth conquering, and to conquer" (Rev. 6:1–2).

## Pre-Wrath View

The Pre-Wrath view identifies this rider as the Antichrist (Rosenthal, *Pre-Wrath Rapture,* p. 142), and presents the following argument. If all seven seals are expressions of God's wrath, then with the breaking of the first seal God would be the one responsible for a false religious system and the rise of the Antichrist. God's house would be divided and opposing itself if Christ were to turn loose the dominant ruler of the seventieth week, who will be energized and controlled by God's great enemy, Satan, and who will blaspheme God, declare himself to be God, desolate Israel, and wage war against the saints. In addition, to think that the Antichrist could gain control of the world once God's Day-of-the-Lord wrath begins is unreasonable (ibid.).

## Critique

We should note four things by way of response.

First, God's house would not be divided and opposing itself if Christ's turning the Antichrist loose would serve God's sovereign purpose. Was God's house divided and opposing itself when God turned over His righteous servant Job to be attacked by Satan (Job 1:8–12; 2:3–6)? Did God have a sovereign purpose for doing that?

When God raised up the pharaoh who severely abused Israel (Exod. 9:16; Rom. 9:17) and hardened that pharaoh's heart so that he refused to obey God's command to let Israel go (Exod. 9:1, 12; 10:1), didn't God have a sovereign purpose for that, although it appeared to oppose His will?

In spite of the fact that God despises the practices of homosexuality, lesbianism, murder, and the hatred of Himself, didn't He turn ancient Gentiles over to these practices as an expression of His wrath against them because they had willfully rejected His revelation to them (Rom. 1:18–32)? Was God thereby opposing Himself by giving up people to practices that He despises?

These are examples of how God, because of His sovereign purposes, does things that might seem to oppose Himself. Parallel to these examples is the truth that God, in spite of the fact that He will despise the Antichrist, will have Christ turn him loose to conquer the world through the breaking of the first seal because He will have sovereign purposes for that action.

Second, God indicated that His Spirit strove (Gen. 6:3) with lawless mankind (vv. 5, 11–13) in the days before the Noachic flood. The word translated "strive" means "to govern"; "it embodies the idea of government, in whatever realm" (Culver, *"din,"* in *Theological Wordbook of the Old Testament,* 1:188). The use of this word for the Holy Spirit indicates that He has one of the same functions as government—the restraint of lawlessness in the world (Rom. 13:3–6; 1 Peter 2:13–14). Thus, the Holy Spirit's restraint of lawlessness has been a significant factor in the administration of God's rule over the world. Because this work of the Spirit belongs to the administration of God's rule over the world, and because God is sovereign, only God has the authority to remove that restraint.

Second Thessalonians 2 reveals that the Antichrist will be characterized by lawlessness. In verse 3, the Greek word translated "sin" in the expression *that man of sin* means "lawlessness" (Arndt and Gingrich, *"anomia,"* in *A Greek-English Lexicon of the New Testament,* p. 71). Thus, the expression *that man of lawlessness* indicates that the Antichrist will be the ultimate expression of human lawlessness. In verse 8, the Greek word translated "wicked" in the expression *that wicked* literally means "lawless one" (*"anomos,"* ibid.) and refers to the Antichrist as the epitome of human lawlessness.

In 2 Thessalonians 2:6–8, Paul indicated that the mystery of lawlessness (the Greek word translated "iniquity" in the expression *the mystery of iniquity* in v. 7 literally means "lawlessness" [*"anomia,"* ibid.]) was already working in his day. Nevertheless, some restraint (the Greek word translated "what witholdeth" in v. 6 literally means "the restraining" [*"katecho,"* ibid., p. 423]) was preventing the Antichrist, the ultimate expression of that lawlessness, from being revealed until the right time. Furthermore, Paul declared that the person causing that restraint would continue it until he, as the restrainer, would "be taken out of the way" (v. 7). Once the restrainer would be removed, the lawless one—the Antichrist—would be revealed (v. 8).

As we noted earlier, because God's Holy Spirit has the function of restraining lawlessness, and because the Antichrist will be the ultimate expression of human lawlessness, Paul was indicating in 2 Thessalonians 2:6–8 that the restraining work of the Holy Spirit is the restraint that prevents the Antichrist from being revealed until the right time. The Holy Spirit will continue that restraining work until He, as the restrainer, is removed, at which time the Antichrist will be revealed.

As we also noted earlier, because only God has the authority to remove the Holy Spirit's restraint, and because the Antichrist will be revealed once that restraint is removed, we can conclude that the Antichrist will be turned loose through divine activity to conquer the world.

Third, in Zechariah 11:15–17, God declared that He would raise up a "foolish" and "idol" shepherd. God's description of this shepherd helps to identify him. The Hebrew word translated "foolish" (v. 15) refers to a person who is morally perverted, insolent (rude, disrespectful, insulting), and impatient with discipline. He does not fear God. He thinks that his own way is without error, and he is overbearing in his attitude because he thinks that he has all of the answers (Goldberg, *"ewil,"* in *Theological Wordbook of the Old Testament,* 1:19).

These characteristics will be true of the Antichrist. He will be morally perverted, for he will lie (2 Thess. 2:11) and kill godly people (Dan. 7:21, 25; Rev. 13:7). He will be insolent toward God and will not fear Him, for he will speak monstrous, blasphemous things against Him (Dan. 11:36; Rev. 13:5–6). The Antichrist will be impatient with discipline and think that his own way is without error, for he "shall do according to his will" (Dan. 11:36). He will be overbearing in his attitude and think that he has all of the answers, for he "shall exalt himself, and magnify himself" (v. 36) and will "think to change times and laws" (7:25).

This shepherd will also be an "idol" shepherd (Zech. 11:17). The Hebrew word translated "idol" means "something worthless (particularly as an object of worship), gods, idols" and "is used primarily in Scripture to describe vain objects of worship, i.e. the gods of this world" (Scott, *"elil,"* in *Theological Wordbook of the Old Testament,* 1:46). These worthless gods or idols "even included people in whom men trusted but who were deceitful and of no value (Job 13:4; Isa. 19:3; Zech. 11:17)" (ibid.). Thus, the shepherd of Zechariah 11:15–17 will be a person who, through deceit, will convince people to put their trust in him as a god, even though he is not a god.

This characteristic will be true of the Antichrist. Despite the fact that he will be a man, he will claim to be God (Dan. 11:36–37; 2 Thess. 2:4). He will use "lying wonders," (2 Thess. 2:9) "all deceivableness of unrighteousness" (v. 10; "every kind of wicked deception" [Arndt and Gingrich, *"apate,"* in *A Greek-English Lexicon of the New Testament,* p. 81]), and a "lie" (v. 11) to convince people to put their trust in him as God. Many people will believe his false claim, place their trust in him, and worship him as God (2 Thess. 2:11; Rev. 13:3–4, 8).

Zechariah 11:16 says that instead of shepherding the people of Israel in a loving, caring way, the foolish, idol shepherd will decimate them cruelly for his own selfish purposes. This characteristic, too, will be true of the Antichrist. During the second half of the seventieth week of Daniel 9, he will desolate the people of Israel (Dan. 9:27; 12:11; Matt. 24:15–23).

All of these characteristics indicate that the foolish, idol shepherd of Zechariah 11:15–17 will be the Antichrist. In light of this fact, to note that God declared that He will raise up the foolish, idol shepherd is important (Zech. 11:16). Concerning the meaning of the Hebrew verb translated "raise up" in this specific verse, Brown, Driver, and Briggs stated the following: "Raise up, bring on the scene" (*"quwm,"* in *A Hebrew and En-*

*glish Lexicon of the Old Testament,* pp. 878–79). Because this evil shepherd will be the Antichrist, God thereby indicated that He will bring the Antichrist on the world scene.

Fourth, God will have specific sovereign purposes for bringing the Antichrist onto the world scene. One purpose will be the judgment of Israel. In Zechariah 11, God foretold the future judgment of Israel because it would reject its good Shepherd, the Messiah (vv. 10–14). As part of that judgment God will send Israel a false shepherd (the Antichrist) who, as noted earlier, will try to annihilate the nation (vv. 15–17; cf. Dan. 9:27). Thus, God's bringing the Antichrist onto the world scene will be a form of His wrath upon Israel.

A second purpose will be the repentance of Israel. For centuries, Israel's rebellion against God and His Messiah has been so stubborn and persistent that nothing short of the severest persecution in Israel's history will break that rebellion and bring the nation to genuine repentance.

Earlier, we noted that the future unparalleled time of Great Tribulation will not end until God has completely shattered the obstinate rebellion of Israel against Himself (Dan. 12:6–7). God will bring the Antichrist on the world scene to play a major role in shattering that rebellion. He will use the Antichrist's desolation of the nation (including his part in drawing the armies of the nations against Israel by the end of the seventieth week, Rev. 16:12–16) as a means of backing Israel so tightly into a corner that it will have no means of escape from total annihilation unless it repents. At that darkest time in its entire history, the nation will repent (Zech. 12:2, 10–13:1).

A third purpose will be the judgment of the world. Isaiah 3:1–15 indicates that sometimes God judges rebellious people by removing good leaders or rulers and giving them oppressive rulers. Thus, God sometimes gives people the kind of rulers they deserve.

During the seventieth week, God will inflict on the rebellious world a ruler who will be the ultimate expression of its own spirit of lawlessness. As we noted earlier, the Antichrist will be the epitome of human lawlessness. That rebellious nature will make him an oppressive, dictatorial tyrant who will subject the world to his self-centered whims. Under the Antichrist, the world will suffer the horrible consequences of the same spirit of lawlessness that prompts it to rebel against God. Thus, God's bringing the Antichrist on the world scene will be a form of His wrathful judgment of the rebellious world.

A fourth purpose will be the exposure of the world's unbelief. God will bring the Antichrist on the world scene and permit him to make his claim to be God in order to demonstrate mankind's unbelief. That unbelief will be graphically displayed through the great multitudes of people who will believe the Antichrist's lie and worship him (2 Thess. 2:10–12; Rev. 13:3–8). This exposure of unbelief will demonstrate the reason for God's wrath being poured out upon the world.

A fifth purpose will be the instigation of the final showdown between Christ and Satan's forces and the resultant defeat of Satan's forces. When God brings the Antichrist on the world scene, it will cause the conflict of the ages between God and Satan's forces to rise to the peak of intensity (Rev. 6–18). This event will be God's way of setting the stage for the grand climax of that conflict when Christ will come out of heaven as God's victorious conqueror to crush Satan's forces (19:11–20:3). Just as God raised up a pharaoh (who despised and stubbornly resisted Him and tried to annihilate His people) for the purpose of demonstrating His awesome power through him and thereby impressing the world with Himself (Exod. 9:16; Rom. 9:17), so He will bring the Antichrist on the world scene for a similar purpose.

Thus, God will have several sovereign purposes for turning the Antichrist loose on the world as an expression of His wrath when Christ breaks the first seal. In conjunction with this event, the following statement by Gustav Stahlin is significant: "The Bible regards many pagan peoples and rulers as executors of God's wrath. They are this even when, like the devil, they consciously fight against God and His people. . . . This is the picture of political powers in Rev." (*"orge,"* in *Theological Dictionary of the New Testament,* 5:441).

## Observations Related to the Second Seal

### Description of the Second Seal

When Christ breaks the second seal, the rider who goes forth on a red horse is given a great sword and power to remove peace from the earth. This will bring great carnage with people killing one another (Rev. 6:3–4). This description indicates that when the second seal is broken, great warfare will be brought to the world. This situation is equal to the wars and rumors of wars, nation rising against nation, and kingdom against kingdom in Christ's Matthew 24:6–8 statement about the beginning of birth pangs.

### Pre-Wrath View

Because the Pre-Wrath view asserts that no wrath of God exists in the first six seals, it argues that this warfare, which obviously involves human activity, is totally the wrath of man (Rosenthal, *Pre-Wrath Rapture,* pp. 142, 173, 181).

### Critique

We should note two points by way of response.

First, this warfare obviously will involve extensive human activity; however, the Scriptures clearly indicate that the wars of nations are often the weapons of God's wrath. For example, God declared that "an assembly of great nations" would be "the weapons of his indignation" and "wrath," even His Day-of-the-Lord wrath, against Babylon (Isa. 13:1–5, 9, 17–19; Jer. 50:9, 13, 25). God raised up Syria and Philistia as instruments of His anger against Israel (Isa. 9:11–12). He used Assyria as "the rod" of His anger, indignation, and wrath against Israel (Isa. 10:5–6). And He brought the Babylonians to war against Judah and Jerusalem as an expression of His wrath (2 Chron. 36:16–17; Ezra 5:12; Jer. 32:28–32).

In line with this view, Johannes Fichtner wrote that the Old Testament presents the view that God sometimes "vents His wrath through earthly powers. . . . Yahweh delivers up the people of His anger to the Assyrian. . . . The nations are also instruments of His wrath against other nations to execute judgment" ("*orge*," in *Theological Dictionary of the New Testament*, 5:400).

The following statements of 2 Chronicles 15:5–6 are very relevant at this point: "And in those times there was no peace to him that went out, nor to him that came in, but great vexations were upon all the inhabitants of the countries. And nation was destroyed of nation, and city of city: for God did vex them with all adversity."

Numerous other passages (including Isa. 51:17–20; 65:12; and Jer. 16:4–10; 24:10) indicate that God uses the sword as an instrument of His anger and judgment. Indeed, in line with the rider of the second seal being given "a great sword," Isaiah 26:20–27:1 signifies that, in the day of the Lord's indignation, when He will "punish the inhabitants of the earth for their iniquity," He will use "his sore and great and strong sword" as an instrument of punishment.

In light of these observations, we can draw the following conclusion. The fact that the warfare of the second seal will involve extensive human activity does not require the conclusion that the warfare will not be an expression of God's wrath.

Second, note that the great sword and the power to take peace from the earth were "given" to the rider on the red horse. This statement means that the rider was not the source of these things; their source was a higher authority. Because Christ is the one who breaks the second seal and thereby instigates what transpires, one can conclude that He is that higher authority. Thus, the warfare of the second seal has a divine source. In line with this fact, Robert L. Thomas asserted that the great sword and power to take peace from the earth were given to the rider "by authority from heaven," and, therefore, the rider "is an agent appointed by God for a specific purpose" (*Revelation 1–7*, pp. 427–28).

## Observations Related to the Third Seal

### Description of the Third Seal

When Christ breaks the third seal, a rider on a black horse comes forth holding a pair of balances in his hand (Rev. 6:5–6). Verse 6 indicates that food is the commodity to be weighed in the balance, and money will buy only one-eighth the normal quantity of food (Vine, *"choinix,"* in *An Expository Dictionary of New Testament Words,* 3:52–53). This implies that prices will be very high because of a scarcity of food. Thus, when the third seal is broken, it will bring famine to the world. This situation equals the famines in Christ's statement in Matthew 24:7–8 about the beginning of birth pangs.

### Pre-Wrath View

Because the Pre-Wrath view asserts that no wrath of God exists in the first six seals, it argues that this famine is totally the wrath of man, the result of man's warfare that began with the second seal (Rosenthal, *Pre-Wrath Rapture,* pp. 142, 173, 181).

### Critique

When Christ breaks the third seal, a voice in the midst of the four beasts speaks (Rev. 6:6). The person speaking determines the prices of the food and sets limits on the famine. In other words, that person administers the famine. Revelation 4 reveals that God sits on the throne in the midst of the four beasts, and Revelation 5:6 portrays Christ as a Lamb standing in the midst of the four beasts. In light of this fact, the voice in the midst of the beasts must belong to either God or Christ. Therefore, either God or Christ, not mankind or Satan, will administer the famine associated with the third seal.

Many Scriptures teach that God uses famine as an expression of His wrath against rebellious mankind (e.g., Jer. 21:5–7, 9; 44:8, 11–13; Ezek. 5:11–17; 7:3, 8, 14–15). For this reason, Johannes Fichtner referred to "Yahweh's wrath, which finds expression in drought and famine" (*"orge,"* in *Theological Dictionary of the New*

*Testament,* 5:400). In light of this fact and the fact that either God or Christ will administer the famine associated with the third seal, this famine apparently will involve an outpouring of divine wrath.

## Observations Related to the Fourth Seal

### Description of the Fourth Seal

When Christ breaks the fourth seal, the rider who comes forth on a pale horse is Death. He is followed by a partner, Hell (Rev. 6:7–8). Together, they are given power to inflict death upon one-fourth of the world's population through means of the sword, hunger (famine), death (in this context referring to pestilence [Arndt and Gingrich, *"thanatos,"* in *A Greek-English Lexicon of the New Testament,* pp. 351–52]), and beasts.

### Pre-Wrath View

Because the Pre-Wrath view asserts that no wrath of God exists in the first six seals, it argues that these fourth-seal causes of death are further results of man's warfare that began with the second seal. In other words, their source is man's wrath, not God's (Rosenthal, *Pre-Wrath Rapture,* pp. 142, 173, 181).

### Critique

We must observe six points by way of response.

First, the Hebrew Old Testament used six major words for the anger or wrath of God (Van Groningen, *"qesep,"* in *Theological Wordbook of the Old Testament,* 2:808).

Second, John used the Old Testament extensively in Revelation. Henry Barclay Swete claimed that 278 of the 404 verses in Revelation contain references to the Old Testament (*The Apocalypse of St. John,* p. cxl). More than half of these references come from the Psalms, Isaiah, Ezekiel, and Daniel (ibid., p. cliii). Twenty-nine Old Testament references are from Ezekiel (ibid., n.). Concerning John's use of the Old Testament in Revelation, Swete declared that there are "references in which it is clear that he has in view certain books and passages, and is practically quoting from them" (ibid., pp. cliii–cliv).

Third, scholars recognize that when John wrote Revelation 6:8 concerning the sword, famine, pestilence, and beasts of the fourth seal, he had in view Ezekiel 5:17 and 14:21. For example, Swete indicated this correlation between Revelation 6:8 and Ezekiel 14:21 (ibid., p. cxliv). In addition, Wilhelm Michaelis asserted that Revelation 6:8 is "unmistakenly influenced by the fourfold series" in Ezekiel 5:17 "and especially" by the sword, famine, beast, and pestilence in Ezekiel 14:21 (*"romphaia,"* in *Theological Dictionary of the New Testament,* 6:996).

Ezekiel 5:17 states, "So will I send upon you famine and evil beasts, and they shall bereave thee; and pestilence and blood shall pass through thee; and I will bring the sword upon thee. I the LORD have spoken it." Ezekiel 14:21 says, "For thus saith the Lord GOD; How much more when I send my four sore judgments upon Jerusalem, the sword, and the famine, and the noisome beast, and the pestilence, to cut off from it man and beast?"

Fourth, the context of Ezekiel 5:17 (vv. 12–16) indicates that the famine, beasts, pestilence, and sword of that passage are expressions of God's wrath. Verses 13 and 15 use two of the six major Old Testament words for the anger or wrath of God noted earlier (the words *hema,* translated as "fury" and "furious rebukes," and *ap,* translated as "anger"). The Hebrew word *hema* refers to "a burning and consuming wrath," and *ap* refers to "anger" (Van Groningen, *"qesep,"* in *Theological Wordbook of the Old Testament,* 2:808).

The context of Ezekiel 14:21 indicates that the sword, famine, beast, and pestilence of that passage are also expressions of God's burning and consuming wrath. Verse 19 uses the Hebrew word *hema* (translated as "fury").

Fifth, note that the two Hebrew words *(hema* and *ap)* that are used for the expressions of God's wrath in the two Ezekiel passages upon which the fourth seal of Revelation 6:8 is based are also used for expressions of God's Day-of-the-Lord wrath against Israel and the Gentiles.

In Ezekiel 7, both *hema* ("fury," v. 8) and *ap* ("anger," vv. 3, 8) are used for "the day of the wrath of the LORD" (v. 19; cf. vv. 10, 12) against Israel (v. 2). This wrath involves the sword, famine, and pestilence (v. 15).

In Zephaniah 2, *ap* ("anger") is used for "the day of the LORD's anger" (vv. 2–3) against Israel ("nation not desired," v. 1) and the Gentiles (vv. 4–15). Zephaniah 3:8 uses *ap* ("anger") for "the day that I rise up to the prey" against the nations, the kingdoms, and all the earth. This must refer to God's gathering of the armies of all of the Gentile nations of the world at the end of the seventieth week for His Day-of-the-Lord wrathful judgment as described in Joel 3 and Zechariah 12–14.

In Isaiah 13, *ap* ("anger") is used for "the day of the LORD" (vv. 6, 9) and "the day of his fierce anger" (v. 13) against Babylon (vv. 1, 19) through the Medes (v. 17). This wrath involves the darkening of the stars, sun, and moon (v. 10), and birth pangs (v. 8).

Ezekiel 38 uses *hema* ("fury," v. 18) and *ap* ("face," v. 18) for "that day" (v. 19) when God will pour out His wrath upon the armies of six nations that will attack Israel with a massive military invasion (vv. 1–16). This outpouring of divine wrath will involve the sword (v. 21), pestilence (v. 22), and beasts (39:4).

This invasion and judgment are to occur after a restoration of Jews to their homeland (38:8, 12) and when they feel so safe and secure that they will have no defenses of their own for their protection (vv. 8, 11, 14). Israel, which began to be restored to its homeland in 1948, will feel safe and secure as the result of establishing a binding covenant with the Antichrist at the beginning of the seventieth week (Dan. 9:27). But the Antichrist will turn against Israel in the middle of the seventieth week and will desolate it throughout the second half of that seven-year period. Thus, Israel will feel safe and secure only during the first half of the seventieth week. In light of this fact, the invasion of Israel and divine judgment of its attackers (Ezek. 38) must take place during the first half of the seventieth week. Thus, there will be an outpouring of God's *hema* and *ap* wrath during the first half of the seventieth week, and it will involve the sword, pestilence, and beasts.

Psalm 2 uses *ap* for God's "wrath" (v. 5) and Christ's "wrath" and "anger" (v. 12) that will be poured out on the Gentile rulers and their armies at Armageddon at Christ's Second Coming after the seventieth week.

Isaiah 34 uses *hema* ("fury," v. 2) for "the day of the LORD's vengeance" (v. 8) against all nations and their armies (v. 2). This wrath will involve cosmic disturbances (v. 4).

Isaiah 63 uses *hema* ("fury," vv. 3, 5, 6) and *ap* ("anger," vv. 3, 6) for Christ's treading of the Gentiles in the winepress (vv. 2–3, 6) in "the day of vengeance" (v. 4) at His coming. Revelation 14:14–20 relates Christ ("the Son of man," v. 14) to "the great winepress of the wrath of God" (v. 19), and Revelation 19:11–21 indicates that, at His Second Coming, Christ "treadeth the winepress of the fierceness and wrath of Almighty God" (v. 15).

Ezekiel 30 uses *hema* ("fury," v. 15) for "the day of the LORD" (v. 3) wrath against Gentiles (vv. 3–5) through Babylon (vv. 10–11, 24–25). This wrath involves the sword (vv. 4–6, 11, 17, 24–25) and birth pangs ("great pain," vv. 4, 9, 16).

Psalm 110:5 uses *ap* ("wrath") for Christ (the Lord at the LORD's right hand, vv. 1, 5) striking through Gentile kings "in the day of his wrath" at His coming (cf. Ps. 2; Rev. 19:11–21).

These passages demonstrate that the words *hema* and *ap* are used for the Day-of-the-Lord wrath in the Old Testament; that the Day-of-the-Lord wrath involves the sword, famine, pestilence, beasts, and human agents (such as the Medes and Babylon); that the Day-of-the-Lord wrath will come upon Israel and the Gentiles; and that some of the Day-of-the-Lord wrath will transpire during the first half of the seventieth week.

We can conclude, then, that the Day-of-the-Lord wrath includes *hema* and *ap* wrath, the same kind of wrath referred to in the contexts of Ezekiel 5:7 and 14:21, which involves the sword, famine, pestilence, and beasts. Thus, the sword, famine, pestilence, and beasts of Ezekiel 5:7 and 14:21 are expressions of the Day-of-the-Lord kind of wrath.

In light of this fact and the fact, as noted earlier, that John had Ezekiel 5:7 and 14:21 in view when he wrote about the fourth seal in Revelation 6:8, we can conclude that the sword, famine, pestilence, and beasts of the fourth seal also are expressions of the Day-of-the-Lord wrath. This conclusion seems to be confirmed by the fact that, in Ezekiel 14:21, God called the sword, famine, pestilence, and beasts "my four severe judgments" (NASB).

Sixth, the fact that the power to inflict death on one-fourth of the world's population "was given unto" Death and Hell indicates that they did not have the authority in and of themselves to do this. A higher authority gave them that authority. In Revelation 1:18, Christ declared that He has "the keys of hell and of death." This statement indicates that He has absolute, sovereign control over Death and Hell and, therefore, is the one who gave them the authority to kill one-fourth of the world's population. This truth, together with the fact that Christ is the one who breaks the fourth seal and thereby instigates what transpires, signifies that the fourth seal is an expression of divine wrath.

## Observations Related to the Fifth Seal

### Description of the Fifth Seal

Revelation 6:9–11 indicates that the fifth seal is related to believers who have been martyred because of their faithful witness and declaration of God's Word. John saw the souls of martyred saints under the altar in heaven.

### Pre-Wrath View

Because the Pre-Wrath view asserts that no wrath of God exists in the first six seals, it makes the following claims. The fifth seal involves only the wrath of man (Rosenthal, *Pre-Wrath Rapture*, pp. 142–43, 181). When the fifth seal is broken, the Great Tribulation and the martyrdom of believers begins in the middle of the seventieth week (ibid., pp. 179, 183). Because believers will refuse to give allegiance to the Antichrist and to worship him, he and his forces will put them to death (ibid., pp. 142–43). Thus, the breaking of the fifth seal instigates and depicts the martyrdom of God's people (ibid., pp. 142–43, 183). Because the breaking of the fifth seal instigates and depicts the martyrdom of God's people, to say that the fifth seal is the wrath of God is to make God responsible for the killing of His own people, who have been faithful to Him (ibid., pp. 142–43).

**Critique**

We should note two points by way of response.

First, note what John saw—and what he did not see—when Christ broke the fifth seal. Revelation 6:9–11 indicates that John did *not* see believers being martyred when the fifth seal was broken. Instead, he saw the disembodied souls of believers who had been slain already. The verb form translated "were slain" (v. 9) is in the Greek perfect tense. H. E. Dana and Julius R. Mantey explain the significance of the perfect tense as follows:

> The perfect is the tense of complete action. . . . It implies a process, but views that process as having reached its consummation and existing in a finished state. The point of completion is always antecedent to the time implied or stated in connection with the use of the perfect. (*A Manual Grammar of the Greek New Testament,* p. 200)

This fact means that the slaying of this particular group of believers had already been completed before John saw their souls under the altar in heaven. Archibald Thomas Robertson, America's premier Greek authority of the twentieth century, indicated that the verb form translated "were slain" in Revelation 6:9 represents action that was completed before the action of the main verb "saw" in John's statement, "I saw" (*A Grammar of the Greek New Testament in the Light of Historical Research,* pp. 909–10, 1118).

The fact that John did not see believers being slain, but instead saw the disembodied souls of saints who had been slain before he saw them, forces the conclusion that these believers were killed before the fifth seal was broken. Thus, the breaking of the fifth seal does not instigate or cause the martyrdom of believers. In addition, this fact means that the fifth seal can involve the wrath of God without making God responsible for the killing of His own people.

Second, obviously the killing of these saints during the seventieth week will involve the evil activity of Satan's forces as they wage war against God by attacking His people (Dan. 7:21, 25; Rev. 13:7). In light of this killing by Satan's forces before the fifth seal is broken, the fifth seal will be related to the wrath of God in two ways.

1. The fifth seal will reveal one reason why Satan's forces will deserve more divine wrath poured out on them through the remaining seals, trumpets, and bowls.
2. The martyred saints of the fifth seal asked God how long He would delay His judgment of those who had killed them.

In this question, they addressed God as *despotes* ("Lord," Rev. 6:10). The ancient Greeks used this word politically to refer to not only people who intruded into a land already occupied by someone else to take possession of it but also an absolute ruler who had "an unlimited possibility of the exercise of power unchecked by any law" (Rengstorf, *"despotes,"* in *Theological Dictionary of the New Testament,* 2:44). In the Greek Bible, this word is used to emphasize God's authority and omnipotence (unlimited power), especially as revealed through His acts in history (ibid., pp. 45, 47).

In light of these usages, when the martyred saints addressed God as *despotes,* that term had the following significance in the context of the fifth seal. The first four seals will involve revelations of God's *despotes* authority and omnipotence in history because they will involve outpourings of God's wrath on Satan's domain, which Satan and his forces will not be able to check. Through these outpourings, God will begin His intrusion into the world already occupied by Satan and his forces to take eventual possession of it from them.

The martyred saints of the fifth seal will be living and dying during the first four seals. Thus, before they are martyred, they will witness various aspects of this revelation of God's *despotes* authority and omnipotence against His enemies. Having thereby observed the fact that God has begun to exercise His *despotes* authority and omnipotent power against Satan's domain, once they have been martyred, they will ask God how long He will delay using this authority and power specifically to avenge their blood against those who killed them. The answer to their question (v. 11) signifies that God will assure these martyred saints that He will use His *despotes* authority and power to avenge their blood through further outpouring of His wrath, once all of the saints who are to be martyred have been killed.

Note that, in the Greek text of verse 11, the expression translated "that they should rest yet for a little season" is a purpose clause, indicating that this expression is not part of God's answer to their question. Instead, it expresses the purpose for God's answer. For the purpose of enabling these troubled saints to rest for a little season, God will respond that He will delay avenging their blood only until all of the saints who are to be martyred have been killed. Thus, God's answer will assure them that He certainly will avenge their blood.

In light of this fact, we can conclude that the second way in which the fifth seal will be related to the wrath of God is by its guarantee of further outpouring of God's wrath after the first four seals.

## Observations Related to the Sixth Seal

### Description of the Sixth Seal

When Christ breaks the sixth seal, dramatic cosmic disturbances and a great earthquake that causes significant geological changes take place. These terrifying events cause unregenerate people of all social classes to flee to the mountains to hide in the dens and the rocks (Rev. 6:12–17). They cry out to the mountains and rocks, "Fall on us, and hide us from the face of him that sitteth on the throne, and from the wrath of the Lamb: For the great day of his wrath is come; and who shall be able to stand?" (vv. 16–17).

### Pre-Wrath View

The Pre-Wrath view asserts that not until the opening of this sixth seal does God begin to intervene actively in the affairs of mankind (Rosenthal, *Pre-Wrath Rapture,* pp. 140–41). But the major thesis of the Pre-Wrath view is as follows: the Day-of-the-Lord wrath does not begin until the seventh seal is opened (ibid., pp. 110, 137, 153, 173). The view is built upon—and, therefore, is dependent upon—that thesis. Thus, to be consistent with its major thesis, the Pre-Wrath view teaches that the sixth seal does not involve the wrath of God (ibid., p. 171). This point means, then, that the dramatic cosmic disturbances and great earthquake are not expressions of God's wrath.

### Critique

Three points indicate that the sixth seal will involve an outpouring of God's wrath.

First, the magnitude of the earthquake and cosmic disturbances that will occur when Christ breaks the sixth seal (Rev. 6:12–14) forces the conclusion that this event will be an awesome expression of the wrath of God, not the work of unregenerate mankind.

Second, these traumatic phenomena of the sixth seal will cause all classes of unregenerate people (the mighty as well as the lowly) to hide in the dens and rocks of the mountains and plead with the mountains and rocks to fall on them and hide them from the face of God and the wrath of the Lamb (vv. 15–16). Their interpretation of the significance of these events will be, "The great day of his wrath is come; and who shall be able to stand?"

(v. 17). These responses clearly indicate that unregenerate man-kind will be convinced that these cataclysmic phenomena are expressions of God's wrath directed against them. They will not regard these catastrophic events to be expressions of man's wrath.

Third, Franz Delitzsch indicated that the sixth seal is based upon the prophecy in Isaiah 2:10–22 (*Biblical Commentary on the Prophecies of Isaiah,* 1:126). That prophecy foretold the time when people, including the proud and lofty, will flee to hide in the holes of the rocks and caves of the earth "for fear of the LORD, and for the glory of his majesty, when he ariseth to shake terribly the earth" (v. 19). Isaiah described what John saw in conjunction with Christ's breaking of the sixth seal of Revelation 6:12–17. Thus, Isaiah was foretelling the sixth seal. Isaiah indicated that he was writing about the Day of the Lord (v. 12), and that "in that day" people will "go into the clefts of the rocks, and into the tops of the ragged rocks, for fear of the LORD, and for the glory of his majesty" (vv. 20–21). Thus, the language of Isaiah's prophecy signifies that the sixth seal will be *within* (not *before*) the Day of the Lord and, therefore, will involve the Day-of-the-Lord wrath of God.

**Pre-Wrath View**

Note the following two points regarding the Pre-Wrath view's rebuttal of what has been seen in the critique immediately above.

First, the Pre-Wrath view asserts that the aorist tense of the Greek verb translated "is come" in the expression *for the great day of his wrath is come* refers to an expected event that is future (Rosenthal, *Pre-Wrath Rapture,* pp. 165–66). In other words, during the sixth seal, the wrathful Day of the Lord is about to come, but it does not begin until the seventh seal is broken (ibid., pp. 164–66, 180).

Second, the Pre-Wrath view claims that, in conjunction with the sixth seal, the apostle John told his readers that "the great day of his wrath is come" (ibid., p. 167). It thereby gives the impression that John is saying that the wrathful Day of the Lord is about to begin.

**Critique**

Note the following two points by way of response to this rebuttal.

First, it was not the apostle John who said that "the great day of his wrath is come." Instead, John simply recorded what the unregenerate, who will be alive on earth at the time, will say when the traumatic events of the sixth seal take place. Be sure to note this distinction because the unregenerate often draw wrong conclusions concerning the works of God. Their conclusion regarding the events of the sixth seal possibly will be wrong. Archibald Thomas Robertson wrote of one exegete who "holds that this language about the great day having come 'is the mistaken cry of men in terror caused by the portents which are bursting upon them.' There is something, to be sure, to be said for this view which denies that John commits himself to the position that this is the end of the ages" (*Word Pictures in the New Testament*, 6:347).

Second, also possible is the prospect that the conclusion of the unregenerate regarding the events of the sixth seal will be correct. In light of that possibility, note that the aorist tense verb translated "is come" in the expression *the great day of his wrath is come* is in the indicative mood with the augment. Usually that kind of aorist tense verb refers to the occurrence of an event in the past, not in the future, unless its context clearly indicates otherwise (Dana and Mantey, *A Manual Grammar of the Greek New Testament*, pp. 193–94). Robertson states, "It is true that in the expression of past time in the indicative and with all the other moods, the aorist is the tense used as a matter of course" (*A Grammar of the Greek New Testament in the Light of Historical Research*, p. 831).

Robert L. Thomas indicates that for that kind of aorist tense verb to refer to "something future or something about to happen, . . . Some contextual feature must be present to indicate clearly these exceptional usages. No such feature exists in the context of the sixth seal, so these special uses are not options here" (*Revelation 1–7*, p. 460). Because this point is true, Thomas concluded that "the verb in Rev. 6:17 must be a constative aorist looking back in time to the point in the past when the great day of wrath arrived" (ibid.).

In light of this past time significance of the verb in Revelation 6:17, if the conclusion of the unregenerate regarding the events of the sixth seal will be correct, then their statement that "the great day of his wrath is come" has two possible meanings.

First, it could mean that the wrathful Day of the Lord has already been in effect through the earlier seals, but it is not until the disturbances of the sixth seal, which obviously are caused by God, that the unregenerate recognize that what they have been experiencing with the earlier seals was actually the Day-of-the-Lord wrath. In line with this view, Thomas, referring to the events of the earlier seals, stated, "The rapid sequence of all these events could not escape public notice, but the light of their true explanation does not dawn upon human conscious- ness until the severe phenomena of the sixth seal arrive" (ibid., p. 458).

Second, we noted in an earlier chapter that the seventieth week of Daniel 9 will have two levels of tribulation or birth pangs. The first half of that seven-year period will consist of the less severe tribulation or beginning of birth pangs. The sec- ond half will consist of the very severe "great tribulation," or hard labor birth pangs.

In light of these two levels of tribulation or birth pangs for the seventieth week, the statement of the unregenerate regard- ing the events of the sixth seal could have the following signifi- cance. The unregenerate will recognize that the Day-of-the-Lord wrath consists of more than one level of severity. The less se- vere level of God's Day-of-the-Lord wrath will take place dur- ing the first half of the seventieth week. But the very severe level of His Day-of-the-Lord wrath will take place during the second half of the seventieth week, beginning with the break- ing of the sixth seal. Once the unregenerate have begun to experience the terrifying disturbances that follow the breaking of the sixth seal, they will recognize that the very severe level

of God's Day-of-the-Lord wrath began when the sixth seal was
broken. Thus, just as Christ assigned the term "great" to the
very severe level of tribulation of the second half of the seventieth week, in contrast with the less severe level of tribulation
of the first half of the seventieth week, so the unregenerate will
assign the term "great" to the very severe level of the Day-of-
the-Lord wrath of the second half of the seventieth week, in
contrast with the less severe level of the Day-of-the-Lord wrath
of the first half of the seventieth week.

**Pre-Wrath View**

The Pre-Wrath view teaches that the cosmic disturbances,
which will begin in conjunction with the breaking of the sixth
seal, will be a prelude or precursor to the beginning of the Day
of the Lord with its wrath (Rosenthal, *Pre-Wrath Rapture*, pp.
153, 159, 164–66, 167, 169, 170, 171, 173, 179). In other words,
those disturbances will be a forewarning to the unregenerate
that they should flee for protection to the rocks and mountains,
because the Day-of-the-Lord wrath is about to come with the
opening of the seventh seal (ibid., p. 164).

**Critique**

Note two points in response to this teaching.

First, in 1 Thessalonians 5:2, the apostle Paul taught that the
Day of the Lord will come like "a thief in the night." In other
words, it will begin suddenly and unexpectedly, when the unregenerate are unprepared. A thief depends upon the element
of surprise for success. He does not give his intended victims a
forewarning of his coming. Paul's point is that the unregenerate will be given no forewarning that the Day of the Lord is
about to come. This fact rules out the sixth seal and all of the
other seals of Revelation as being forewarnings of the beginning of the Day of the Lord.

Second, Paul taught that the Day of the Lord will begin at the
same time that the unregenerate will claim that they have "peace
and safety" in the world (Arndt and Gingrich, *"hotan"* and

*"asphaleia,"* in *A Greek-English Lexicon of the New Testament,* pp. 592, 118; 1 Thess. 5:3). George Milligan pointed out that the tense and mood of the Greek verb translated "shall say," together with the Greek word translated "when" in the statement "when they shall say, Peace and safety," indicate *"coincidence of time* in the events spoken of: It is 'at the very moment when they are saying.'" (*St. Paul's Epistles to the Thessalonians,* p. 65).

By contrast, the Pre-Wrath view has the Day of the Lord beginning, not at the same time that the unregenerate will claim that they have peace and safety, but at the same time that they will be hiding in the rocks and mountains in absolute terror.

## Conclusion

In light of our observations related to the seals of the scroll in Revelation, we can draw the following conclusion: all seven seals are expressions of God's Day-of-the-Lord wrath, and, therefore, the Pre-Wrath view is wrong in its assertion that the Day-of-the-Lord wrath does not begin until the breaking of the seventh seal.

# CHAPTER FIVE

# Issues Related to the Second Coming

## Pre-Wrath View

The Pre-Wrath view teaches the following things concerning the Second Coming of Christ. The future return of Christ will be singular (Rosenthal, *Pre-Wrath Rapture,* pp. 222–23). Thus, there will be only one Second Coming (ibid., p. 221). The Second Coming will consist of a series of events (ibid., p. 217). Those events will include the Rapture of the church (ibid., pp. 110, 153, 217, 219, 221), the Day-of-the-Lord judgment of the unsaved (ibid., pp. 217, 222), and Christ's return in glory to receive His kingdom (ibid., pp. 146, 222). Although the Second Coming will consist of this series of events, it will be one inclusive unit (ibid., p. 221). Nowhere does the Bible even imply two separate future comings of Christ (ibid., p. 222).

## Critique

Despite its assertion that only one future coming of Christ will occur, the Pre-Wrath view teaches four future comings of Christ within the boundaries of the one Second Coming.

The first of these comings will take place between the sixth and seventh seals immediately after the Great Tribulation has ended but before the end of the seventieth week. At this coming Christ will rapture His bride (the Old Testament saints and the church saints) from the earth and take it to heaven. Christ will remain in heaven for the rest of the seventieth week (Van Kampen, *The Sign*, pp. 304, 422–23, and the chart at the end of *The Sign*).

The second of these comings will take place immediately after the end of the seventieth week and at the beginning of a thirty-day reclamation period. Christ will descend physically from heaven to the earth to bring the salvation of Israel (the Israelite survivors of the seventieth week) and to reclaim the rule of the earth for God (ibid., pp. 331, 423, and the chart at the end of *The Sign*). Sometime after the sixth day of the thirty-day reclamation period, Christ will return to heaven, where He will remain for approximately twenty-four days (ibid., p. 344, and the chart at the end of *The Sign*).

The third of these comings will take place after the seventh bowl judgment at the end of the thirty-day reclamation period. Christ will come back physically to the earth with His holy angels to defeat Antichrist and his forces at Armageddon (ibid., pp. 344, 360, 369, 423, and the chart at the end of *The Sign*). Then there will be a forty-five-day restoration period (ibid., pp. 370–77, and the chart at the end of *The Sign*). At the close of these forty-five days, Christ will return to heaven to deliver the kingdom of earth to God and to receive the rule of the whole earth from God (ibid., pp. 377–79).

The fourth future coming will take place several days after Christ receives the rule of the whole earth from God. On the first day of the Millennium, He will descend permanently to the earth with His bride (the Old Testament saints and the church saints) to rule His worldwide millennial kingdom (ibid., pp. 378, 394, 423).

**Pre-Wrath View**

The Pre-Wrath view teaches that the Second Coming (the "parousia") will include Christ's continuous presence for the rapturing of the church and for the administration of His Day-of-the-Lord judgments upon the unsaved (Rosenthal, *Pre-Wrath Rapture*, p. 217).

**Critique**

The Pre-Wrath view teaches that the Second Coming will begin with the Rapture long before the end of the seventieth week (ibid., p. 153) and that the Day-of-the-Lord judgments will begin on the same day as the Rapture (ibid., pp. 115, 196, 219) and will continue through the rest of the seventieth week and the thirty-day reclamation period after the end of the seventieth week (Van Kampen, *The Sign*, pp. 360, 369, and the chart at the end of *The Sign*).

But, as we noted earlier, the view also teaches that, from the time of the Rapture to the end of the Day-of-the-Lord judgments, Christ's movements will be as follows: After He raptures the church from the earth, He will take it to heaven, where He will remain for the rest of the seventieth week. After the end of the seventieth week and at the beginning of the thirty-day reclamation period, Christ will descend from heaven to the earth. After the sixth day of the reclamation period, He will return to heaven and remain there for approximately twenty-four days. At the end of the thirty-day reclamation period, Christ will come back to the earth.

In light of these movements of Christ between heaven and earth during the span of time covered by the Second Coming, how can the Second Coming include His continuous presence?

**Pre-Wrath View**

The Pre-Wrath view teaches that once the church is raptured and taken to heaven by Christ, it is to remain forever with Him (Rosenthal, *Pre-Wrath Rapture*, p. 296). As we noted earlier, it also asserts that the church will return to the earth with Christ on the first day of the Millennium. The view seems to imply that, once Christ takes the church to heaven at the Rapture, the church will remain in heaven until it returns to the earth with Christ on the first day of the Millennium.

## Critique

The Pre-Wrath view is correct in its teaching that once the church is raptured and taken to heaven by Christ, it is to remain forever with Him. The apostle Paul indicated that this will be so. In 1 Thessalonians 4:17, after talking about church saints being caught up together to meet Christ in the air, Paul declared, "and so shall we ever be with the Lord." This statement means that once the church meets Christ in the air at the Rapture, it will go wherever He goes.

This biblical truth poses a problem for the Pre-Wrath view. If it is true that the church will remain in heaven from the time Christ takes it there at the Rapture until it returns to earth with Him on the first day of the Millennium, then the view has a conflict between two of its teachings—the teaching that, during that span of time, Christ will go back and forth between heaven and earth several times and the teaching that once the church is raptured to heaven, it will go wherever He goes. If the church will go wherever Christ goes, and if Christ will go back and forth between heaven and earth several times, then how will the church remain in heaven during that span of time?

## Pre-Wrath View

The Pre-Wrath view teaches the following concerning the beginning of the Second Coming. The Second Coming will begin after the cosmic disturbances that will result from the breaking of the sixth seal (Rev. 6:12–14) and before the Day-of-the-Lord wrath begins with the breaking of the seventh seal (Rev. 8:1; Rosenthal, *Pre-Wrath Rapture,* pp. 110, 153).

The Second Coming of Christ will begin with the Rapture (Rosenthal, *Pre-Wrath Rapture,* p. 219; Van Kampen, *The Sign,* pp. 291, 423), and the Day of the Lord will begin immediately thereafter on the same day (Rosenthal, *Pre-Wrath Rapture,* pp. 117, 196, 219). Christ's coming will be "unannounced and unexpected" by the unsaved (ibid., p. 221). The unsaved will have "no sense of impending judgment" (ibid., p. 219).

The Pre-Wrath view also teaches that the cosmic disturbances of the sixth seal will be a precursor of the Rapture of the church and the Day of the Lord (ibid., pp. 153, 164–66), that those cosmic disturbances will signify to the unsaved that they should flee to the mountains for protection (ibid., p. 165), and that they will flee before the Day of the Lord begins (ibid., pp. 90, 170).

### Critique

That the cosmic disturbances of the sixth seal will cause the unsaved to flee to the mountains for protection is true. Revelation 6:12–16 clearly indicates that fact. But, if it were true that those cosmic disturbances will be a precursor of the Rapture of the church and the Day of the Lord, and that that precursor will cause the unsaved to flee, and if it were true that the Second Coming will begin with the Rapture, then it would also be true that the cosmic disturbances of the sixth seal would be a precursor of the Second Coming as well as of the Rapture. Because a precursor is an event that precedes another event and signifies the approach of that other event (*The American College Dictionary,* s.v. "precursor"), this would mean that the cosmic disturbances would alert the unsaved beforehand that the Second Coming was near. In light of this prospect, how could Christ's coming be "unannounced" and "unexpected" by the unsaved? And, in light of the reaction of the unsaved to the cosmic disturbances, how can one say that the unsaved will have "no sense of impending judgment" before the Second Coming begins?

### Pre-Wrath View

The Pre-Wrath view teaches that the abomination of desolation spoken of in Daniel 9:27 will begin in the middle of the seventieth week when the Antichrist will take his seat in Israel's future temple, make his blasphemous claim that he is God, and demand that the world worship him as God (Van Kampen, *The Sign*, pp. 325–26). Furthermore, it teaches that once the Antichrist begins these oppressive actions in the middle of the seven-year seventieth week, he will be allotted 1,290 days to continue (ibid.). Since chronology in the Bible is based upon the lunar calendar system of 360 days in a year, 1,290 days would equal three and one-half years (3.5 x 360 = 1,260 days) plus an additional 30 days. In other words, the Antichrist will be able to continue through the 1,260 days of the second half of the seventieth week and the additional 30 days of the reclamation period beyond the end of that week (ibid.). At the end of the additional 30 days, Christ will return to the earth and judge the Antichrist with destruction (ibid., pp. 326, 360).

## Critique

The Pre-Wrath view is correct in its teaching that the Antichrist will begin his oppressive actions in the middle of the seven-year seventieth week. However, its teaching that once he begins these actions he will be given 1,290 days to continue before he is destroyed contradicts two biblical factors.

First, Revelation 13:4–6 indicates that once the Antichrist starts his blasphemies, begins to be worshiped, and instigates his persecution of the saints in the middle of the seventieth week, he will be given power to continue forty-two months. In the lunar calendar system of the Bible, a month consists of 30 days; therefore, 42 months consists of 1,260 days or three and one-half years. Thus, Revelation 13:4–6 indicates that Antichrist will be given power to continue for 42 months, or 1,260 days (to the end of the seventieth week). By contrast, the Pre-Wrath view teaches that he will be given power to continue for 43 months, or 1,290 days (for an additional 30 days beyond the end of the seventieth week).

Second, Daniel 7:25–26 indicates that once the Antichrist starts his blasphemies, he will be given the power to continue for three and one-half "times" (three and one-half years), and then he will be judged (v. 26). By contrast, the Pre-Wrath view teaches that he will be given the power to continue for three and one-half years and an additional 30 days (1,290 days), and then he will be judged.

### Pre-Wrath View

The Pre-Wrath view teaches that Christ will "render Antichrist useless, or paralyzed," or "handcuffed" at the beginning of His Second Coming, after the cosmic disturbances of the sixth seal, part way through the second half of the seventieth week (Van Kampen, *The Sign,* p. 496 n. 3, and the chart at the end of *The Sign*). This event will cut short the Great Tribulation that will be caused by the Antichrist. However, Antichrist will not be destroyed at this time (ibid.). He will not be destroyed until thirty days after the end of the seventieth week (ibid., pp. 326, 360).

### Critique

This teaching presents at least two problems. First, the Scriptures indicate that when the sixth bowl judgment will be unleashed, the Antichrist will play a key role in prompting the rulers of all of the Gentile nations of the world to gather with their military forces to Armageddon for the battle "of the great day of God Almighty" (Rev. 16:12–16). Thus, he will be actively exercising great worldwide influence one seal, seven trumpets, and six bowls after the time that, according to the Pre-Wrath view, he was rendered useless, paralyzed, or handcuffed by Christ.

Second, the Scriptures indicate that after the Gentile rulers and armed forces of the world have gathered together to Armageddon, Antichrist will lead them in warfare against Christ and His army (Rev. 19:19–20). How could the Antichrist be actively exercising influence of such magnitude if earlier he was rendered useless, paralyzed, or handcuffed?

### Pre-Wrath View

The Pre-Wrath view teaches that several military campaigns will occur during and after the seventieth week. It calls the first of these "the Jerusalem Campaign" and indicates that it will begin in the middle of the seventieth week when the Antichrist will attack Jerusalem and set himself up in the temple as God. This event will begin the Great Tribulation of the fifth seal (Van Kampen, *The Sign,* pp. 192, 263). Some of the references given for this first campaign are Ezekiel 38:8-9, 11, 16; Zechariah 13:8; 14:2; and Matthew 24:15-21 (ibid., pp. 192-93).

The Pre-Wrath view calls the second campaign "the Jehoshaphat Campaign" (ibid., p. 262) and indicates that it will happen just before the sign of the end of the age (the cosmic disturbances of the sixth seal [ibid., p. 258]) and just before the Day of the Lord will begin (ibid.). This event will involve the gathering of the nations that surround Israel for a second attack against Jerusalem, and some of the references given for this second campaign are Joel 3:1-2, 9, 11-16, and Zechariah 12:4, 6; 14:2 (ibid., pp. 262-64). Thus, this action will be a separate campaign from the Jerusalem Campaign and will take place at a later time. This Jehoshaphat Campaign will be a precursor to the Second Coming of Christ and the Day of the Lord (ibid., p. 263).

## Critique

Note two facts concerning this teaching regarding the Jerusalem and Jehoshaphat Campaigns. First, the Pre-Wrath view gives references from the same section of Zechariah (chaps. 12-14) for both of these proposed campaigns. In fact, it uses the same verse (Zech. 14:2), which describes all nations battling against Jerusalem, for both campaigns. If these are separate campaigns at two different times, how can the same passage be used for both events?

Second, the Pre-Wrath view teaches that the Jehoshaphat Campaign will happen *before* the cosmic disturbances of the sixth seal and will be a precursor to the Second Coming of Christ and the Day of the Lord. Earlier, we noted that, according to the Pre-Wrath view, the Second Coming will be "unannounced and unexpected" by the unsaved (Rosenthal, *Pre-Wrath Rapture,* p. 221) and that the unsaved will have "no sense of impending judgment" (ibid., p. 219). A precursor is an event that precedes another event and signifies the approach of that other event (*The American College Dictionary*, s.v. "precursor"). In light of this fact, if the Jehoshaphat Campaign were a precursor to the Second Coming and the Day of the Lord, this point would mean that it would alert the unsaved beforehand that the Second Coming and Day of the Lord were imminent. How, then, could Christ's coming be "unannounced" and "unexpected" by the unsaved, and how can it be said that the unsaved will have "no sense of impending judgment" before the Second Coming begins?

## Pre-Wrath View

The Pre-Wrath view teaches that the Jehoshaphat Campaign will happen just before the cosmic disturbances of the sixth seal (Van Kampen, *The Sign*, pp. 258, 262). It identifies this campaign with the battling of the armies of all nations against Jerusalem described in Zechariah 14:2 (ibid., p. 262).

## Critique

The identification of this proposed Jehoshaphat Campaign with the battling against Jerusalem described in Zechariah 14:2 poses a problem for the Pre-Wrath view. Zechariah 14:3 indicates that Christ will return in His Second Coming to fight against these armed forces while they are in the process of attacking Jerusalem. Thus, Zechariah 14:2-3 reveals that the armies (including the commanders and soldiers) of all of the Gentile nations of the world will be on the field of battle against Jerusalem when Christ returns in His Second Coming.

According to the Pre-Wrath view, because Christ will not come until after the cosmic disturbances of the sixth seal, this fact would mean that although the Jehoshaphat Campaign would begin *before* the cosmic disturbances, it would still be going on *after* those disturbances when Christ returns in His Second Coming. Otherwise, no forces would exist for Him to fight against.

This view conflicts, however, with the fact that in response to the cosmic disturbances of the sixth seal, "the chief captains" (*"chiliarchoi,"* literally "the leader of a thousand soldiers" [Arndt and Gingrich, *A Greek-English Lexicon of the New Testament,* p. 890]) and "the mighty men" (*"ischuros,"* literally "mighty in war" [ibid., p. 384]) will hide in the dens and rocks of the mountains in terror (Rev. 6:12–16). Thus, if the Second Coming of Christ were to begin right after the cosmic disturbances of the sixth seal, the military commanders and soldiers would be hiding in terror in the mountains in fulfillment of Revelation 6:12–16. They would not be battling against Jerusalem in fulfillment of Zechariah 14:2–3.

### Pre-Wrath View

The Pre-Wrath view teaches that the second future coming of Christ within the boundaries of the one Second Coming will take place immediately after the end of the seventieth week and at the beginning of a thirty-day reclamation period. It claims that Christ will come at that time for the spiritual salvation of Israel. When Christ will become visible to the Israelite survivors of the seventieth week, they "shall look upon" Christ "whom they have pierced" and will repent of their rejection of Him and be saved in fulfillment of Zechariah 12:10 (Van Kampen, *The Sign,* pp. 328–29, 331, 423).

### Critique

The context of Zechariah 12:10 indicates that this future salvation of the Israelite survivors of the seventieth week will take place when the armies of all of the Gentile nations of the world are battling against Jerusalem (see Zech. 12:2–3, 8–9; 14:2). But we noted earlier that the Pre-Wrath view gives references from this same context (Zech. 12:4, 6; 14:2) for its proposed Jehoshaphat Campaign, which it claims will happen before the cosmic disturbances of the sixth seal (Van Kampen, *The Sign,* pp. 262–64).

Because Zechariah indicates that the spiritual salvation of the Israelite survivors of the seventieth week will take place when

the armies of all of the Gentile nations of the world are battling against Jerusalem, and because the Pre-Wrath view claims
that that battling against Jerusalem will happen before the cosmic disturbances of the sixth seal, how then can the Pre-Wrath
view teach that this spiritual salvation of the Israelite survivors
will take place immediately after the end of the seventieth week
(which, according to its understanding, will be one seal and
seven trumpets after the cosmic disturbances of the sixth seal)?

# CHAPTER SIX

# Matthew 24 and the Second Coming

### The Setting—Matthew 24:1–3

On one occasion when Christ left the temple in Jerusalem, His disciples came to Him to show Him the buildings of the temple complex. No doubt they, like other Jews, were proud of the temple and wanted Christ to be impressed with its magnificence. It was classified as one of "the marvels" of the world of Emperor Augustus (Durant, *Caesar and Christ,* p. 533).

Christ shocked the disciples by warning that all of these buildings of the temple would be destroyed in the future. His warning prompted them to ask Him some questions, one of which was as follows: "What shall be the sign of thy coming, and of the end of the world?" (literally, "of the age"; Matt. 24:3). They were referring to the end of the current age that precedes the coming messianic age, when Christ, as the Kinsman-Redeemer and the last Adam, will administer God's rule over the entire earth.

# The Sign

## Pre-Wrath View

The Pre-Wrath view claims that this "sign" question was actually two questions—"What shall be the sign of thy coming?" and "What shall be the sign . . . of the end of the age?"—and that, therefore, the disciples' question signified that there will be two future signs (Van Kampen, *The Sign*, pp. 256–59).

According to the Pre-Wrath view, the first sign, the sign of the end of the age, will consist of the cosmic disturbances of the sixth seal (Rev. 6:12–13), the same cosmic disturbances to which Christ referred in Matthew 24:29 (ibid., pp. 256–60). This first sign will serve as a warning to the unsaved that the Day-of-the-Lord judgment is imminent (ibid., p. 268).

The second sign, the sign of Christ's coming to which He referred in Matthew 24:30, will immediately follow the cosmic disturbances of the first sign (ibid., pp. 256, 259, 267) and will consist of an unparalleled burst of supernatural light (ibid., p. 268).

## Critique

We should note two points concerning these teachings of the Pre-Wrath view. First, the "sign" question that the disciples asked was not in actuality two questions. The Greek construction of the disciples' question is the kind to which the Granville Sharp Rule applies (Dana and Mantey, *A Manual Grammar of the Greek New Testament*, p. 147; see also Archibald Thomas Robertson's reference to Matthew 24:3 as an example of this kind of construction [*A Grammar of the Greek New Testament in the Light of Historical Research*, p. 787]). This point means that their question in Matthew 24:3 indicated both that Jesus' Second Coming and the end of the age will be the same event (His coming will end the current age) and that, therefore, the sign of His coming will also be the sign of the end of the current age.

Second, the Pre-Wrath view teaching that the sign of the end of the age will serve as a warning to the unsaved that the Day-of-the-Lord judgment is imminent (Van Kampen, *The Sign,* p. 268) contradicts its other teaching that the unsaved will have "no sense of impending judgment" before the Day of the Lord begins (Rosenthal, *Pre-Wrath Rapture,* p. 219).

## Cosmic Disturbances

### Pre-Wrath View

The Pre-Wrath view teaches that the Second Coming of Christ foretold in Matthew 24:30 will take place shortly after the cosmic disturbances of the sixth seal (Rev. 6:12–14; Rosenthal, *Pre-Wrath Rapture,* pp. 110, 153). It bases this teaching on two suppositions.

First, according to Matthew 24:29–30, the Second Coming of Christ will take place shortly after cosmic disturbances. The Pre-Wrath view believes that the cosmic disturbances of Matthew 24:29 are those associated with the sixth seal in Revelation 6:12–14 (ibid., p. 110).

In light of this belief, the Pre-Wrath view reasons as follows. Because the Second Coming of Christ foretold in Matthew 24:30 will take place shortly after cosmic disturbances, and because the cosmic disturbances of Matthew 24 are those associated with the sixth seal, then the Second Coming of Christ of Matthew 24:30 must take place shortly after the cosmic disturbances of the sixth seal (Rev. 6:12–14).

Second, according to Matthew 24:29, the cosmic disturbances of that verse will take place immediately after the Great Tribulation but shortly before Christ's Second Coming of Matthew 24:30. The Pre-Wrath view believes the cosmic disturbances of the sixth seal will cut short or end the Great Tribulation (Van Kampen, *The Sign,* pp. 258–59, 264, 295). In light of this belief, the Pre-Wrath view reasons as follows. Because the cosmic disturbances of Matthew 24 will take place immediately after the Great Tribulation but shortly before Christ's Second Coming of Matthew 24:30, and because the cosmic disturbances of the sixth seal will cut short or end the Great Tribulation, then the cosmic disturbances of Matthew 24 and the sixth seal must be the same, and, therefore, the Second Coming of Christ of Matthew 24:30 must take place shortly after the cosmic disturbances of the sixth seal (Rev. 6:12–14).

## Critique

This Pre-Wrath view teaching that the Second Coming of Christ will take place shortly after the cosmic disturbances of the sixth seal is based on two questionable beliefs.

1. It is based on the belief that the Great Tribulation will not last to the end of the seventieth week because it will be cut short by the sixth seal with its cosmic disturbances part way through the second half of the seventieth week. But in an earlier chapter, we saw biblical evidence to the effect that the Great Tribulation will last to the end of the seventieth week.
2. It is based on the belief that the cosmic disturbances of Matthew 24:29 are those associated with the sixth seal in Revelation 6:12–14 (Rosenthal, *Pre-Wrath Rapture*, p. 110). That belief presents several problems.

The first problem with that belief is that the cosmic disturbances of Matthew 24:29 will take place "after" the Great Tribulation. In other words, they will not begin until after the Great Tribulation has ended. This point means, therefore, that the cosmic disturbances of Matthew 24 will not cut short or end the Great Tribulation. For the cosmic disturbances of Matthew 24:29 to cut short or end the Great Tribulation, the Great Tribulation would have to continue until those cosmic disturbances began.

By contrast, the Pre-Wrath view teaches that the cosmic disturbances of the sixth seal will cut short or end the Great Tribulation. In light of this contrast, how can the cosmic disturbances of Matthew 24:29 be those associated with the sixth seal of Revelation 6:12–14? To nullify this contrast, the Pre-Wrath view changes the wording of Matthew 24:29 by stating that its cosmic disturbances "will occur *after* the tribulation—or more correctly, *when* the tribulation is cut short" (Van Kampen, *The Sign*, p. 259). It has to change the wording of the biblical text to make the disturbances of Matthew 24:29 correspond with its view of the sixth seal disturbances.

The second problem with the Pre-Wrath view belief is that Revelation 6:12–17 indicates that, in response to the cosmic disturbances of the sixth seal, people of all classes will flee in terror to hide in the dens and rocks of the mountains and will plead with the rocks and mountains to fall on them. By contrast, Matthew 24 does not indicate that response to its cosmic disturbances.

The third problem with the Pre-Wrath view belief is the fact that the cosmic disturbances of the sixth seal are not the only cosmic disturbances foretold in the Bible. More cosmic disturbances will occur after those of the sixth seal in Revelation 6. A third of the sun, moon, and stars will be darkened at the fourth trumpet judgment (Rev. 8:12). The sun will be darkened by smoke from the abyss at the fifth trumpet (9:1–2). The sun will scorch people on the earth with fire and fierce heat when the fourth bowl will be poured out (16:8–9).

In addition, the Scriptures indicate that the sun, moon and stars will be darkened once the armies of the Gentile nations will have gathered together in Israel to wage war (Joel 3:1–2, 9–15). The Pre-Wrath view calls this Joel 3 gathering of the armies "the Jehoshaphat Campaign" and claims that this campaign will happen just before the cosmic disturbances of the sixth seal (Van Kampen, *The Sign*, pp. 258, 262). It thereby equates the cosmic disturbances of Joel 3 with those of the sixth seal and indicates that this warfare will take place before the Second Coming of Christ (ibid., p. 263). The Pre-Wrath view identifies this Joel 3 campaign with the battling of the armies of all nations against Jerusalem described in Zechariah 14:2 (ibid., p. 262).

This identification of the Joel 3 campaign with the Zechariah

14:2 battling against Jerusalem poses a problem for the Pre-Wrath view's equating of the Joel 3 cosmic disturbances with those of the sixth seal. Zechariah 14:3 indicates that Christ will return in His Second Coming to fight against these armed forces while they are in the process of attacking Jerusalem. Thus, Zechariah 14:2–3 reveals that the armies (including the commanders and soldiers) of all of the Gentile nations of the world will be on the field of battle against Jerusalem when Christ returns in His Second Coming.

Because the Pre-Wrath view teaches that Christ will not come until *after* the cosmic disturbances of the sixth seal, this would mean that, although the Joel 3 campaign would begin *before* those cosmic disturbances, it would still be going on *after* them when Christ returns in His Second coming; otherwise, no forces would exist against which He would fight.

This position conflicts, however, with the fact that, in response to the cosmic disturbances of the sixth seal, the military commanders and soldiers of the world will hide in the dens and rocks of the mountains in terror (Rev. 6:12–16). According to the Pre-Wrath view, that is where they will be when Christ will return in His Second Coming after the sixth seal disturbances.

We should note, then, the following contrast: The military commanders and soldiers of the Joel 3–Zechariah 14 campaign will be on the field of battle against Jerusalem when Christ will return in His Second Coming *after* the cosmic disturbances of Joel 3. But the military commanders and soldiers of Revelation 6:12–16 will be hiding in terror in the mountains *after* the cosmic disturbances of the sixth seal.

In light of this contrast, we can conclude that the cosmic disturbances of Joel 3 are not the cosmic disturbances of the sixth seal of Revelation 6. This fact means, then, that another future disturbance of the sun, moon, and stars will occur in addition to the disturbance of the sun, moon, and stars of the sixth seal. It also means that the Matthew 24:29 cosmic disturbances could be the Joel 3 cosmic disturbances, not the sixth seal disturbances.

# COSMIC DISTURBANCES
## OF THE 70TH WEEK

Beginning of
70th Week

7 Seals

6th Seal Cosmic Disturbances

70th Week

7 Trumpets

4th Trumpet Cosmic Disturbances

5th Trumpet Cosmic Disturbances

7 Bowls

4th Bowl

End of
70th Week

Joel 3 Cosmic Disturbances

NARROW DAY OF THE LORD

## The End of the Age

### Pre-Wrath View

The Pre-Wrath view teaches that the end of the age is the same phenomenon as the Day of the Lord. Thus, it will start at the beginning of Christ's Second Coming after the cosmic disturbances of the sixth seal (Rev. 6:12–16) and will end at the Battle of Armageddon thirty days after the end of the seventieth week. This view means that the end of the age will include the seven trumpet and seven bowl judgments (Van Kampen, *The Sign,* pp. 282, 423).

### Critique

This teaching of the Pre-Wrath view indicates that the end of the age will be a period of time consisting of a series of events that will begin between the middle and the end of the seventieth week and will continue through the thirty-day period beyond the end of the seventieth week. In other words, the end of the age will not be a onetime event, the conclusion of the current pre-messianic age, at a specific point in time. This teaching poses several problems.

First, we noted earlier that the construction of the disciples' question in Matthew 24:3 indicated that the Second Coming and the end of the age will be the same event with the same sign. In other words, the current pre-messianic age will end, not begin, when Christ will come out of heaven. Thus, the end of the age will be a onetime event at a specific point in time. It will not be an extended period of time.

Second, in Christ's Matthew 24 answer to the disciples' question, He indicated that at His coming that will end the current pre-messianic age, He will return as the Son of Man in the clouds of heaven (Matt. 24:29–30). Christ thereby related His future Matthew 24 coming to Daniel 7:13–14.

Daniel 7:13–14 ascribed the designation "the Son of man" to the Messiah and indicated that, as the Son of Man, the Messiah will use the clouds of heaven as His chariot (cf. Ps. 104:1–3).

Daniel 7:13–14 also revealed that when the Messiah, as the Son of Man, will use the clouds of heaven as His chariot, God will give Him the rule of the whole earth.

Because Christ related His Matthew 24 coming to Daniel 7:13–14, He thereby indicated that His Matthew 24 coming, which will end the current age, will take place at the time portrayed in that Old Testament passage. Because Daniel 7:13–14 portrayed the time when God will give the Messiah, as the Son of Man, the rule of the whole world, this means that Christ's Matthew 24 coming and the end of the current age will take place when God will give Him the rule of the whole world. In other words, the end of the current pre-messianic age will take place at the point in time when God will give Christ the rule of the whole world.

Contrary to this position, the Pre-Wrath view divorces Christ's Matthew 24 coming and the end of the age from Daniel 7:13–14. It teaches that Christ's Matthew 24 coming and the beginning of the end of the age will take place shortly after the cosmic disturbances of the sixth seal (Rosenthal, *Pre-Wrath Rapture,* pp. 110, 153), that the end of the age will end at the Battle of Armageddon (seven trumpet and seven bowl judgments after the Matthew 24 coming [Van Kampen, *The Sign,* pp. 423–24]), but that God will not give Christ the rule of the whole earth (in fulfillment of Daniel 7:13–14) until forty-five days after the end of the age will terminate at the Battle of Armageddon (ibid., pp. 369, 377–79).

Third, Christ signified that His Matthew 24 coming will be with power (v. 30). The Greek word translated "power" was used in statements that express "the hope and longing that God will demonstrate His power in a last great conflict, destroying His enemies" and establishing "His dominion" (Grundmann, *"dunamis,"* in *Theological Dictionary of the New Testament,* 2:295). The fact that Christ used this word to describe His Matthew 24 coming indicates that the purpose of that coming will be to destroy His enemies in a last great conflict (the Battle of Armageddon) and to establish God's theocratic kingdom dominion over the entire earth ( Joel 3:1–2, 9–21; Zeph. 3:8–20; Zech.

12–14; Rev. 16:12–16; 19:11–20:6). Because Christ's Matthew 24 coming will end the current age, this point means that the Battle of Armageddon, the end of the age, and the establishment of the millennial kingdom will all take place in conjunction with His Matthew 24 coming.

Contrary to this position, the Pre-Wrath view teaches the following. The Matthew 24 coming and the beginning of the end of the age will take place shortly after the cosmic disturbances of the sixth seal (Rosenthal, *Pre-Wrath Rapture*, pp. 110, 153), but the end of the age will not end until the Battle of Armageddon (two comings of Christ after the Matthew 24 coming; Van Kampen, *The Sign*, pp. 423–24, and the chart at the end of *The Sign*), and the millennial kingdom will not begin until forty-five days after the end of the age will terminate at Armageddon (ibid., pp. 369, 377–79). To express it another way, the millennial kingdom will not begin until the third coming of Christ after the Matthew 24 coming (ibid., the chart at the end of *The Sign*).

Fourth, Matthew 24:30–31 refers to the coming of the Son of Man "with power and great glory" together with His angels. Matthew 25:31 states, "When the Son of man shall come in his glory, and all the holy angels with him, then shall he sit upon the throne of his glory." The language of these passages makes two facts obvious. First, both of these passages refer to the same coming of Christ. Thus, Matthew 25 is referring to Christ's Matthew 24 coming. Second, Matthew 25:31 picks up chronologically where Matthew 24:30 ends.

In light of these two obvious facts, we can conclude the following. In Matthew 25:31 Christ indicated that His sitting upon a throne to rule the earth in the millennial kingdom will begin in conjunction with His Matthew 24 coming shortly after the end of the Great Tribulation. The fact that the Matthew 25 passage is referring to the time when Christ will begin His rule at the beginning of the Millennium is signified further by His title of King (vv. 34, 40; cf. Zech. 14:9) and the entrance of the righteous into their inheritance of the kingdom (v. 34; cf. Dan. 7:18, 22, 27).

Because the end of the age will take place at the Matthew 24 coming of Christ, and because Christ's rule of the earth and the millennial kingdom will begin in conjunction with His Matthew 24 coming, then Christ's rule of the earth and the millennial kingdom will begin in conjunction with the end of the age.

Contrary to this position, the Pre-Wrath view teaches the following. Matthew 24:30–31 and Matthew 25:31 refer to two different comings of Christ. The Matthew 24 coming will take place shortly after the cosmic disturbances of the sixth seal (Rosenthal, *Pre-Wrath Rapture,* pp. 110, 153), but the Matthew 25 coming will not take place until the beginning of the Millennium, seven trumpets, seven bowls, and an additional forty-five days after the Matthew 24 coming (Van Kampen, *The Sign,* pp. 273, 387–90, and the chart at the end of *The Sign*). The end of the age will begin when the Matthew 24 coming will take place, and it will end forty-five days before the Matthew 25 coming at the beginning of the Millennium (ibid., the chart at the end of *The Sign*). Because the end of the age will end forty-five days before the Millennium will begin, Christ's rule of the earth and the millennial kingdom will not begin in conjunction with the end of the age.

## The End of the Age and Matthew 13:24–43

In Matthew 13:24–30 Christ taught the parable of the tares. He told about a man who sowed good seed (wheat) in his field. Later, his enemy sowed tares among that wheat. As a result, the wheat and the tares sprang up and began to grow together. When the man's servants noticed what had happened, they reported the situation to him and asked if they should go into the field during the growing season and root up the tares from among the wheat. The man replied that they should not do that because, while rooting out the tares, they might also root out the wheat. Instead, they were to let the wheat and the tares grow together throughout the growing season. Then, in the time of harvest, the man would tell the reapers, "Gather ye together first the tares, and bind them in bundles to burn them: but gather the wheat into my barn" (v. 30).

Sometime after Christ taught this parable, His disciples asked Him to interpret it (v. 36). He interpreted it as follows. The man who sowed the good seed (wheat) is the Son of Man (Christ). The field into which the wheat was sown is the world. The wheat represents the children of the kingdom (the righteous). The tares represent the Devil's children (his spiritual brood—the unsaved; see 1 John 3:8–10). Thus, the enemy who sowed the tares in the field is the Devil. The harvest is the end of the world (literally, "the end of the age," the same terms as the disciples used in their question about the end of the age in Matt. 24:3). The reapers are the angels (vv. 37–39).

After Christ identified these elements of the parable, He said,

> As therefore the tares are gathered and burned in the fire; so shall it be in the end of this world. The Son of man shall send forth his angels, and they shall gather out of his kingdom all things that offend, and them which do iniquity; And shall cast them into a furnace of fire: there shall be wailing and gnashing of teeth. Then shall the righteous shine forth as the sun in the kingdom of their Father. (vv. 40–43)

### Pre-Wrath View

The Pre-Wrath view interprets the field into which the wheat and the tares are sown as being the kingdom of heaven. It does this by claiming that the wheat and the tares grow together "within the kingdom of heaven" (Van Kampen, *The Sign*, p. 465) and that Satan plants the tares "in the kingdom of heaven" (ibid., p. 466).

### Critique

This interpretation has three problems. First, Christ did not interpret the field as the kingdom of heaven. Instead, He said,

"The field is the world" (the *kosmos;* v. 38). Thus, the Pre-Wrath view differs with Christ in the interpretation of the field.

Second, statements that Jesus made about the world (the *kosmos*) indicate that He did not equate the world of this current pre-messianic age with the kingdom of heaven. His declaration, "My kingdom is not of this world" (John 18:36) indicates that the kingdom of heaven is not to be identified with the world of the current pre-messianic age. Christ asserted that the world hated Him and that its works were evil (John 7:7). The kingdom of heaven would not hate Christ or be characterized by evil works. He pronounced woe upon the world (Matt. 18:7), but He did not pronounce woe upon the kingdom of heaven. He called Satan "the prince of this world" (John 12:31; 14:30). The Greek word translated "prince" means "ruler" (Arndt and Gingrich, *"archon,"* in *A Greek-English Lexicon of the New Testament,* p. 113). Surely, the Lord would never call Satan the ruler of the kingdom of heaven.

Christ indicated that His believers are physically present *in* the world, but are not *of* the world (John 15:19; 17:11, 14, 16). This fact means that although they are physically present in the world, they are not identified with the world of this current pre-messianic age. Instead, they are identified with the kingdom of heaven. This latter teaching of Christ sheds light on those who are identified as the wheat in the parable of the tares. The fact that Christ calls this "good seed" that He sowed in the "field" (the world) "the children of the kingdom" indicates that although they are physically present in the world, they are identified with the kingdom of heaven, not with the world of this current pre-messianic age. This contrast of identification indicates a contrast between the kingdom of heaven and the world. All of these statements by Christ imply that the kingdom of heaven is not to be equated with the world of the current pre-messianic age.

Third, the parable of the tares portrays Satan, the enemy of Christ, sowing tares in the same field as Christ's wheat with the intention of destroying the wheat. The parable thereby implies that the current pre-messianic age is characterized by warfare between two kingdoms—the kingdom of heaven and the kingdom of Satan (Eph. 6:12; Col. 1:13). It also indicates that the field of battle where the warfare between these two kingdoms is waged is the world of this current age. A field of battle is not the same as the combatants who wage war in that field. Thus, the field of the parable is to be identified with the world of this current pre-messianic age, not with the kingdom of God, one of the kingdoms waging war in that field.

### Pre-Wrath View

In its treatment of the parable of the tares, the Pre-Wrath view presents the following sequence: first, the tares will be separated from the wheat; next, the wheat will be gathered into the barn; and, then, the tares will be burned (Van Kampen, *The Sign*, pp. 465–66). The view, therefore, has the wheat being gathered into the barn *before* the tares are burned. The Pre-Wrath view's interpretation of this sequence is as follows: the righteous (the wheat) will be raptured into heaven (the barn) between the sixth and seventh seals *before* the wicked (the tares) will be burned (*before* they will enter the Day-of-the-Lord wrath) with the breaking of the seventh seal (ibid.).

### Critique

This interpretation has two problems. First, its sequence is based upon a questionable assumption related to one part of the parable. In Matthew 13:30, the householder says, "Gather ye together first the tares, and bind them in bundles to burn them: but gather the wheat into my barn." On the basis of this statement, the Pre-Wrath view assumes that although the tares were to be gathered and bound before the gathering of the wheat into the barn, the tares would not be burned until after the gathering of the wheat into the barn. One difficulty with this assumption is that although the householder's statement indicated that the tares were to be gathered and bound before the gathering of the wheat into the barn, it did not signify when the tares were to be burned in relationship to the gathering of the wheat into the barn.

Another difficulty with the Pre-Wrath view's assumption is that the focus of the householder's statement is upon the different destinies of the wheat and the tares—the tares are to be burned, but the wheat is to be gathered into the barn. The focus is not upon the timing of the burning of the tares in relation to the gathering of the wheat into the barn. The fact that the householder commanded that the tares be gathered first and bound in preparation for burning before he commanded the wheat to be gathered into the barn seems to indicate that his primary focus was upon the destiny of the tares. His primary concern was that the fruit of his enemy's evil activity in his field be eliminated. The fact that Christ's disciples called the parable "the parable of the tares of the field," (v. 36) not the parable of the wheat and the tares, seems to imply that they understood the primary focus and concern to be the destiny and elimination of the tares.

Second, the sequence in Christ's interpretation of the parable of the tares conflicts with that in the Pre-Wrath view's interpretation. In Jesus' interpretation of the householder's statement, the first item He addressed was the judgment destiny of the wicked in the end of this current pre-messianic age. Christ's angels will gather the wicked out of His kingdom and cast them into a furnace of fire (vv. 40–42).

After addressing that matter, Christ said, "Then shall the righteous shine forth as the sun in the kingdom of their Father" (v. 43). The Greek word translated "then" in this latter statement is a time word. It can refer to either an event that takes place *at the same time as* another event in the same context, or to an event that takes place *after* another event in the same context (Arndt and Gingrich, *"tote,"* in *A Greek-English Lexicon of the New Testament,* p. 831). It cannot, however, refer to an event that takes place *before* another event in the same context. This fact conflicts with the Pre-Wrath view's interpretation that the righteous (the wheat) will be raptured into heaven (the barn) *before* the

wicked (the tares) will be burned (*before* they will enter the Day-
of-the-Lord wrath).

### Pre-Wrath View

The Pre-Wrath view equates the burning of the tares with
God's wrathful Day-of-the-Lord judgment upon the wicked on
the earth after the Matthew 24 Second Coming of Christ (Van
Kampen, *The Sign,* pp. 179, 310, 311, 361, 465–66).

### Critique

The Pre-Wrath view is correct when it teaches that God's
wrathful Day-of-the-Lord judgment will come upon the wicked
(the unsaved) on the earth. Revelation 3:10 declares that that
time of judgment will come upon "all the world, to try them
that dwell upon the earth" (cf. Rev. 8:13; 11:10; 16:1; and the
numerous references in Revelation chapters 6–18 to the disas-
trous things upon "the earth"). Thus, Revelation makes clear
that God's Day-of-the-Lord wrath will come upon the wicked
while they are living upon the earth, not while they are located
somewhere else.

The Pre-Wrath view is wrong, however, in equating the burning of the tares with God's Day-of-the-Lord judgment upon the
wicked, and in its teaching that the Day-of-the-Lord judgment
will take place after Christ's Matthew 24 Second Coming. Christ's
interpretation of the burning of the tares (Matt. 13:40–42) poses
a problem for this equation and teaching of the Pre-Wrath view.
It poses a problem for at least two reasons.

First, Christ said that at the end of the current pre-messianic
age, He, as the Son of Man, "shall send forth his angels, and
they shall gather out of his kingdom all things that offend, and
them which do iniquity" (v. 41). Earlier in this chapter, we noted
the following facts: Jesus indicated that His Matthew 24 coming
as the Son of Man in the clouds of heaven with His holy angels
will end the current pre-messianic age (Matt. 24:3, 29–31a) and
will occur when God gives Him the kingdom of the whole world
("the kingdom under the whole heaven," Dan. 7:27) to rule over

as His representative (last Adam) on earth in fulfillment of Daniel 7:13–14. The fact that God will give the kingdom of the whole world to Christ indicates that it is the Father's kingdom. Only the one who owns the kingdom would have the authority to give it to another. But the fact that God the Father will give it to Christ to rule over as His representative signifies that the kingdom thereby also becomes Christ's kingdom while it continues to belong to the Father.

In another chapter, we noted that Christ's second responsibility as mankind's Kinsman-Redeemer is as follows: at His Second Coming, He must evict Satan and all of Satan's forces from the earth and then take tenant possession of the planet. In other words, Christ must rid the earth of Satan and his entire kingdom *before* He restores God's theocratic kingdom rule to it.

In light of these facts, Christ's interpretation of the burning of the tares is significant in that just as the primary focus and concern of the householder in the parable of the tares was the elimination of the fruit (the tares) of his enemy's activity in his field, so Christ's primary focus and concern at His Second Coming at the end of this current pre-messianic age will be the elimination of the fruit (all of the unsaved who are alive on the earth at that time) of His enemy's (Satan's) activity in the world that God the Father has just given Him to rule. Thus, when Christ comes as the Son of Man in the clouds of heaven, He "shall send forth his angels, and they shall gather out of his kingdom" (Matt. 13:41) that He has just received all of the human members of Satan's kingdom. This action will be part of His Kinsman-Redeemer activity of evicting Satan's kingdom from the earth.

We noted earlier that the field in which the unsaved (the tares) are located during the current pre-messianic age is the world that Christ will have as His kingdom at His Second Coming. In light of this fact, when His angels gather all of the unsaved who are alive on the earth "out of his kingdom," they will remove them from the world. Not one human member of Satan's kingdom will be left on the earth to go into the next period of world history after Christ's Matthew 24 Second Coming. This fact conflicts with the Pre-Wrath view, which equates the burning of the tares with God's wrathful Day-of-the-Lord judgment upon the wicked on the earth after Christ's Matthew 24 Second Coming. That view requires that the wicked be left on the earth for a period of time after that coming of Christ.

This view has a second problem. After Christ indicated that His angels will remove the unsaved (the tares) from His kingdom on the earth, He then stated that they "shall cast them into a furnace of fire" (v. 42). The sequence and language of His interpretation implies that this fiery place of judgment is not on the earth. By contrast, the Pre-Wrath view regards it as being on the earth during the Day of the Lord, when the angels of Revelation reap the tares by blowing the seven trumpets and pouring out the seven bowls upon the earth (Van Kampen, *The Sign,* pp. 179, 309–12). Note, however, that in Revelation these angels are blowing trumpets and pouring out bowls upon the people and places where they are, not gathering them out from where they are and then casting them into a furnace of fire as the parable of the tares indicates (Matt. 13:30, 41–42).

### Pre-Wrath View

The Pre-Wrath view teaches that the gathering of the wheat into the barn in the time of harvest in the parable of the tares (v. 30) is a reference to the Rapture of the church from the world before the Day-of-the-Lord wrath will begin (ibid., pp. 290, 465–66). It also teaches that at the Rapture the church will be taken into heaven (ibid., pp. 294–97), thereby equating the barn in the parable with heaven (ibid., p. 489).

### Critique

In His interpretation of the parable, Jesus equated the harvest with the end of the current pre-messianic age (v. 39). Then He indicated one of the results of the end of the age—"Then shall the righteous shine forth as the sun in the kingdom of their Father" (v. 43). Christ thereby signified that, in conjunction with the harvest (the end of the age), the righteous (the wheat) will enter God the Father's kingdom, the kingdom that He will give to Christ at His Matthew 24 Second Coming to establish and rule over on the earth as His representative. Thus, contrary to the Pre-Wrath view, Christ equated the barn in the parable of the tares with the future theocratic kingdom of the Millennium, not with heaven. In addition, contrary to the Pre-Wrath view, He equated the gathering of the wheat into the barn with the entrance of the righteous into the future, earthly theocratic kingdom of the Millennium, not with the Rapture of the church into heaven. After Christ, as the Kinsman-Redeemer, evicts Satan's kingdom (including his unsaved tares) from the earth, Christ will establish God's theocratic kingdom on the earth. All of the righteous (the wheat) who are alive on the earth at the end of the current pre-messianic age will then enter directly into that kingdom.

**Pre-Wrath View**

The Pre-Wrath view divides all of the unsaved in the parable of the tares into two groups—first, counterfeit believers who identify themselves with the church and refuse to worship the beast and receive his mark ("all things that offend," Matt. 13:41), and second, the rest of the unsaved ("them which do iniquity," v. 41). Although the view teaches that both of these groups (all of the unsaved) will be cast into a furnace of fire, it claims that only the first group (the counterfeit believers) are the tares (Van Kampen, *The Sign*, pp. 361, 438–39, 465–66).

**Critique**

This division of all of the unsaved into two groups by the Pre-Wrath view has two problems. First, it requires the conclusion that three kinds of plants were sowed in the field: wheat (the saved), tares (counterfeit believers), and another kind (the rest of the unsaved). By contrast, the parable actually mentions only two kinds of plants: wheat (the saved) and tares (all of the unsaved).

Second, this view has the tares and another group cast into a furnace of fire. The parable has only the tares cast into a furnace.

### Conclusion

Note the important point that in the parable of the tares Christ taught a particular order of events for the people who will be alive on the earth at the time of His Matthew 24 Second Coming. At that time, all of the unsaved (the tares) will be removed from the earth in judgment, but all of the saved (the wheat) will be left on the earth to enter the next period of history, the Millennium.

## The End of the Age and Matthew 13:47–50

In Matthew 13:47–50, Christ taught the parable of the dragnet. He talked about a net that was cast into the sea and gathered every kind of fish. When the net was full, the fishermen drew it to shore, sat down, and separated the good fish and the bad fish. They "gathered the good into vessels, but cast the bad away" (v. 48).

Christ interpreted this parable as follows: "So shall it be at the end of the world: the angels shall come forth, and sever the wicked from among the just, and shall cast them into the furnace of fire: there shall be wailing and gnashing of teeth" (vv. 49–50).

### Pre-Wrath View

The Pre-Wrath view bases its interpretation of this parable on Christ's statement that the fishermen "gathered the good into vessels, but cast the bad away" (v. 48). Because Christ referred to the good being gathered into vessels *before* He referred to the bad being cast away, the Pre-Wrath view concludes that He was teaching the following order: at the time of Christ's Matthew 24 Second Coming at the end of the age, the saved (the good fish) will be raptured to heaven *before* the unsaved (the bad fish) enter God's wrathful Day-of-the-Lord judgment (are cast away; Van Kampen, *The Sign*, pp. 484–85).

## Critique

This interpretation poses several problems. First, its conclusion concerning the order that Christ was teaching is based upon a questionable assumption. Because in the parable Christ referred to the good being gathered into vessels *before* He referred to the bad being cast away, the Pre-Wrath view assumes that He was thereby teaching the chronological order in which the saved and the unsaved will be dealt with in conjunction with His Matthew 24 Second Coming.

Note, however, that although in the parable Christ referred to the good being gathered into vessels *before* He referred to the bad being cast away, He did not use any time words that would indicate a chronological order for the gathering of the good and the casting away of the bad. In light of this lack of time words, the apparent purpose of Jesus' statement was not to present a chronological order, but rather to emphasize the separate destinies of the good and the bad, with particular focus on the destiny of the bad—the good will be kept, but the bad will be cast away.

Christ's interpretation of the parable of the dragnet poses a second problem for the Pre-Wrath view. In its interpretation, the Pre-Wrath view has the saved being raptured to heaven *before* the unsaved enter the Day of the Lord. Thus, according to that view, at Christ's Matthew 24 Second Coming at the end of the age, it is the saved who will be separated from the unsaved by being taken from the earth by rapture to heaven, and the unsaved will be left on the earth to enter the next period of history.

By contrast, in His interpretation, Christ indicated that at the end of the current pre-messianic age (the Greek word translated "world" in v. 49 means "age," just as it did in the parable of the tares), His angels "shall come forth, and sever the wicked from among the just, and shall cast them into the furnace of fire" (vv. 49–50a). The Greek word translated "sever" has the general meaning of "separate, take away," and specifically means "take out" in verse 49 (Arndt and Gingrich, *"aphoridzo,"* in *A Greek-English Lexicon of the New Testament*, p. 126).

We must note three facts from Christ's interpretation. First, it is the unsaved, not the saved, who will be taken out or removed at the end of the age. Second, when the unsaved are taken out, they will be removed "from among" the saved. These two events indicate that the saved will be left when the unsaved are removed. Third, when the unsaved are taken out, they will be cast into the furnace of fire. Thus, their taking out will result in judgment. Therefore, in Christ's interpretation, the order, the means, and the result of separation between the unsaved and the saved are the opposite of the order, the means, and the result in the Pre-Wrath view.

### Conclusion

Through His interpretation of the parable of the dragnet, Christ once again taught a particular order of events for the people who will be alive on the earth at the time of His Matthew 24 Second Coming. It is the same order that He taught through His interpretation of the parable of the tares. At His coming, all of the unsaved will be taken from the earth in judgment, but all of the saved will be left on the earth to enter the next period of history, the Millennium.

## Matthew 24:37–41

Having already talked about His Second Coming at the end of the current pre-messianic age after the Great Tribulation (Matt. 24:3, 21, 29–30), Jesus declared, "But as the days of Noe were, so shall also the coming of the Son of man be" (v. 37). Through that declaration, He indicated that the order of events at His Second Coming will be the same as the order of events in Noah's day. Christ then described the order of events in Noah's days as follows: "For as in the days that were before the flood they were eating and drinking, marrying and giving in marriage, until the day that Noe entered into the ark, and knew not until the flood came, and took them all away" (vv. 38–39a).

At the end of this description of the order of events in Noah's day, Christ said, "so shall also the coming of the Son of man be" (v. 39b). He thereby indicated a second time that the order of events at His Second Coming will be the same as the order of events in Noah's day.

Finally, Christ gave two specific examples of the order of events at His Second Coming: "Then shall two be in the field; the one shall be taken, and the other left. Two women shall be grinding at the mill; the one shall be taken, and the other left" (vv. 40–41). Through these examples, Christ indicated that one of the ways in which the order of events at His Second Coming at the end of the current pre-messianic age will be the same as the order of events in Noah's day is as follows: just as in Noah's day some people were taken at the time of the Flood and others were left, so at Christ's Second Coming, some people will be taken and others will be left.

In light of this comparison between the order of events in Noah's time and the order of events at Christ's Second Coming, we must ask some questions. In Noah's day at the time of the Flood, who are the people who were taken, and who are those who were left? At Christ's Second Coming at the end of the age, who are the people who will be taken, and who are those who will be left?

**Pre-Wrath View**

The Pre-Wrath view presents the following line of reasoning. In Matthew 24:37–41, Christ taught that, at His Second Coming, God will employ the same destiny principle for the saved and the unsaved that He employed for Noah and the unsaved in the days of Noah. It is the principle of God's rescuing His saved people *before* He destroys the unsaved.

Just as God rescued Noah and his family through means of the ark *before* He destroyed the unsaved of Noah's day through the Flood, so at Christ's Second Coming God will rescue the saved through means of their rapture to heaven *before* He destroys the unsaved through the Day-of-the-Lord judgment. In light of this, one can conclude that the people who will be *taken* from the field and the mill at Christ's Second Coming will be

the saved. They will be taken from the earth by rapture before
the Day-of-the-Lord wrath begins.

In addition, just as God *left* the unsaved of Noah's day outside the ark to be *taken* from the earth through the judgment
of the Flood, so at Christ's Second Coming the unsaved will be
*left* on the earth to be *taken* from it through the Day-of-the-Lord
judgment. This prompts the conclusion that the people who
will be *left* in the field and at the mill at Christ's Second Coming will be the unsaved. They will be *left* on the earth after the
Rapture of the saved so as to be *taken* from the earth through
the Day-of-the-Lord judgment (Van Kampen, *The Sign*, pp. 64,
186, 282–84).

**Critique**

This Pre-Wrath view interpretation of Christ's teaching in
Matthew 24:37–41 has five problems. First, that interpretation
is based upon the foundation of the Pre-Wrath view's understanding of such events as the length and nature of the Great
Tribulation and the Day of the Lord, the relationship of the
Great Tribulation to the Day of the Lord, the use of the word
*wrath*, the significance of the seals, the significance of the sixth
seal, the cosmic disturbances, the nature of the Second Coming, the future military campaigns, the number of signs, the
end of the age, and the interpretation of the parables of the
tares and the dragnet. In this critique of the Pre-Wrath Rapture view, we have seen that its understanding of these events
has significant problems. These problems prompt the conclusion that its interpretation of Christ's teaching in Matthew
24:37–41 is based upon a faulty foundation.

Second, Christ's focus in verses 37–39a was upon the pre-
flood practices and destiny of the unsaved people of Noah's
day, not upon the principle of God's rescuing His saved people
*before* He destroys the unsaved. Christ focused His comments
on the following facts: instead of preparing for the coming judgment of the Flood, the unsaved people of Noah's day devoted
their attention to the normal activities of life. Because they did

not know the time that the judgment would come, they were ignorant of the deadline by which they needed to be prepared. As a result, when the judgment came, they had no time to prepare for it. They were caught totally unprepared to escape God's judgment. "The flood came, and *took* them all away" (v. 39, emphasis mine). The Greek word for *all* indicates that not one unsaved person was *left* on the earth to enter the period of history after the Flood. This was the situation or order of events when the Flood came.

Christ did refer to "the day that Noe entered into the ark" (v. 38). But the fact that Christ introduced that reference with the Greek word translated "until" indicates that the purpose of that reference was to identify the time that the unsaved stopped devoting their attention to the normal activities of life. It was not for the purpose of focusing on the destiny of Noah.

After focusing upon the pre-flood practices and the destiny of the unsaved people of Noah's day, Christ said, "so shall also the coming of the Son of man be" (v. 39b), thereby indicating that the situation or order of events at His Second Coming will be the same as it was when the Flood came. Instead of preparing for the coming judgment at Christ's Second Coming, the unsaved people of that time will devote their attention to the normal activities of life. Because they will not know the time when Christ will come with judgment (Matt. 24:36), they will be ignorant of the deadline by which they need to be prepared. As a result, when Christ will come with judgment, they will have no time to prepare for it. They will be caught totally unprepared to escape God's judgment. Christ will come, and all of them will be *taken* away in judgment. Not one unsaved person will be *left* on the earth to enter the next period of history (the Millennium) after Christ's Second Coming. This will be the situation or order of events when Christ will come in His Second Coming at the end of the current pre-messianic age.

In light of what has been seen, one can conclude that the people who will be *taken* from the field and the mill at Christ's Second Coming (vv. 40–41) will be all of the unsaved who are

alive on the earth at that time. They will be taken from the earth
in judgment. By contrast, the Pre-Wrath view teaches that the
people who will be *taken* from the field and the mill at the Second Coming will be all of the saved who are alive on the earth
at that time. They will be taken from the earth by rapture before the Day-of-the-Lord judgment will begin.

Third, the Pre-Wrath view makes the Rapture of the saved
to heaven at the Second Coming of Christ parallel to the rescue of Noah and his family, but the two events are not parallel.
In the Rapture, the saved will be taken from the earth, but in
the rescue of Noah and his family, they were not taken from
the earth. Instead, they were *left* on the earth to go into the
next period of history after the Flood. In light of this fact, one
can conclude that the people who will be *left* in the field and at
the mill at Christ's Second Coming will be all of the saved who
will be alive on the earth at that time. They will be left on the
earth to go into the next period of history, the Millennium.
By contrast, the Pre-Wrath view teaches that the people who
will be *left* in the field and at the mill at Christ's Second Coming will be all of the unsaved who are alive on the earth at
that time. They will be left on the earth after the Rapture of
the saved so as to be taken from the earth through the Day-
of-the-Lord judgment.

Thus, a proper understanding derived from this study of Matthew 24:37–41 is as follows: in that passage, Christ taught that
at His Second Coming all of the unsaved people will be *taken*
from the earth in judgment, and all of the saved will be *left* on
the earth to enter the millennial kingdom.

Fourth, this understanding of the Matthew 24 teaching of
Christ agrees with His interpretations of the parables of the
tares and the dragnet of Matthew 13, which we examined earlier. In that examination, we saw that Christ's interpretations
of those parables conflicted with the Pre-Wrath view's interpretations of them.

Fifth, Luke 17:37 substantiates this understanding of Christ's
Matthew 24 teaching. In Luke 17:26–36, Luke recorded the same

teaching of Christ that Matthew recorded in Matthew 24:37–41. However, in Luke 17:37, Luke recorded something that Matthew did not record—a question that Christ's disciples asked Him after He talked about people being *taken* from the bed, the mill, and the field and other people being *left* at those places at His Second Coming (vv. 34–36). The disciples asked Christ, "Where, Lord?"

Note the important fact that the disciples were not asking, "Where will those who will be *left* be?" It would not have been necessary for them to ask for the location of the people who will be left, for it would have been obvious that they will be left in the same bed, mill, and field where they were before the other people were taken away. Instead, the disciples were asking, "Where will those who will be *taken* be?" They wanted to know where those people will be taken at Christ's Second Coming.

Christ's answer to the disciples' question is *very* significant, because it identifies who will be *taken* from the bed, mill, and field at His Second Coming. He answered, "Wheresoever the body is, thither will the eagles be gathered together" (v. 37). The Greek word translated "eagles" refers to vultures (Arndt and Gingrich, *"aetos,"* in *A Greek-English Lexicon of the New Testament,* p. 19). According to Arndt and Gingrich, in this particular verse, the Greek verb translated "will . . . be gathered together" refers to the gathering "of birds of prey around a dead body" (*"episunago,"* ibid., p. 301).

Christ's answer indicates that those people who will be *taken* from the bed, mill, and field at His Second Coming will be taken into the realm of death. Death will be part of God's judgment upon them, and vultures will eat their dead bodies (cf. Rev. 19:17–18, 21). The fact that the bodies of those who will be *taken* at the Second Coming will be eaten by vultures signifies that those who will be *taken* from the bed, mill, and field will not be church saints *taken* from the earth by rapture, as the Pre-Wrath view claims. When the Rapture takes place, the bodies of church saints will be changed into immortal, resurrection type bodies and transported from the earth to meet Christ in the air (1 Cor.

15:51–53; 1 Thess. 4:13–17). Thus, Christ's answer indicates that the unsaved people are those who will be *taken* from the bed, mill, and field at His Second Coming. They will be taken from the earth in judgment.

## Pre-Wrath View

The Pre-Wrath view rejects the understanding that the Flood taking and the Second Coming taking are the same kind of taking, namely, a taking in judgment. It teaches that the Flood taking (Matt. 24:39) is a taking of the unsaved in judgment, but the Second Coming taking (Matt. 24:40–41) is a taking of the saved to heaven by rapture (Van Kampen, *The Sign*, pp. 282–84, 485). It bases this distinction upon the use of two different Greek verbs for these takings in the biblical text. It draws attention to the fact that the Greek verb translated "took" in the expression "the flood came, and took them all away" (Matt. 24:39) is *airo* and that the Greek verb translated "taken" in the expressions "the one shall be taken" in Matthew 24:40–41 and Luke 17:34–36 (referring to those taken from the bed, mill, and field at the Second Coming) is *paralambano* (ibid., p. 485).

The Pre-Wrath view points out that these two Greek verbs have different meanings, and that Christ used the verb *paralambano* in His John 14:3 promise to come again and receive *(paralambano)* His saved ones to Himself so that they could be where He is. The Pre-Wrath view claims that this was a promise to come and rapture the church (ibid., pp. 283–84, 485). On the basis of these different verbs with different meanings and the fact that Christ used the same verb *(paralambano)* for the Rapture and the taking of people from the bed, mill, and field at His Second Coming, the Pre-Wrath view makes two assumptions. First, the Flood taking and the Second Coming taking are not the same kind of taking. Second, the taking of people from the bed, mill, and field at Christ's Second Coming is the taking of saved people from the earth by rapture. It is not the taking of unsaved people from the earth by judgment (ibid.).

## Critique

This teaching of the Pre-Wrath view is correct on three points. First, it is true that two different Greek verbs are used for the Flood taking and the Second Coming taking. The verb used for the Flood taking is *airo,* and the verb used for the Second Coming taking is *paralambano.*

Second, also true is the fact that these two verbs have different meanings. Arndt and Gingrich signify that although in some passages the verb *airo* is used for lifting up and taking a person or thing along in a positive sense (Matt. 4:6; 11:29), in Matthew 24:39, where it is used for taking away the unsaved by the Flood, it contains "no suggestion of lifting up" and has the negative sense of removal "by force, even by killing" (*"airo,"* in *A Greek-English Lexicon of the New Testament,* p. 24). The verb *airo* sometimes referred to taking by an impersonal agency. Arndt and Gingrich also assert that in Matthew 24:40–41, where *paralambano* refers to the taking of people away from the field and the mill at Christ's Second Coming, that verb means to "take (to oneself), take with or along" (*paralambano,* ibid., pp. 624–25).

Third, that *paralambano* is the verb used in John 14:3 for Christ's taking up or receiving saved people to Himself in the Rapture of the church is correct.

However, the Pre-Wrath proponents should not assume that because two different Greek verbs with different meanings are used for the Flood taking and the Second Coming taking that they are not referring to the same kind of taking, namely, a taking in judgment. The use of two different verbs with different meanings does not require that assumption.

1. The fact that two different verbs with two different meanings are used in Matthew 24:39–41 does not automatically mean that they refer to two different kinds of taking events. The Bible sometimes uses two different words to refer to the same event. For example, in 2 Kings 2, both the Hebrew words *alah* (v. 1) and *laqach* (vv. 3, 5) are used for the same event—the taking up of Elijah into heaven.

2. Note the important fact that the same two verbs, *airo* and *paralambano*, that are used in Matthew 24:39, 40–41, are also used in John 19:15–16 for the same event—the taking of Christ for crucifixion. In the cry of the crowd, "Away with him, away with him, crucify him" (v. 15), the Greek word translated "away" is the verb *airo*. Thus, the crowd literally shouted, "Take, take, crucify him." Verse 16 states that "they took" *(paralambano)* Christ to crucify Him. Because these two verbs are used for the same negative event in John 19:15–16, we are not required to conclude that they are used for two different kinds of taking in Matthew 24:39–41, one negative (judgment) and one positive (the Rapture).

3. The two different verbs with different meanings are used in Matthew 24 for a specific reason. When God judged the unsaved of Noah's day, He used an impersonal agency (flood waters) to administer that judgment. He did not use personal agents to take the unsaved away with them to their place of judgment. In light of this fact, the Bible used the verb *airo*, which sometimes referred to taking by an impersonal agency, for the Flood taking (v. 39).

   By contrast, in Christ's interpretation of the parables of the tares and dragnet (examined earlier in this chapter), He indicated that at His Second Coming at the end of the age, He will send forth His angels to gather to themselves all of the living unsaved to take into judgment (Matt. 13:37–42, 49–50). Because personal agents (angels) will be used to take away the unsaved into judgment, the Bible used the verb *paralambano*, which involves the idea of a personal being or beings taking other persons with them (Matt. 24:40–41).

The Pre-Wrath proponents should not assume that just because the same verb *(paralambano)* appears in Christ's statements concerning the Rapture (John 14:3) and the taking of people from the bed, mill, and field at His Second Coming (Matt.

24:40–41; Luke 17:34–36) that the taking of people from the bed, mill, and field at His Second Coming is the taking of saved people from the earth by rapture. The appearance of that same verb in more than one of Christ's statements does not require the assumption that He was referring to the same event in all of those passages. The verb *paralambano* appears in Christ's statement about an unclean spirit taking seven more wicked spirits with him into a man (Matt. 12:45). It appears again in His statement about a person taking one or two witnesses with him when he confronts a person about a grievance (Matt. 18:16). In neither of these instances is *paralambano* referring to a taking by rapture. In light of the fact that the verb *paralambano* appears in statements of Christ that are totally unrelated to the Rapture, we are not required to assume that its appearance in His statement about people being taken from the bed, mill, and field at His Second Coming is a reference to His taking of saved people from the earth by rapture.

In addition, note that in Matthew 24:40–41 and Luke 17:34–36 Christ did not say that those who will be taken from the bed, mill, and field will be taken by Him. By contrast, in His John 14:3 rapture statement He said, "I will come again, and receive you unto myself."

## The Rapture and the Second Coming

### Pre-Wrath View

The Pre-Wrath view teaches that Christ's Second Coming (the coming described in Matthew 24 and Luke 17) will begin with and on the same day as the Rapture (Rosenthal, *Pre-Wrath Rapture,* p. 219; Van Kampen, *The Sign,* pp. 291, 423, 434).

### Critique

A major problem with this view is the fact that the order of events at the Second Coming will be the reverse of the order of events at the Rapture. At the Rapture, all of the saved living on the earth at that time will be taken from the earth to meet

Christ in the air and be taken to heaven (John 14:2–3; 1 Thess. 4:13–17), and all of the living unsaved will be left on the earth to enter the next period of history. By contrast, our study of the parables of the tares and dragnet, Matthew 24:37–41 and Luke 17:37 indicated that Christ taught the following order of events for His Second Coming: all of the unsaved living on the earth at that time will be taken from the earth in judgment, and all of the living saved will be left on the earth to enter the next period of history, the Millennium. This reverse order prompts the conclusion that the Rapture and the Second Coming of Christ must be two separate events, taking place at two separate, distinct times in the future.

A second problem with this Pre-Wrath view is the fact that neither Matthew 24 nor Luke 17 specifically refers to the Rapture or explicitly states that it will occur at the Second Coming. In fact, no biblical passage explicitly states that.

## Matthew 24:31

In the context of Matthew 24:37–41 (which we have just examined), Christ stated that when He will come in His Second Coming after the Great Tribulation (vv. 30–31), He "shall send his angels with a great sound of a trumpet, and they shall gather together his elect from the four winds, from one end of heaven to the other" (v. 31).

### Pre-Wrath View

The Pre-Wrath view teaching concerning this statement is as follows: the elect in this passage are the believers who make up the church; therefore, this statement concerning Christ's elect being gathered together is a reference to the Rapture of the church. Thus, Christ was teaching that the church will be raptured from the earth to heaven at His Second Coming after the Great Tribulation. This position agrees with the Pre-Wrath view's interpretations of Matthew 24:37–41 and the parables of the tares and dragnet (Van Kampen, *The Sign*, pp. 284, 289–91, 487–89).

## Critique

Contrary to this Pre-Wrath view teaching, every part of Christ's Matthew 24:31 statement is derived from Old Testament passages that relate exclusively to the nation Israel, not to the church. These passages provide significant reasons for concluding that the gathering together of the elect refers not to the Rapture of the church, but to the gathering of Jews who are alive on the earth at Christ's Second Coming after the Great Tribulation.

First, the term *elect* is not used exclusively for church saints in the Bible. Many Old Testament passages reveal that God made the nation of Israel His elect, or chosen, people in contrast with all other nations. For example, concerning Israel's relationship to God, 1 Chronicles 16:13 states, "O ye seed of Israel his servant, ye children of Jacob, his chosen ones." In Isaiah 45:4, God called the nation "Israel mine elect."

In Deuteronomy 7:6, Moses said to the people of Israel, "For thou art an holy people unto the LORD thy God: the LORD thy God hath chosen thee to be a special people unto himself, above all people who are upon the face of the earth."

In light of this and other similar statements in Deuteronomy, Gottfried Quell wrote that Deuteronomy "established the concept of election in the sense of the designation of Israel as the people of God" (*"eklegomai,"* in *Theological Dictionary of the New Testament,* 4:163). He also asserted that with regard to election, "the nations did not experience what Israel experienced" (ibid., p. 164).

Moses told the people of Israel that God's choice of them to be His elect nation was not based on the size of the nation (Deut. 7:7). Instead, God had a twofold basis for that choice. First, because He delighted in Abraham, Isaac, and Jacob, the fathers of the nation Israel, to love them, He chose to make their physical descendants the special objects of His love (Deut. 7:8; 10:15). Second, because God would be faithful to the oath that He had sworn to the fathers of the nation, He chose their physical descendants to be His elect nation (Deut. 7:8). In that oath, God swore that He would keep the Abrahamic covenant in effect with the physical descendants of Abraham, Isaac, and Jacob forever (Exod. 32:13; Luke 1:55, 72–73).

This second basis for God's choice of Israel to be His elect nation emphasizes God's faithfulness to His sworn word. Because God is faithful to His word, He will keep the Abrahamic covenant in effect with the nation of Israel forever. In line with this view, the words of Psalm 105:8–10 are significant: "He hath remembered his covenant for ever, the word which he commanded to a thousand generations. Which covenant he made with Abraham, and his oath unto Isaac; and confirmed the same unto Jacob for a law, and to Israel for an everlasting covenant."

God elected Israel to be the nation with whom He would keep the Abrahamic covenant in effect forever. He swore an oath to keep that covenant in effect with Israel forever. To keep that oath, God must keep Israel as His elect nation forever. Thus, God's faithfulness to His sworn word guarantees Israel's permanent position as God's elect nation.

King David indicated that God's election of Israel for a unique relationship with Himself was not a temporary arrangement. In 2 Samuel 7:23–24, David said, "And what one nation in the earth is like thy people, even like Israel, whom God went to redeem for a people to himself, . . . For thou hast confirmed to thyself thy people Israel to be a people unto thee for ever." David did not qualify the permanence of this unique relationship. He did not say that it would remain in effect as long as the nation did certain things.

Note the important fact that all of these statements identify the entire nation, not just its saved members, as God's "chosen," His "elect."

Second, in Matthew 24:31, Christ talked about His elect being gathered "from the four winds, from one end of heaven to the other." Arndt and Gingrich stated that, in Matthew 24:31, this expression concerning the winds refers to "the four directions, or cardinal points" ("*anemos*," in *A Greek-English Lexicon of the New Testament*, p. 64).

In light of this fact, we should note three other facts from the Old Testament. First, because of Israel's persistent rebellion against God, He declared that He would scatter the Jews "into all the winds" (Ezek. 5:10, 12) or "toward all winds" (Ezek. 17:21). In Zechariah 2:6, God stated that He scattered them "abroad as the four winds of the heaven." Concerning the expression "the four winds" in the Old Testament, J. Barton Payne wrote, "The 'four winds,' *ruhot,* describe the four quarters or four directions of the world (Jer. 49:36; Ezek. 37:9)" (*"riah,"* in *Theological Wordbook of the Old Testament,* 2:836). Thus, in the Old Testament, it had the same meaning as that noted earlier in Matthew 24:31. God did scatter the Jews all over the world.

The second fact to be noted from the Old Testament is that God also declared that in the future Israel would be gathered from the east, west, north, and south, "from the ends of the earth" (Isa. 43:5–7). We should also note that, in the context of this promise, God called Israel His "chosen" (vv. 10, 20).

The third fact to be noted from the Old Testament is that just as Christ indicated that the gathering of His elect from the four directions of the world will take place in conjunction with the sound of a "great trumpet" (the literal translation of the Greek text of Matt. 24:31), so Isaiah 27:13 teaches that the scattered children of Israel will be gathered to their homeland in conjunction with the blowing of "a great trumpet" (NIV; the literal translation of the Hebrew).

Franz Delitzsch stated that this teaching in Isaiah refers to "the still living *disapora*" being "gathered together by the signal of God" (*Biblical Commentary on the Prophecies of Isaiah,* 1:461). Delitzsch also indicated that Assyria and Egypt, referred to in this passage, represent all the lands of exile (ibid.).

Referring to Isaiah 27:13, Gerhard Friedrich wrote that in that future eschatological day, "a great horn shall be blown" and the exiled will be brought back by that signal (*"salpigx,"* in *Theological Dictionary of the New Testament,* 7:84). Friedrich asserted that in conjunction with the blowing of the great trumpet of Isaiah 27:13 "there follows the gathering of Israel and the return of the dispersed to Zion" (ibid., p. 80).

Note the significant fact that Isaiah 27:13, which foretells this future gathering of Israel, is the only specific reference in the Old Testament to a "great" trumpet (Glasson, *The Second Advent*, p. 199).

Although Isaiah 11:11-12 does not refer to a great trumpet, it is parallel to Isaiah 27:13, for it refers to the same gathering of Israel (ibid.; Delitzsch, *Biblical Commentary on the Prophecies of Isaiah*, 1:461). In its context, this passage indicates that when the Messiah (a root of Jesse) comes to rule and transform the world as an "ensign" (a banner), He will gather together the scattered remnant of His people Israel "from the four corners of the earth" (Isa. 11:1, 10-12).

In light of the fact that Isaiah 27:13 and 11:11-12 refer to the same gathering of Israel, Glasson wrote,

> In the O.T. and also in later Jewish writings two things are associated with the gathering of the dispersed: the trumpet and the ensign (or standard). The following prayer still appears in the Jewish Daily Prayer Book: Sound the *great trumpet* for our freedom; lift up the *ensign* to gather our exiles, and gather us from the four corners of the earth. Blessed art thou, O Lord, who gatherest the banished ones of thy people Israel. (*The Second Advent*, pp. 198-99; the prayer quoted from *Authorized Daily Prayer Book of the United Hebrew Congregations of the British Empire*, trans. S. Singer, p. 48)

In their New Year service, in which their prayer is almost identical to this one, Jews quote Isaiah 27:13 and 11:12 (ibid., p. 199).

In the *Apocalypse of Abraham*, an ancient piece of Jewish literature that was written sometime between 200 B.C. and 200 A.D., the following statement was made: "Then will I blow the trumpet from the winds and send forth mine elect . . . he then summons my despised people out of all nations" (ed. G. H. Box, 31:1f.; quoted by Friedrich, *"salpigx,"* in *Theological Dictionary of the New Testament*, 7:84).

The Old Testament passages that we have considered correspond precisely with Christ's statement in Matthew 24:31. This fact indicates that Christ derived His statement from Old Testament passages that relate exclusively to the nation of Israel, not to the church.

Another reason for believing that Matthew 24:31 refers to the gathering of Israel is the fact that its context is Jewish in nature. It refers to the destruction of Israel's second temple in Jerusalem (vv. 1–2), the abomination of desolation that will take place in Israel's future temple in Jerusalem in the middle of the seventieth week (v. 15; cf. Dan. 9:27), the urgency of the inhabitants of Judea fleeing to the mountains when the abomination of desolation takes place (vv. 16–20), and the Sabbath day (v. 20).

In addition, Matthew 25:31–32 refers to another gathering of people at Christ's Second Coming with His angels. This gathering will involve Gentiles, not Jews (the Greek words translated "nations" mean "Gentiles" [Arndt and Gingrich, *"ethnos,"* in *A Greek-English Lexicon of the New Testament,* p. 217]). The context makes clear that all Gentiles (both saved and unsaved) who will be alive on the earth at that time will be gathered. Because the Bible never calls all Gentiles God's "elect," this gathering cannot be the gathering of the Lord's "elect" referred to in Matthew 24:31. It must be a totally separate gathering, even though both gatherings will take place in conjunction with Christ's Second Coming with His angels.

Because the Matthew 24:31 and 25:31–32 gatherings are separate from each other, and because the chapter 25 gathering will involve all Gentiles (both saved and unsaved), then the 24:31 gathering must involve all Jews (both saved and unsaved) who will be alive on the earth at Christ's Second Coming.

**Pre-Wrath View**

The Pre-Wrath view argues against this understanding of Matthew 24:31 by contending that 24:30–31 describes the exact same event as the 1 Thessalonians 4:15–17 Rapture passage.

To demonstrate that this is so, proponents point out the following four parallels between the two passages.

1. Both passages relate events that will transpire at the coming *(parousia)* of Christ (Matt. 24:27, 30–31; 1 Thess. 4:15).
2. Both passages have Christ's coming being announced with a trumpet (Matt. 24:31; 1 Thess. 4:16).
3. Both passages have Christ coming "in the clouds" (Matt. 24:30; 1 Thess. 4:17).
4. The Matthew 24 passage has angels gathering Christ's elect together (v. 31); parallel to this, the 1 Thessalonians 4 passage has the church saints being "caught up together" to meet Christ in the air.

The fact that the expression "caught up together" is in the passive voice implies that other beings will catch up the church saints and take them to Christ. Because Christ taught in the parable of the tares that He will send forth His angels as reapers to gather the wheat (the church saints) into His heavenly barn, one can conclude that Christ's angels are the beings who will catch up the church saints together to meet Christ in the air in fulfillment of the 1 Thessalonians 4 Rapture passage.

On the basis of these parallels, the Pre-Wrath view argues that Matthew 24:30–31 and 1 Thessalonians 4:15–17 are describing the same rapture event. It claims, therefore, that Matthew 24:30–31 is referring to the Rapture of the church, not the future gathering of Israel (Van Kampen, *The Sign*, pp. 284, 289–91, 487, 489).

### Critique

The Pre-Wrath view presents what it perceives to be parallels between Matthew 24:30–31 and 1 Thessalonians 4:15–17. We should note, however, that significant contrasts exist between the two passages.

1. First Thessalonians 4:14 refers to dead saints coming with Christ from heaven when He comes to rapture the church.

Matthew 24:30–31 says nothing about dead saints coming with Christ at His Second Coming when He will send His angels to gather His elect.

2. First Thessalonians 4:16 indicates that when Christ will come to rapture the church, His coming will be accompanied by a shout. Matthew 24:30–31 says nothing about a shout accompanying Christ's Second Coming after the Great Tribulation.

3. First Thessalonians 4:16 indicates that an archangel will be involved with Christ's coming to rapture the church. Matthew 24:30–31 makes no reference to an archangel.

4. First Thessalonians 4:16 teaches that dead believers will be resurrected from the dead when Christ comes to rapture the church. Matthew 24:30–31 is totally silent concerning resurrection of the dead.

5. First Thessalonians 4:17 signifies that believers will be caught up from the earth when Christ comes to rapture the church. Matthew 24:31 refers to the elect being gathered together, but it gives no hint of their being caught up from the earth at Christ's Second Coming.

6. First Thessalonians 4:17 indicates that believers will meet Christ in the air as a result of their being caught up from the earth when He comes to rapture the church. Matthew 24:31 gives no indication of the elect meeting Christ in the air as a result of their being gathered together at His Second Coming.

7. First Thessalonians 4 refers to Christ as "Jesus" (v. 14) and "Lord" (vv. 15–17), but not as "the Son of man," in conjunction with His coming to rapture the church. Matthew 24:30–31 refers to Christ as "the Son of man" but not as "Jesus" and "Lord," in conjunction with the elect being gathered at His Second Coming.

8. Matthew 24:30 refers to "the sign" of the Son of Man appearing in heaven in conjunction with Christ's Second Coming. First Thessalonians 4 makes no reference to His sign in conjunction with His coming to rapture the church.

9. Matthew 24:30 indicates that all the tribes of the earth

will mourn in response to the sign of the Son of Man appearing in heaven in conjunction with Christ's Second Coming. First Thessalonians 4 is totally silent concerning any mourning in conjunction with Christ's coming to rapture the church.

10. Matthew 24:30 states that all of the tribes of the earth "shall see the Son of man coming" in His Second Coming. First Thessalonians 4 says nothing about the tribes of the earth seeing Christ coming when He comes to rapture the church.

11. Matthew 24:31 teaches that Christ will send His angels (plural) to gather His elect in conjunction with His Second Coming. First Thessalonians 4 refers to only one archangel; it contains no reference to a group of angels in conjunction with Christ's coming to rapture the church. This lack of reference to a group of angels in this Rapture passage is interesting in light of the following promise of Christ in the John 14 Rapture passage: "I will come again, and receive [paralambano] you unto myself" (v. 3).

    We noted earlier that the Greek verb *paralambano* means to "take (to oneself), take with or along" (Arndt and Gingrich, *A Greek-English Lexicon of the New Testament,* pp. 624–25). In light of this meaning, Arndt and Gingrich indicate that in John 14:3 Christ promised, "I will take you to myself" (ibid., p. 625). The language of this promise may indicate that Christ Himself, not angels, will perform the action of catching up the church saints to meet Him in the air at the Rapture. Certainly the Lord Himself would have the power necessary to do this apart from angelic agents.

12. Matthew 24:31 refers to the elect being gathered "from [literally "out of"] the four winds, from one end of heaven to the other." First Thessalonians 4 makes no reference to the church saints being gathered "out of the four winds, from one end of heaven to the other."

13. Admittedly, both passages involve a trumpet in conjunc-

tion with Christ's coming, but they do not both have a trumpet announcing Christ's coming, as the Pre-Wrath view claims. First Thessalonians 4:16 has Christ's descent from heaven announced "with the trump of God," but Matthew 24:31 has Christ's angels being sent with the sound of a great trumpet to gather together His elect.

14. Admittedly, both passages refer to clouds in conjunction with Christ's coming, but they do not both have Christ coming "in the clouds," as the Pre-Wrath view claims. Matthew 24:30 has Christ, as the Son of Man, "coming in [literally "on"] the clouds of heaven," but 1 Thessalonians 4:17 has the church saints being caught up "in the clouds" to meet Christ in the air.

In addition to these significant contrasts, one should note that the Pre-Wrath view bases part of its teaching concerning 1 Thessalonians 4:15–17 upon its interpretation of the parable of the tares. It interprets the gathering of the wheat into the barn as a reference to the church's Rapture to heaven. It thereby equates the barn of that parable with heaven. As we noted earlier, Christ equated the barn with the future millennial kingdom, not with heaven.

The contrasts between Matthew 24:30–31 and 1 Thessalonians 4:15–17 and the fact that the Pre-Wrath view bases part of its teaching concerning the Thessalonians passage upon its faulty interpretation of the parable of the tares militate against the following conclusions of the Pre-Wrath view: Matthew 24:30–31 is referring to the same rapture event as is 1 Thessalonians 4:15–17; therefore, Matthew 24:30–31 is referring to the Rapture of the church, not to the future gathering of Israel.

### Pre-Wrath View

The Pre-Wrath view presents another argument against Matthew 24:31 referring to a gathering together of Israel at Christ's Second Coming after the Great Tribulation. It contends that the Greek word *eklektos* (which is translated "elect," and means "chosen out, selected, to be chosen as a recipient of special privilege") is never used for the nation of Israel in the New Testament. Instead, it is used for the church, the collective body of all believers (Jews and Gentiles) in Jesus Christ. Therefore, the gathering of the elect in Matthew 24:31 is a reference to the Rapture of the church at the Second Coming of Christ, not to the gathering of Israel (Rosenthal, "The Great Tribulation," p. 9; Van Kampen, *The Sign,* pp. 489–90).

## Critique

Granted, the Greek word *eklektos,* which is translated "elect," is not used for the nation of Israel in the New Testament. However, the Greek word *ekloge* is translated "election" and means "selection, election, choosing" (Arndt and Gingrich, *"ekloge,"* in *A Greek-English Lexicon of the New Testament,* p. 242). This word is also used in the New Testament for not only Jewish believers in Jesus Christ (Rom. 11:5, 7) but also the nation of Israel (Rom. 11:28).

In Romans 11:28, the apostle Paul wrote the following concerning unbelieving Israel: "As concerning the gospel, they are enemies for your sakes: but as touching the election, they are beloved for the fathers' sakes." Then, in verse 29, Paul told why the nation of Israel continues in God's election even while they are enemies with regard to the gospel: "For the gifts and calling of God are without repentance."

The Greek word translated "without repentance" in Paul's statement means "irrevocable, of something one does not take back" (Arndt and Gingrich, *"ametameletos,"* in *A Greek-English Lexicon of the New Testament,* p. 44).

The statements of several New Testament scholars shed light on the significance of Paul's comments.

Concerning Paul's statement in verse 28, John Murray wrote,

It must be observed that the two clauses refer to relationships of God to Israel that are contemporaneous. Israel are both "enemies" and "beloved" at the same time, enemies as regards the gospel, beloved as regards the election. . . . "The election" in this instance is not the same as that in 11:6, 7. In the latter the election belongs only to the remnant in distinction from the mass who had been rejected and hardened and so denotes the particular election which guarantees the righteousness of faith and salvation. But in this instance Israel as a whole are in view, Israel as alienated from the favour of God by unbelief. The election, therefore, is the election of Israel as a people and corresponds to the "people which he foreknew" in verse 2, the theocratic election. This is made apparent also by the expression "for the fathers' sake." It is another way of saying what had been said in terms of the firstfruit and the root in verse 16. "Beloved" thus means that God has not suspended or rescinded his relation to Israel as his chosen people in terms of the covenants made with the fathers. (*The Epistle to the Romans,* pp. 100–101)

With regard to Paul's statement in verse 29, Murray asserted the following:

"The gifts and the calling of God" have reference to those mentioned in 9:4, 5 as the privileges and prerogatives of Israel. That these "are not repented of" is expressly to the effect that the adoption, the covenants, and the promises in their application to Israel have not been abrogated. The appeal is to the faithfulness of God (cf. 3:3). The veracity of God insures the continuance of that relationship which the covenants with the fathers instituted. (Ibid.)

James M. Stifler said, "Israel in their relation to the Gospel are 'enemies [regarded as such by God] for your sakes.' . . . But Israel in their relation to their own election by God as His people are 'beloved for the fathers' sakes,' Abraham, Isaac, and

Jacob. The election here does not refer to the elect remnant now in the church, but to God's choice of the Jewish nation as His own (Deut. 7:6)" (*The Epistle to the Romans,* p. 197).

Concerning Paul's statement in verse 29, Stifler wrote that the gifts are Israel's "own peculiar possessions, already enumerated (9:4, 5). The 'calling' is the act of God in which He chose them for His people. These gifts and this calling are 'without repentance' on God's part; He will never recall them" (ibid.).

Gottlob Schrenk signified that Paul used the Greek word *ekloge* "for the election of all Israel in the fathers, R. 11:28. . . . Here the reference is not to a part (cf. R. 9:11; 11:5, 7) but to the whole people" (*"ekloge,"* in *Theological Dictionary of the New Testament,* 4:179).

Everett F. Harrison wrote, "Even though under the gospel economy Israelites as such are considered enemies (by God) for the sake of the Gentiles, yet all the time, when viewed from the standpoint of their national election, they are loved of God for the sake of the fathers (cf. v. 16). God's promises are irrevocable and time will prove it" ("Romans," in *The Expositor's Bible Commentary,* 10:124).

Concerning Paul's statement in verse 29, Harrison said, "The gifts of God are doubtless the special privileges of Israel mentioned in 9:4, 5. They bear witness to the reality of the calling—the summons of Israel to a unique place in the purpose of God. By being first in the Greek sentence, the word 'irrevocable' (v. 29) is emphatic" (ibid., p. 125).

Thus, in line with what the Old Testament teaching that we examined earlier indicated, the apostle Paul in the New Testament emphasized that God's calling of Israel to be His elect nation is *irrevocable.* Although the nation is in a state of unbelief with regard to God and His current program, God will never take back that election. Israel is still God's elect nation and will continue to be so forever.

Commenting on this emphasis by Paul, Christian Maurer, using the term "this holiness" to refer to Israel's position as

God's elect nation, wrote, "This holiness, which is grounded in the act of God encompassing the whole existence and history of Israel, cannot be set aside by even the most radical and culpable perversion" (*"rhiza,"* in *Theological Dictionary of the New Testament,* 6:989).

The apostle Peter's comments in Acts 3 support this fact. Peter was speaking to a crowd of men in the temple. He identified his hearers as "ye men of Israel" (v. 12) and declared that they were guilty of having delivered up, denied, and killed God's Son, Jesus (vv. 13–15). Despite this worst of all possible sins against God, Peter indicated that they were still "the children . . . of the covenant which God made with [Israel's] fathers," Abraham, Isaac, and Jacob (v. 25). They were still related to the Abrahamic covenant that associates Israel with God as His elect nation.

## Conclusion

The truths that we have seen concerning Matthew 24:31 prompt the following conclusion: contrary to the claims of the Pre-Wrath view, this verse refers to the gathering of Israel from the whole world in conjunction with the Second Coming of Christ after the Great Tribulation. It does not refer to the Rapture of the church.

We should note two final facts concerning this future gathering of Israel. First, in Ezekiel 20, God foretold that in the future He will gather the people of Israel out of the countries where they are scattered and will bring them into a wilderness, where He will plead with them before they enter the land of Israel (vv. 34–37). Although God will gather all of the people of Israel (the unsaved rebels and transgressors together with the saved) out of the countries where they are scattered, the unsaved will not be allowed to enter the land of Israel. They will be purged "out from among" the nation before it enters the land of Israel (v. 38). As a result, the nation of Israel that will enter the land of Israel at that time will consist totally of saved people.

Apparently, this gathering of all of the people of Israel out of the countries where they are scattered is the gathering of the elect nation of Israel to which Christ referred in Matthew 24:31. Also apparent is that the purging of the unsaved rebels and transgressors from among the nation will be part of the following order of events: the gathering out of Christ's kingdom "all things that offend, and them which do iniquity" of the parable of the tares (Matt. 13:41), the severing of "the wicked from among the just" of the parable of the dragnet (v. 49), and the taking of people from the bed, mill, and field (Matt. 24:40–41; Luke 17:34–36), all at the Second Coming of Christ after the Great Tribulation.

Second, despite the dramatic return of significant numbers of the people of Israel to their ancient homeland since Israel was reestablished there as a nation-state in 1948, only about one-third of all of the Jews in the world were located there by the beginning of the year 2000. Approximately two-thirds of them were still scattered among the nations of the world. This fact means that the greatest gathering of Israel from its scattering is yet future. Apparently, that is the gathering foretold in Ezekiel 20:34–38 and Matthew 24:31.

# CHAPTER SEVEN

# The Great Multitude

## Introduction

Between the breaking of the sixth and seventh seals, the apostle John saw "a great multitude, which no man could number, of all nations, and kindreds, and people, and tongues." This multitude "stood before the throne, and before the Lamb" in heaven. The persons of this multitude were "clothed with white robes" and had "palms in their hands." They "cried with a loud voice, saying, Salvation to our God which sitteth upon the throne, and unto the Lamb" (Rev. 7:9–10).

One of the twenty-four elders in heaven told John that the persons of this multitude "are they which came out of great tribulation, and have washed their robes, and made them white in the blood of the Lamb" (Rev. 7:13–14).

The Greek text indicates that they came out of "the great tribulation." This means that this great multitude consisted of people who were present on the earth during the specific Great Tribulation to which Christ referred in Matthew 24:21. Earlier in our study, we saw that the Great Tribulation will begin in the middle of the future seven-year seventieth week of Daniel 9.

The major issue that we must address in this chapter is whether the Pre-Wrath view's identification of this great multitude is correct.

## The Identification of the Great Multitude

### Pre-Wrath View

The Pre-Wrath view identifies the great multitude as God's elect (the persons of all nations, kindreds, people, and tongues for whom Christ died) who have just been raptured to heaven out of the Great Tribulation between the breaking of the sixth and the seventh seals. It consisted of the church saints who were alive on earth at the time of the Rapture and "the dead in Christ" (the Old Testament and church saints who had died before the Rapture; Van Kampen, *The Sign*, pp. 295–301, 391).

One of the arguments the Pre-Wrath view uses to support its conclusion that the great multitude has been raptured to heaven is as follows. In heaven, the persons of the multitude *stood* before God's throne, *wore* white robes, and *held* palms in their hands (Rev. 7:9). This description indicates that they had resurrection bodies in contrast to the bodiless souls of the martyred saints of the fifth seal (Rev. 6:9). Because no believers will have a resurrection body in heaven before the Rapture, and because John did not see the great multitude in heaven until after the sixth seal was broken, one must conclude that the great multitude consisted of the church saints and the Old Testament saints who have just been resurrected and raptured to heaven after the breaking of the sixth seal (ibid., pp. 296–98).

### Critique

This argument of the Pre-Wrath view is based upon a questionable assumption—that because the persons of the great multitude stood, wore robes, and held palms in their hands they must be in heaven with resurrection bodies. For several reasons, the fact that these things were true of them does not prove that they had literal, physical, resurrection bodies.

First, when Christ broke the fifth seal, John saw under the altar in heaven the (souls) of saints who had been slain for the Word of God and their testimony (Rev. 6:9). Because they had been slain, they were without physical bodies, and yet they were given white robes to wear (v. 11). Thus, in Revelation the wearing of a white robe in heaven did not require a resurrection body; even bodiless souls could wear such a robe.

Second, when the rich man of Luke 16 died, his body was buried (v. 22) and his soul went to hell (v. 23). Although his soul was without a physical body, Christ ascribed eyes (v. 23) and a tongue (v. 24) to his bodiless soul.

Third, angels are spirit beings by nature (Eph. 6:12; Heb. 1:14). As a result, by nature they do not have physical bodies. (In Ephesians 6:12, the apostle Paul put angels in a different category from those beings who have flesh and blood bodies; in Luke 24:39, Christ stated that a spirit does not have flesh and bones such as He had in His resurrection body.) Despite the fact that angels do not have physical bodies by nature, the Bible ascribes to them wings, faces, feet, and hands (Isa. 6:2, 6; Rev. 10:1–2, 5, 8, 10) and portrays them wearing clothing (Matt. 28:2–3; Mark 16:5; Acts 1:10; Rev. 15:6). Furthermore, in the same heavenly scene in which the persons of the great multitude "stood" before God's throne (Rev. 7:9), all of the angels "stood" around that throne (v. 11). Note the interesting fact that, in both instances, the word translated "stood" is derived from the same Greek verb. Because the angels could stand there without physical bodies, we are not required to conclude that the persons of the great multitude had to have physical resurrection bodies to stand there.

Fourth, God is a Spirit (John 4:24). As a result, He by nature does not have a physical body. Nevertheless, the Bible ascribes to Him a head and hair (Dan. 7:9), eyes and a face (Jer. 16:17), an arm (Isa. 40:10), hands (Heb. 10:31), feet (Nah. 1:3), and a finger (Deut. 9:10), and portrays Him wearing clothing (Dan. 7:9).

All four of these reasons indicate the same truth: although the Bible ascribes such things as hands, feet, faces, tongues, the wearing of clothing, and the act of standing to human, angelic, and divine beings, that fact does not mean that those beings have literal, physical bodies such as resurrected human beings have. Because this conclusion is true, the fact that the persons of the great multitude of Revelation 7 stood, wore robes, and held palms in their hands does not require the conclusion that they were in heaven with literal, physical resurrection bodies.

## Pre-Wrath View

The Pre-Wrath view teaches that the great multitude (the church and the Old Testament saints) did not include the martyred saints whose souls John saw under the altar in heaven when Christ broke the fifth seal. As a result, those martyred saints were neither resurrected nor raptured with the church and the Old Testament saints between the sixth and seventh seals. They were the martyred saints referred to in Revelation 20:4, who "had not worshipped the beast, neither his image, neither had received his mark upon their foreheads, or in their hands," and who "were beheaded for the witness of Jesus, and for the word of God." These saints, who were martyred during the Great Tribulation, will not be resurrected until the first day of the Millennium (Van Kampen, *The Sign*, pp. 296–98, 502).

## Critique

We should note four facts concerning this Pre-Wrath view distinction between the great multitude (the church and the Old Testament saints) and the saints who were martyred during the Great Tribulation.

First, the Pre-Wrath view must maintain this distinction between the great multitude and the saints who were martyred during the Great Tribulation for its view—that the great multitude is the church and the Old testament saints who have just been resurrected and raptured to heaven after the breaking of the sixth seal—to be correct. Because one of the twenty-four elders told John that the great multitude consisted of persons who come out of the Great Tribulation (Rev. 7:14), the Pre-Wrath view cannot have the great multitude come out of the Great Tribulation to heaven by martyrdom instead of by resurrection and rapture.

If the persons of the great multitude were to come out of

the Great Tribulation to heaven by martyrdom, they would do so individually as they were being killed throughout the course of the Great Tribulation, and they would enter heaven as souls without a literal physical body. By contrast, the Pre-Wrath view requires that the persons of the great multitude leave the earth and enter heaven together as one group at one point in time and with resurrection bodies because that is what will happen at the Rapture.

Second, the Pre-Wrath view indicates that the great multitude consisted of *God's elect* for whom Christ died (Van Kampen, *The Sign*, p. 295), including Old Testament and New Testament saints who died before the Rapture of the church (ibid., pp. 299–301). It also refers to the fifth seal saints, whom it claims died by martyrdom during the Great Tribulation before the Rapture as *"God's faithful elect"* (ibid., pp. 463–64). But it asserts that those martyrs were not part of the great multitude that is resurrected and raptured to heaven after the breaking of the sixth seal. Instead, they do not get resurrected until the first day of the Millennium (ibid., pp. 296–98). This position presents the Pre-Wrath proponents with a problem concerning the identification of the great multitude. If the great multitude included *God's elect* who died before the Rapture, and if the fifth seal Great Tribulation martyrs were *God's elect* who died before the Rapture, then the great multitude should include the fifth seal Great Tribulation martyrs. That this is a problem is seen from the fact that the Pre-Wrath view acknowledges that it does not know the reason for this distinction (ibid., p. 392).

Third, biblical revelation concerning the nature and membership of the church indicates that all persons who come to a saving knowledge of Christ while the church is on the earth belong to the church and its destiny. In light of this fact, because the destiny of the church includes the Rapture, all persons who come to a saving knowledge of Christ while the church is on the earth will go to heaven in the Rapture. Contrary to this position, the Pre-Wrath view has its fifth seal martyrs saved and martyred while the church is on the earth, but it teaches

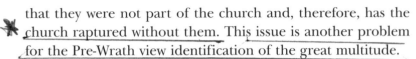

that they were not part of the church and, therefore, has the church raptured without them. This issue is another problem for the Pre-Wrath view identification of the great multitude.

Fourth, that the Pre-Wrath view equates its fifth seal martyrs (Rev. 6:9) with the martyrs of Revelation 20:4 is questionable. Granted, in both passages the martyrs were slain for their witness and for the Word of God (the same Greek word is translated "testimony" in 6:9 and "witness" in 20:4), but also true is that some additional comments are said about the martyrs of 20:4 that are not said about those of 6:9. First, 20:4 specifically states that its martyrs were beheaded. In contrast, 6:9 does not identify the method(s) of execution used for its martyrs. It simply states that they "were slain." Second, 20:4 describes its martyrs as those "which had not worshipped the beast, neither his image, neither had received his mark upon their foreheads, or in their hands." In contrast, 6:9 says nothing to this effect concerning its martyrs.

These two contrasts have significance in light of two other factors. First, earlier in this study, we saw the Pre-Wrath view's teaching that the breaking of the fifth seal begins both the Great Tribulation and the martyrdom of believers in the middle of the seventieth week, but we also saw that that teaching is erroneous. When Christ broke the fifth seal, John did not see believers being martyred. Instead, he saw in heaven the disembodied souls of believers who already had been slain during the first four seals (Rev. 6:9). Thus, the martyrs of Revelation 6:9 were killed before the Great Tribulation began, before the beast and his image began to be worshiped, and before the beast's mark began to be placed on the foreheads or hands of people. In contrast, Revelation 20:4 indicates that its martyrs were killed during the Great Tribulation, when people were worshiping the beast and his image and receiving his mark.

Second, in Revelation 6:11, God informed the Revelation 6:9 martyrs that they were not the total number of believers who were to be killed. More believers were to be martyred beyond the time that God stated this. The fact that God stated this in conjunction with the fifth seal implied that more believers would be martyred beyond the fifth seal.

In light of these two items, this critique concludes that the two additional comments about the Revelation 20:4 martyrs in contrast with the Revelation 6:9 martyrs signify the following: contrary to the Pre-Wrath view, the martyrs of Revelation 20:4 are not to be equated with those of Revelation 6:9. The martyrs of Revelation 6:9 were killed during the first four seals within the first half of the seventieth week, before the Great Tribulation, the worship of the beast and his image, and the placing of his mark on people began. In contrast, the martyrs of Revelation 20:4 were killed after the fifth seal during the Great Tribulation in the second half of the seventieth week, when people were worshiping the beast and his image and receiving his mark. They were the additional believers whom God said in Revelation 6:11 were to be killed. This distinction poses another problem for the Pre-Wrath view identification of the great multitude because, as we noted earlier, it cannot have the great multitude consisting of people who come out of the Great Tribulation to heaven by martyrdom instead of by rapture.

### Pre-Wrath View

In light of the elder's statement that the great multitude came out of the Great Tribulation (Rev. 7:14), the Pre-Wrath view declares that the great multitude came "out from within" the Great Tribulation (Van Kampen, *The Sign*, p. 492).

### Critique

In light of that declaration, the Pre-Wrath view has three problems. First, that declaration implies that all of the persons of the great multitude were living on the earth during the Great Tribulation. It rules out that the great multitude could include within itself people who lived and died before the Great Tribulation began and who, therefore, were never in the Great Tribulation. That declaration thereby conflicts with the Pre-Wrath view teaching that the great multitude included Old Testament saints and church saints who died before the Rapture took them to heaven. All of the Old Testament saints and many of the church saints who died before the Rapture would have died before the Great Tribulation began and, therefore, would never have been in the Great Tribulation.

Second, closely related to this first problem is another. If the great multitude includes the church saints that just came "out from within" the Great Tribulation by means of the Rapture, as the Pre-Wrath view teaches, then one must conclude that this was only a partial rapture of the church. It would include only those church saints who had lived on the earth during the Great Tribulation. It would not include the church saints who had lived and died before the Great Tribulation began and who, therefore, were never in the Great Tribulation. In contrast, the Bible teaches that when the Rapture takes place, the entire church will be taken from the earth to heaven.

Third, the Pre-Wrath view contradicts itself concerning when the Rapture will take place and, therefore, when the great multitude will be taken from the earth to heaven. On the one hand, in line with its declaration that the great multitude came "out from within" the Great Tribulation by means of the Rapture, it asserts that the Rapture will take place *during* the Great Tribulation (Van Kampen, *The Sign,* pp. 299, 301). On the other hand, because the Pre-Wrath view teaches that the Rapture and the Second Coming of Christ will take place at the same time (ibid., pp. 291, 423), and because Christ taught that His Second Coming will take place *after* the Great Tribulation (Matt. 24:21, 29–30), the Pre-Wrath view states that the Rapture will take place *after* the Great Tribulation (ibid., pp. 259, 293, 295).

**Pre-Wrath View**

The Pre-Wrath view claims that Revelation 7 seems to indicate that the great multitude arrived in heaven suddenly as a complete group, all at one point in time, as would be true if it came there by means of the Rapture. It did not arrive there progressively over a period of time, as would be true if it came there through martyrdom during the course of the Great Tribulation (ibid., pp. 295, 490).

This view asserts that the Greek present tense participle translated "came" in the elder's statement "These are they which came out of the great tribulation" (Rev. 7:14) does not signify action that continues over a period of time. It offers the following support for that assertion. First, the context of the present tense participle determines whether it should be translated "come" (which does not signify continuing action) or "are coming" (which does signify continuing action). The context of the elder's statement in Revelation 7:14 does not permit the translation that signifies continuing action. Thus, the elder was not saying that the great multitude was in the process of increasing in number through means of martyrdom (ibid., p. 491).

Second, the Pre-Wrath view claims that, over the course of several centuries, all reputable translators and groups of translators have rendered the present tense participle in Revelation 7:14 as "come," "came," or "have come" but not as "coming." In contrast with those reputable translators, a few individual twentieth-century translators, without the counsel of a group of qualified scholars, have rendered the participle as "coming." But many of them were allowing their bias in favor of the pretribulation Rapture view, not the biblical context, to determine their translation (ibid., 491).

Third, the Pre-Wrath view quotes, as support for its view concerning the present tense participle in Revelation 7:14, statements from the unpublished *Exegetical Digest of Revelation 4–7* by Robert L. Thomas (Van Kampen, *The Sign*, p. 491)

### Critique

We should note several points concerning the Pre-Wrath view treatment of the present tense participle in the elder's Revelation 7:14 statement. First, its quotation of statements from the *Exegetical Digest of Revelation 4–7* by Robert L. Thomas gives the impression that Dr. Thomas agrees with its view that the context of Revelation 7:14 does not permit the translation that signifies continuing action. However, in his exegetical commentary, *Revelation 1–7,* which was published later than the first book advocating the Pre-Wrath view, Dr. Thomas clearly indicated that he disagreed with the Pre-Wrath view on this issue.

Contrary to that view, Dr. Thomas gave reasons for concluding that the present tense participle in Revelation 7:14 does express continuing action in that context. Concerning the elder's statement in that verse, he said, "The usual force of the present tense is to portray continuous action. The Semitic-style construction of the statement favors allowing this sense here" (*Revelation 1–7,* p. 495). Concerning the relationship of the present tense participle to verbs in the context, he wrote, "The participle's parallelism with the finite verbs serves to emphasize the durative force of its present tense: 'those who are in the process of coming'" (ibid., p. 496). Regarding the tense of the verb in the elder's Revelation 7:13 question "whence came they?" concerning the great multitude, Dr. Thomas stated that it "does not necessarily imply that their number is complete and negate the idea that they are still arriving" (ibid.). He indicated that the verbs in the verse 14 expressions "have washed their robes" and "made them white" do not "negate the durative notion of the participle" (ibid.). Then he said, "The present participle gives the impression that the persecution of the saints will be a prolonged process that from John's standpoint was partly past and partly future (cf. 6:9–11)" (ibid.).

Finally, Dr. Thomas specifically declared that the Pre-Wrath view of the great multitude's departure out of the Great Tribulation "can be dismissed because it neglects the ongoing nature of the departure indicated by the present participle *erchomenoi* and rests on an unwarranted distinction between the Great Tribulation and the day of the God's wrath" (ibid., p. 497 n. 119).

Second, the Pre-Wrath view's comments concerning different translators implied that historically all competent, reputable language scholars have rejected the notion that the present tense participle referred to a continuing process of people being martyred over a period of time and the notion that the great multitude consisted of martyrs. Only incompetent language scholars of the twentieth century have proposed those notions. Many of those incompetent scholars proposed them because of a pretribulation Rapture view bias, not because of the biblical text.

Note that this Pre-Wrath view implication is inaccurate. During the twentieth century, a number of competent, reputable language scholars who were not advocates of the pretribulation Rapture view proposed views contrary to what the Pre-Wrath view advocates. For example, Archibald Thomas Robertson, who has been regarded as the premier twentieth-century Greek language scholar of America, wrote that the present tense participle in Revelation 7:14 is a "present middle participle with the idea of continued repetition" (*Word Pictures in the New Testament*, 6:352).

R. H. Charles, another outstanding Greek language scholar of the twentieth century, came to the same conclusion as Robertson. He claimed that the combination of the present tense participle with the two verbs ("washed" and "made") in the same verse (Rev. 7:14) is a Semitic type construction that gives the sense of continuous action to the participle (*The Revelation of St. John*, 1:213). Then, when discussing the continuous action significance of the participle in the elder's statement, Charles said, "The martyrs are *still* arriving from the scene of the Great Tribulation" (ibid.).

Two competent, reputable European language scholars who wrote articles for the *Theological Dictionary of the New Testament* (the most authoritative, exhaustive work on the Greek language of the New Testament published in the twentieth century) expressed views contrary to that advocated by the Pre-Wrath view. Joachim Jeremias concluded that the great multitude of Revelation 7 consisted of martyrs (*"hades,"* 1:149), and Heinrich Schlier wrote, "Rev. 7:14 should also be quoted in this context. The martyrs before the throne of God, whom the divine sees coming out of great tribulation, have also suffered the sufferings

of Christ. They are the host of those who in the tribulation of
the last time have been washed, not in their own blood, but in
the blood of the Lamb" (*"thlibo, thlipsis,"* in *Theological Dictionary of the New Testament*, 3:144).

In response to the elder's question "What are these which
are arrayed in white robes?" (Rev. 7:13), John expressed igno-
rance concerning the identification of the persons in the great
multitude (v. 14). If, as the Pre-Wrath view teaches, the great
multitude included all of the church saints, then it seems strange
that John, as one of the church's apostles and part of its foundation (Eph. 2:20), did not recognize at least some of the persons in the multitude. This factor is especially true in light of
the following considerations. In Revelation 7, John was observ-
ing a preview of something that would take place in the future
beyond his lifetime. If that preview portrayed the great multitude consisting of not only the Old Testament saints but also
all of the church saints, then it also portrayed, as part of the
great multitude, John, the other apostles, and church saints
whom John knew personally during his lifetime because they,
too, were church saints. In light of this fact, if the great multitude were what the Pre-Wrath view says, then surely John would
have recognized himself, the other apostles, and other church
saints in the great multitude. The fact that John did not identify any of the persons in the great multitude implies that it
did not include all of the church saints.

J. A. Seiss wrote the following concerning John's inability to
identify the great multitude:

> If they represent the finally complete Church, did he
> not know that the Church was to be thus exalted and
> glorified? Was he so ignorant of the character and des-
> tiny of that chosen body of which he was an apostle and
> a chief, as not to know it, or whence it came, upon en-
> countering it in heaven? Would it not be a sorry im-
> peachment of his apostolic character and enlightenment,
> besides very stupid and unreasonable, to proceed on

such an assumption, or on anything which involves it? The manifest fact that he was perplexed and in doubt with reference to these palm-bearers, and that the Elder interfered to solve his questionings, proves that they are not the Church proper, but . . . a body of saved ones, with a history and place peculiarly their own, and not as yet exactly understood by the apostle. (*The Apocalypse*, pp. 172–73)

## Conclusion

In light of the problems associated with the Pre-Wrath view identification of the great multitude in Revelation 7, one can conclude that its identification is wrong. The great multitude did not consist of the Old Testament saints and the church saints who had just been raptured to heaven between the sixth and seventh seals.

# CHAPTER EIGHT

# The Day of the Lord

## Introduction

In earlier chapters of this critique, we observed several of the Pre-Wrath view teachings concerning the Day of the Lord and noted problems associated with those teachings. This chapter will focus on more of its teachings on the same subject. But to understand better the issues involved, we must first look at the significance of the Day of the Lord.

## The Significance of the Day of the Lord

The Bible teaches that God created the universe for His own sovereign purposes (Rev. 4:11). As a result, the heavenly and earthly realms are owned and ruled by God (1 Chron. 29:11–12; 2 Chron. 20:6; Pss. 47:2; 103:19; 135:6; Isa. 40:12–26; Jer. 10:7, 10; Dan. 4:17, 34–35, 37; Acts 17:24; 1 Tim. 1:17; Rev. 5:13). As the owner and ruler of the earth, God has His own sovereign purpose for world history and, therefore, for specific events within that history (Isa. 14:24–27; 19:12; 23:9; 46:8–11; Jer. 4:28; 23:20; 26:3; 30:24; 36:3; 49:20; 50:45; 51:29; Lam. 2:8; Rom. 8:28; 9:11, 17; Eph. 1:9–11; 3:10–11; 2 Tim. 1:9; 1 John 3:8).

In the Bible, the expression "the Day of the Lord" (together with other synonymous expressions, such as "that day," "the day of God," etc.) is strongly related to God's rule of the earth and, therefore, to His sovereign purpose for world history and specific events within that history. The Day of the Lord refers to God's special interventions into the course of world events to judge His enemies, accomplish His purpose for history, and thereby demonstrate who He is—the sovereign God of the universe (Isa. 2:10-22; Ezek. 13:5, 9, 14, 21, 23; 30:3, 8, 19, 25-26).

Several scholars have recognized this significance of the Day of the Lord. For example, John A. T. Robinson stated, "In itself, 'the Day of the Lord' is a general and comprehensive expression for the consummation of God's purpose, alike in victory and in judgment" (*Jesus and His Coming,* p. 19).

A. B. Davidson wrote, "It is a day that is a special time; and it is the Day of the Lord, belongs to Him, is His time for working, for manifesting Himself, for displaying His character, for performing His work—His strange work upon the earth" (*The Theology of the Old Testament,* pp. 374-75). Again he said, "It is a manifestation of God—of God as what He is truly, and in the whole round of His being. Hence it displays His whole character, and sees His whole purpose effected" (ibid., pp. 378-79).

J. Barton Payne declared, "The comprehensive phrase, by which the Old Testament describes God's intervention in human history for the accomplishment of His testament is *yom Yahwe,* 'the day of Yahweh'" (*The Theology of the Older Testament,* p. 464). And again he stated, "The 'day' is thus characterized by an observable accomplishment of the general aims of divine providence. It refers to that point in history at which the sovereign God lays bare His holy arm on behalf of His testament and of its heirs, whether in a way that is specifically miraculous, or not" (ibid., p. 465).

## The Pre-Wrath View and the Day of the Lord

### Pre-Wrath View

The Pre-Wrath view teaches that only one Day of the Lord is revealed in the Bible. All passages that give information about the Day of the Lord refer to the future time when God will pour out His wrath upon the unrighteous on earth and upon Antichrist's domain (Van Kampen, *The Sign,* pp. 494–95). The Old Testament prophets knew nothing about more than one distinct Day of the Lord (Rosenthal, *Pre-Wrath Rapture,* p. 129).

## Critique

The Bible definitely foretells a future Day of the Lord when God's wrath will be poured out upon the unrighteous and Antichrist's domain. For example, Isaiah 2:10–22 describes a Day of the Lord that will involve the sixth seal of the future seventieth week of Daniel 9 (Rev. 6:12–17). In addition, the apostle Paul in 1 Thessalonians 5:1–11 referred to a Day of the Lord that was future beyond his time and that would bring sudden, inescapable destruction upon the unsaved of the world. Nothing of its nature has taken place yet, so we must conclude that it is still future.

Despite these references to a future Day of the Lord, and in contrast with the Pre-Wrath view teaching, the Bible indicates that several Days of the Lord have existed in the past in which God demonstrated His sovereign rule by raising up several nations to execute His judgment on other nations. For example, He raised up Babylon to judge the southern kingdom of Judah during the 600s and 500s B.C. (Lam. 1:2; 2:1, 21–22; Ezek. 7:19; 13:5; Zeph. 2:2–3), Babylon to judge Egypt and its allies during the 500s B.C. (Jer. 46:10; Ezek. 30:3), and Medo-Persia to judge Babylon during the 500s B.C. (Isa. 13:6, 9). Concerning Jerusalem's destruction by Babylon in 586 B.C., Gerhard Von Rad wrote, "The overthrow of Jerusalem was a day of Yahweh. It is now past, history rolls on and one can look back upon it" (*"hemera,"* in *Theological Dictionary of the New Testament,* 2:944).

## Pre-Wrath View

According to the Pre-Wrath view, the Day of the Lord is characterized totally by God's wrath against man, not by man's wrath against man (Rosenthal, *Pre-Wrath Rapture,* p. 105).

## Critique

Because God in the past Days of the Lord (which we've just noted) raised up nations to execute His judgment upon other nations, one can conclude that those past Days of the Lord involved human warfare. Several Bible scholars have recognized that this fact was so. For example, Gerhard Von Rad wrote, "The prophets expect the day of Jahweh to bring war in its train" (*Old Testament Theology*, 2:123).

With reference to the judgments associated with the Day of the Lord, A. B. Davidson stated, "Judgment always took place in an external manner, in the form of chastisement at God's hands through His instruments—often in war" (*The Theology of the Old Testament*, p. 374). After indicating that sometimes the Day of the Lord involves a direct miraculous intervention of God, Davidson declared, "But at other times, besides the supernatural gloom and terrors that surround Him when He appears, He is represented as using some fierce, distant nation as the instrument by which He executes His judgment (Is 13, Zeph)" (*A Dictionary of the Bible*, vol. 1, s.v. "eschatology").

Because warfare between nations involves man's wrath against man, one can conclude that past Days of the Lord involved not only God's wrath against man but also man's wrath against man.

### Pre-Wrath View

The Pre-Wrath view claims that, of the various Hebrew words that refer to God's anger or wrath, *ebrah* is by far the strongest, that it is the only word used specifically for God's Day-of-the-Lord wrath, and that, in its context, it is always used for God's Day-of-the-Lord wrath against Gentile nations, not against Israel. The words *chemah, qetseph,* and *charon* are milder words basically referring to discipline but not judgmental wrath (Van Kampen, *The Sign,* p. 464).

### Critique

Two facts conflict with this teaching. First, Old Testament scholar Gerard Van Groningen disagrees with the view that *ebrah* is the strongest of the Hebrew words that refer to God's anger or wrath. He claims that the strongest of these words "probably, are *qesep* which often refers to the Lord's anger, and *hemah* and *haron* both of which refer to a burning and consuming wrath" (*"qesep,"* in *Theological Wordbook of the Old Testament,* 2:808). Note that he is referring to the same three words but with slightly different spellings, which the Pre-Wrath view classifies as the milder words.

Second, the Pre-Wrath view is in error in its claim that in its context the Hebrew word *ebrah* is always used for God's Day-of-the-Lord wrath against Gentile nations, not against Israel. In Ezekiel 7, *ebrah* is used for "the day of the wrath [*ebrah*] of the LORD" (v. 19; cf. vv. 7, 10, 12). In this context, God's wrath is against Israel (vv. 2, 7, 23–24, 26–27). In addition, Zephaniah uses *ebrah* ("wrath," 1:15, 18) for "the great day of the LORD" (1:14) and "the day of the LORD's wrath" (1:18) against all mankind in general (1:2–3), including Judah and Jerusalem (1:4, 10, 12).

Many scholars have recognized the fact that the Bible teaches that both Israel and the Gentiles are subject to God's Day-of-the-Lord wrath. For example, Johannes Fichtner wrote, "The earlier prophets proclaim this judgment not merely on the Gentiles but also on the people of God which has turned aside from Him. In this sense they can speak of the day of Yahweh, the day of wrath, as an eschatological event, Am. 5:18–20; Is. 2:6–21; Zeph. 1:15, 18. For Israel there is no escaping it, except that individuals may be sheltered by timely conversion, Zeph. 2:1–3" (*"orge,"* in *Theological Dictionary of the New Testament,* 5:401, see also pp. 398–99, 403, 438).

**Pre-Wrath View**

The Pre-Wrath view teaches that the Day of the Lord will begin with the breaking of the seventh seal on the same day as the Rapture and will end at the Battle of Armageddon forty-five days before the Millennium will begin (Van Kampen, *The Sign,* pp. 369, 418, 423–24, 435). Thus, the Day of the Lord will not include the Millennium. The total nature of the Day of the

Lord will be characterized by the darkness of terrible divine judgment upon all of the unsaved people of the earth. In contrast with the Millennium, no part of the Day of the Lord will be characterized by blessing. Those who claim that the Day of the Lord will extend through the Millennium have only one Bible verse upon which to base that view. They mistakenly believe that 2 Peter 3:10 (which refers to a future Day of the Lord when "the heavens shall pass away with a great noise, and the elements shall melt with fervent heat, the earth also and the works that are therein shall be burned up") will be fulfilled after the Millennium. In reality, it will be fulfilled before the Millennium through the Day-of-the-Lord trumpet and bowl judgments (Rosenthal, *Pre-Wrath Rapture,* pp. 126–28; Van Kampen, *The Sign,* pp. 392–93).

**Critique**

Contrary to this teaching of the Pre-Wrath view, the Bible indicates that the future Day of the Lord will have at least a twofold nature. First, it will be characterized by darkness and a terrible outpouring of divine wrath upon the world (Joel 2:1–2; Amos 5:18–20; Zeph. 1:14–15; 1 Thess. 5:1–11). Amos 5:18–20 emphasizes that this characterization will be the total nature of the Day of the Lord for God's enemies. It will bring no divine light or blessing to them. Such will be the nature of the Day of the Lord during the seventieth week of Daniel.

Second, the Day of the Lord will also be characterized by light, an outpouring of divine blessing, and the administration of God's rule. The prophet Joel, after talking about the darkening of the sun, moon, and stars and God's Day-of-the-Lord judgment of the armies of the nations gathered in Israel (3:9–16), foretold great divine blessing "in that day" (3:17–21).

In addition, the prophet Zechariah, after discussing the future Day of the Lord, when all nations will war against Jerusalem and the Messiah will come to the earth to fight against the nations (14:1–5), indicated that "that day" will not be characterized totally by either darkness or light; instead, that "one day" will be characterized by both darkness and light. The earlier part of "that day" will be characterized by darkness, and the latter part will be characterized by light (vv. 6–7). In addition, "that day" will be characterized by great blessing (v. 8), and the administration of God's rule over all of the earth (v. 9). Such will be the nature of the Day of the Lord during the Millennium.

Thus, contrary to what the Pre-Wrath view asserts, those who claim that the Day of the Lord will extend through the Millennium have more than one Bible passage upon which to base that view.

Note that numerous scholars have recognized the twofold nature of the Day of the Lord. For example, J. Barton Payne stated that the Day of the Lord involves a twofold pattern of judgment and restoration (*The Theology of the Older Testament*, p. 464).

A. B. Davidson wrote:

> Hence the "Day of the Lord" acquires a double-sided character. It is a day of salvation and judgment, or a day of salvation through judgment . . . a day of salvation behind this. Sometimes one side is prominent and sometimes another . . . Sometimes both sides of the Divine manifestation are brought forward, as in Joel. (*The Theology of the Old Testament*, pp. 377–78)

On the one hand, H. H. Rowley asserted, "This element of judgement [sic] belongs essentially to the thought of the Day of the Lord" ("The Day of the Lord," in *The Faith of Israel*, p. 178). On the other hand, he declared the following:

> From this it follows that in biblical thought the Golden Age has a fundamentally religious basis. It is essentially the Day of the Lord, and what is of importance is that there shall not only be unity of rule, but that all shall be permeated by the spirit of God, so that all life shall reflect his will. It was never conceived in merely eco-

nomic or political terms, but always in moral and spiritual terms, so that it is appropriately thought of as the Kingdom of God, whether the term is found or not. It was the age when peace and justice should be universal amongst men. . . . (Ibid., p. 181)

In all this we should not forget that the Golden Age was always conceived of as the Day of the Lord. . . . All the passages in the Old Testament which present in various ways the vision of the Golden Age, or of the Day of the Lord, are commonly referred to as messianic. . . . (Ibid., p. 187)

It will be seen that all of the elements of the description of the Day of the Lord are to be found here—the universality and permanence of peace, judgment and deliverance, economic bliss, righteous and world-wide dominion. (Ibid., p. 191)

Just as each day of creation and the Jewish day were twofold in nature—a time of darkness ("night") followed by a time of light ("day"; Gen. 1:4–5)—so the future Day of the Lord will be twofold in nature—a period of darkness (divine judgment) followed by a period of light (divine blessing and rule).

As we noted earlier, because the Day of the Lord will demonstrate who God is, for God—who is light and in whom there is no darkness at all (1 John 1:5)—to have His day consist totally of darkness with no period of light—especially considering that the present day of Satan and rebellious mankind is characterized by a rule of darkness (Eph. 6:12; Col. 1:13)—would seem strange.

In addition, because the present day of Satan and rebellious mankind involves their rule of the world system, the future Day of the Lord would not truly be *His* day if it did not involve His rule of the world system during the Millennium. How could the Day of the Lord fully demonstrate who He is—the sovereign

# TWOFOLD NATURE AND TWO PHASES OF THE FUTURE DAY OF THE LORD

THE DAY OF THE LORD

**MILLENNIUM**

light,
divine blessing,
administration of God's rule

1000 years

**70th WEEK**

darkness,
divine wrath

7 years

God of the universe—without the sovereign exercise of His rule in visible form over the entire world? Because it is God's rule, not the rule of Satan and rebellious mankind, that will be administered worldwide throughout the Millennium, that future period of time will not be part of the day of Satan and rebellious mankind. In light of that fact, if the Millennium is not part of the Day of the Lord, then to whose day will the Millennium belong?

## Pre-Wrath View

Malachi 4:5 declares, "Behold, I will send you Elijah the prophet before the coming of the great and dreadful day of the LORD." On the basis of this biblical declaration, the Pre-Wrath view develops the following argument. The book of Revelation foretells the powerful ministry of two unique witnesses (Rev. 11:1–12). Most likely, one of those two witnesses will be the reincarnated Elijah, whom God will send to earth to minister during the second half of the seventieth week of Daniel. Malachi 4:5 indicates that Elijah will be sent before the beginning of the Day of the Lord (Van Kampen, *The Sign*, pp. 231, 442). Because the two witnesses will not be sent until the second half of the seventieth week of Daniel, and because one of those witnesses (Elijah) will be sent before the beginning of the Day of the Lord, then one can conclude that the Day of the Lord will not begin until sometime during the second half of the seventieth week of Daniel (ibid., p. 424). The Day of the Lord will not start at the beginning of the seventieth week, as the pretribulation Rapture view claims (Rosenthal, *Pre-Wrath Rapture*, pp. 117, 155–58).

## Critique

This argument of the Pre-Wrath Rapture view misses the fact that the biblical expression "the Day of the Lord" has a double sense (a broad sense and a narrow sense) in relationship to the future. The broad sense refers to an extended period of time involving divine interventions related at least to the entire seventieth week of Daniel and the thousand-year Millennium. We presented evidence for this view in this critique. Concerning this broad sense, A. B. Davidson wrote, "Though the 'Day of the Lord,' as the expression implies, was at first conceived as a definite and brief period of time, being an era of judgment and salvation, it many times broadened out to be an extended period. From being a day it became an epoch" (*The Theology of the Old Testament*, p. 381).

The narrow sense refers to one specific day—the day on which Christ will return to the earth in His glorious Second Coming with His angels.

Just as the word *day* in Genesis 1:5 has both a broad sense (a twenty-four hour day—"And the evening and the morning were the first day") and a narrow sense (the light part of a twenty-four hour day in contrast with the darkness part—"And God called the light Day, and the darkness he called Night")—so the expression "the day of the Lord" has both a broad and narrow sense in relationship to the future.

The fact that the Bible presents a future Day of the Lord that will be narrowed or limited to one specific day is indicated by the following combination of facts.

First, Revelation 16:12–16 signifies that the armies of all of the nations of the world will not begin to gather in Israel for Armageddon until the sixth bowl is poured out. Note that the pouring out of the sixth bowl and the resultant gathering of the armies will take place after a significant part of the broad Day of the Lord has already run its course.

Second, both Joel 3:9–16 and Zechariah 14:1–5 indicate that, after the armies of the nations have gathered in Israel, "the Day of the LORD cometh" and is "near." Obvious from the language is the fact that this Day of the Lord will not take place until after the armies have gathered in Israel.

Since this Day of the Lord of Joel 3 and Zechariah 14 will not take place until after the armies have gathered in Israel, and since the armies will not begin to gather until after a significant part of the broad Day of the Lord has run its course, then this must be another Day of the Lord that is to come after a significant part of the broad Day has run its course.

This other Day will be one part of the broad Day of the Lord, but a genuine sense exists in which it will be a complete Day of the Lord on its own, different from the broad Day. One difference will be its duration. The broad Day will cover an extended period of time. By contrast, the Joel 3 and Zechariah 14 Day will be narrow or limited in time. Thus, there will be two future Days of the Lord.

Third, both Joel 3 and Zechariah 14 indicate that their Day of the Lord will be the specific time when the Messiah will come to fight against and destroy the armies gathered in Israel. Revelation 19:11–21 signifies that that time will be when Christ comes from heaven to the earth. Thus, the narrow Day of the Lord will be the day on which Christ will come to the earth in His glorious Second Coming.

Note that Joel 3:14–15 indicates that the sun, moon, and stars will be darkened when the narrow Day of the Lord is near. In other words, they will be darkened before the narrow Day comes. Joel 2:31 declares that those heavenly bodies will be darkened "before the great and the terrible day of the LORD come." Obvious from this statement is the fact that Joel 3 and 2 are referring to the same Day of the Lord. We can conclude, then, that the narrow Day of Joel 3 and Zechariah 14 is to be identified with the great and terrible Day of the Lord—the day on which Christ will return to the earth in His glorious Second Coming.

*The Babylonian Talmud* made the following statement concerning the great and terrible Day of the Lord: "This is understood to refer to the advent of the Messiah" (*Shabbath,* 118a, n., p. 580).

In light of this discussion, we should note that the Bible applies the expression "the great and terrible day of the LORD" to the narrow Day, not the broad Day. This fact implies that the narrow Day will differ from the rest of the broad Day in not only duration but also significance. Although the earlier part of the judgment phase of the broad Day will involve a great outpouring of divine wrath upon the domain of Satan and

mankind, the narrow Day will be the grand climax of that judgment phase. Thus, E. W. Bullinger, when referring to the Day
of the Lord of Joel 2:31, said, "It is called 'the great and terrible day of the LORD,' as though it were the climax of the whole
period known as 'the day of the LORD'" (*The Apocalypse or "The
Day of the Lord,"* p. 248).

Along similar lines, C. F. Keil, when referring to the judgment of the narrow Day of Joel 3, declared, "It is the last decisive judgment, in which all the single judgments find their end"
(*The Twelve Minor Prophets,* 1:226).

The narrow Day will be the great and terrible Day of the Lord
because, in contrast with the earlier part of the judgment phase
of the broad Day, the narrow Day will involve the coming of
Christ from heaven to the earth. Therefore, it will do the following things.

- It will expose God's enemies to the actual presence of Christ
  and the fullness of His divine power, glory, judgment, and
  warfare (Matt. 24:29–30; 25:31; Rev. 19:11–12, 15).
- It will bring the angelic armies of heaven against these
  enemies (Matt. 13:40–42, 49–50; 25:31; Rev. 19:14).
- It will end the rule of Satan and rebellious mankind over
  the world system and evict them from the earth (Matt.
  13:40–42, 49–50; 25:41, 46; Luke 17:26–37; Rev. 19:17–20:3),
  thus ending their day on earth forever.

Because the narrow Day of the Lord will bring such a decisive, permanent change to the world, the prophet Joel called
the place where the grand climax of God's judgment will fall
on Satan and rebellious mankind "the valley of decision" (3:14).
Concerning this designation, Keil called it the "valley of the
deciding judgment, from *charats,* to decide, to determine irre-
vocably" (ibid., p. 228).

At least two significant implications derive from the fact that
both a broad Day of the Lord and a narrow Day of the Lord
will occur.

First, as earlier noted, because the narrow Day of Joel 3 and Zechariah 14 will take place *after* a significant part of the broad Day has already run its course, and because the narrow Day will be the day on which Christ will come to the earth in His glorious Second Coming, we can conclude that Christ will come to the earth in His glorious Second Coming after a significant part of the broad Day has already run its course, after a major part of God's Day-of-the-Lord wrath has been poured out upon the world. Christ's Second Coming will not take place before or at the beginning of the outpouring of God's Day-of-the-Lord wrath, as the Pre-Wrath Rapture view claims.

Second, as earlier demonstrated, the expression "the great and terrible day of the Lord" of Joel 2:31 refers to the narrow Day when Christ will come to the earth in His glorious Second Coming. It does not refer to the broad Day.

The prophet Malachi (4:5) referred to the same great and terrible Day of the Lord as Joel. (Malachi used the identical Hebrew words and constructions that Joel used for the great and terrible Day of the Lord in Joel 2:31.) In its comments on Joel 2:31, The International Critical Commentary states, "The clause *before the great and terrible day of Yahweh comes* is the same as in Mal. 3:25 [Engl. 4:5]" (Smith, Ward, and Bewer, *A Critical and Exegetical Commentary on Micah, Zephaniah, Nahum, Habakkuk, Obadiah and Joel,* p. 124).

Because Joel and Malachi were both referring to the same great and terrible Day of the Lord, and because Joel was referring to the narrow Day, we can conclude that Malachi's great and terrible Day of the Lord is also the narrow Day, the day on which Christ will return to the earth in His glorious Second Coming as the grand climax or end of the judgment phase of the broad Day of the Lord.

Malachi declared that God will send "Elijah the prophet before the coming of the great and terrible day of the LORD" (4:5 NASB). Because Malachi was referring to the narrow Day, we can conclude that he was indicating that God will send Elijah before the narrow Day, not before the broad Day when God

# DOUBLE SENSE OF THE FUTURE DAY OF THE LORD

BROAD DAY OF THE LORD

MILLENNIUM

1000 years

great and terrible—
Christ's Second Coming

NARROW DAY OF THE LORD

70th WEEK

divine wrath

7 years

begins to pour out His wrath upon the world. In light of the meaning of the great and terrible Day of the Lord, Malachi's declaration leaves room for Elijah to come and minister after the broad Day of the Lord has begun and, therefore, while the wrath of God is being poured out upon the world. His declaration does not require Elijah to come before the broad Day of the Lord begins (before God begins to pour out His wrath upon the world), as the Pre-Wrath Rapture view claims. Thus, contrary to what the Pre-Wrath view asserts, Malachi's declaration does not militate against the broad Day of the Lord starting at the beginning of the seventieth week of Daniel 9.

**Pre-Wrath View**

The Pre-Wrath view asserts that Matthew 24 and Luke 17 teach that the Day of the Lord will begin on the same day as the Rapture and Christ's Second Coming.

In Matthew 24:37–41, Jesus said,

> But as the days of Noe were, so shall also the coming of the Son of man be. For as in the days that were before the flood they were eating and drinking, marrying and giving in marriage, until the day that Noe entered into the ark, and knew not until the flood came, and took them all away; so shall also the coming of the Son of man be. Then shall two be in the field; the one shall be taken, and the other left. Two women shall be grinding at the mill; the one shall be taken, and the other left.

Luke 17:26–30 records Christ's statements as follows:

> And as it was in the days of Noe, so shall it be also in the days of the Son of man. They did eat, they drank, they married wives, they were given in marriage, until the day that Noe entered into the ark, and the flood came, and destroyed them all. Likewise also as it was in the days of Lot; they did eat, they drank, they bought,

they sold, they planted, they builded; but the same day
that Lot went out of Sodom it rained fire and brimstone
from heaven, and destroyed them all. Even thus shall it
be in the day when the Son of man is revealed.

On the basis of these statements, the Pre-Wrath view claims
the following. Christ was asserting that immediately after Noah
entered the ark, God's wrathful judgment began on the same
day, and immediately after Lot left Sodom, God's wrathful judgment came on that very day. Through these assertions, He was
indicating a principle—that God's wrathful judgment comes
immediately after believers are removed from the place of judgment, even on the very day of their removal.

In light of this principle, when Christ said, "Even thus shall
it be in the day when the Son of man is revealed" (Luke 17:30),
He was indicating that God's Day-of-the-Lord wrathful judgment
will begin immediately after the church has been raptured from
the earth at His coming, even on the very day of His coming.
Thus, in Matthew 24 and Luke 17, Christ was teaching that the
beginning of the Day of the Lord will occur on the same day as
the Rapture and His Second Coming.

One can conclude that those who will be "taken" from the
field and the mill at Christ's coming (Matt. 24:40–41) are the
believers, who will be taken from the earth by rapture. Those
who will be "left" are the unsaved, who will be left on the earth
for the Day-of-the-Lord judgment, which will last for an extended
period of time (the rest of the seventieth week and an additional thirty days) and will include the seven trumpet and seven
bowl judgments (Rosenthal, *Pre-Wrath Rapture*, pp. 139–40, 196,
219–20; Van Kampen, *The Sign*, pp. 280–84, 423–24, and the
chart at the end of *The Sign*).

### Critique

We should note several points regarding this interpretation
of Christ's statements in Matthew 24 and Luke 17. First, this
interpretation has the statements concerning "the day" that

Noah entered into the ark (Luke 17:27) and "the same day" that Lot went out of Sodom (Luke 17:29) parallel to a day to which the biblical texts of Matthew 24 and Luke 17 make no reference, namely, to the day that the church is raptured. Because neither of these texts specifically mentions the church, the Rapture, or the day of the Rapture, the Pre-Wrath Rapture view must draw this parallel by implication on the basis of its beliefs concerning such things as the divisions of the seventieth week, the length of the Great Tribulation, the significance of the sixth seal, the time that the Day of the Lord begins, and the relationship of the Rapture to the Matthew 24 and Luke 17 coming of Christ, not on the basis of explicit textual reference. Thus, it reads more into the Matthew 24 and Luke 17 texts than what those texts specifically state.

In contrast, the biblical text explicitly has "the day" that Noah entered the ark and "the same day" that Lot went out of Sodom parallel to "the day" when the Son of Man is revealed (Luke 17:30), not to an unexpressed day when believers are removed from the place of judgment. In light of this fact, the principle that Christ indicated was as follows: just as judgment came on the day that Noah entered the ark and the day that Lot went out of Sodom, so judgment will come on the day when Christ will come out of heaven. This principle does not include more than the texts express. Although this judgment will undoubtedly be part of the Day-of-the-Lord judgment, the texts do not explicitly indicate that the Day-of-the-Lord judgment will *begin* at this coming of Christ. It could involve an aspect of the Day-of-the-Lord judgment that will come after a major part of the Day of the Lord has already run its course.

Second, the Pre-Wrath view has Noah's entering the ark and Lot's leaving Sodom parallel to the taking of people from the bed, mill, and field at Christ's coming in Matthew 24 and Luke 17. On the basis of this parallel, it interprets the taking as the taking of believers from the earth by rapture. This view presents two problems.

First, this parallel conflicts with the textual parallel that we noted earlier. The biblical text has Noah's entering the ark and Lot's leaving Sodom parallel to Christ's coming from heaven, not to the taking of people at His coming.

The second problem with having Noah's entering the ark and Lot's leaving Sodom parallel to the taking of people at Christ's coming in Matthew 24 and Luke 17 is related to language. The language describing Noah's entering the ark (Matt. 24:38; Luke 17:27) and Lot's leaving Sodom (Luke 17:29) indicates that Noah and Lot performed those actions. No one else performed those actions for them. The text of Genesis says "Noah went in" (7:7) and "In the selfsame day entered Noah" (v. 13). Although angels set Lot outside the city of Sodom (Gen. 19:15–16), they clearly indicated that he was responsible to leave the vicinity of Sodom to escape the coming judgment (vv. 17–22). The fact that Christ's statement in Luke 17:29 used an active voice verb for Lot's leaving Sodom indicates that the Lord was referring to Lot's activity of leaving the vicinity of Sodom, not the angels' activity of setting him outside that city.

In contrast, the language describing the taking of people from the bed, mill, and field at Christ's coming in Matthew 24 and Luke 17 indicates not that the people are taking themselves but that they are being taken by other beings or entities.

This contrast of language militates against the Pre-Wrath view making Noah's entering the ark and Lot's leaving Sodom parallel to the taking of people at Christ's coming in Matthew 24 and Luke 17. Therefore, it also militates against the taking of people being the taking of believers from the earth by rapture.

Third, chapter six of this critique presented other problems associated with the Pre-Wrath view's interpretation of Matthew 24 and Luke 17.

## Conclusion

This chapter has presented reasons for concluding that the following teachings of the Pre-Wrath View are contrary to the Scriptures. Only one Day of the Lord is revealed in the Bible; the Hebrew word *ebrah* is the only word used specifically for

God's Day-of-the-Lord wrath, and it is used for God's Day-of-the-Lord wrath against Gentile nations, not against Israel; the Day of the Lord will not include the Millennium; the content of Malachi 4:5 prompts the conclusion that the Day of the Lord will not begin until sometime during the second half of the seventieth week of Daniel 9; and Matthew 24 and Luke 17 indicate that the Day of the Lord will begin on the same day as the Rapture and Christ's Second Coming.

# CHAPTER NINE

# Second Thessalonians 2

## Introduction

Paul began 2 Thessalonians 2 with the following request of the Thessalonian Christians: "Now we beseech you, brethren, by the coming of our Lord Jesus Christ, and by our gathering together unto him, that ye be not soon shaken in mind, or be troubled, neither by spirit, nor by word, nor by letter as from us, as that the day of Christ is at hand" (vv. 1–2).

This request implies that the Thessalonian Christians were greatly shaken and disturbed. Apparently, some of them had quickly departed from their ability to determine whether reports that had been made to them were true or false. As a result, they had fallen into a constant state of alarm and nervous anxiety.

The last part of verse two reveals the cause of the turmoil. Some person(s) had falsely reported that the Day of the Lord had already begun (the Greek text says, "the Day of the Lord"). Paul used the perfect tense of the Greek verb translated "is at hand." The perfect tense "views action as a finished product" and "signifies action as complete from the point of view of present time" (Dana and Mantey, *A Manual Grammar of the Greek New Testament,* p. 200).

Similarly, James Everett Frame declared that the Greek verb that Paul used does not mean "is coming," "is at hand," or "is near." Instead, it means "has come," "is on hand," or "is present" (*A Critical and Exegetical Commentary on the Epistles of St. Paul to the Thessalonians*, p. 248). Albrecht Oepke (*"enistemi,"* in *Theological Dictionary of the New Testament*, 2:543–44), Leon Morris (*The First and Second Epistles to the Thessalonians*, p. 216), James Moffatt ("The First and Second Epistles to the Thessalonians," in *The Expositor's Greek Testament*, 4:47), and Henry Alford ("The Second Epistle to the Thessalonians," in *The Greek Testament*, 3:289) all asserted that the verb means "to be present." In fact, Alford pointed out that in the other six instances in which that same verb occurs in the New Testament it always has the "sense of *being present*" (ibid.).

Thus, the cause of the Thessalonians' trouble was the false claim that the broad Day of the Lord, about which they had been taught in the past (1 Thess. 5:1–3; 2 Thess. 2:5), had already come and that they were in it (Morris, *The First and Second Epistles to the Thessalonians*, p. 217).

The middle of verse two implies that whoever started this report asserted that it had been communicated originally by Paul and his companions, either through means of a divinely inspired prophetic utterance ("by spirit"), by some oral teaching ("by word"), or by letter (ibid., p. 216). The words translated "as from us" are related to all three of these means of communication (ibid., n. 8). Because Paul and his companions had been the authoritative teachers of the Thessalonians, this assertion that they originated the report that the Day of the Lord had already begun was a very deceptive trick designed to persuade the Thessalonians of the truthfulness of the report (v. 3).

Paul made very clear that he and his companions had nothing to do with the false report. In the next several verses, he completely repudiated it by demonstrating conclusively that the broad Day of the Lord had not come.

In verse one, Paul's language indicated that a significant relationship existed between the request to the Thessalonians and the coming (*parousia*) of Christ and the gathering of the church saints to Him. The apostle wrote, "Now we beseech you, brethren, by the coming of our Lord Jesus Christ, and by our gathering together unto him." To understand this relationship, we must observe three facts.

First, the preposition translated "by" in the expressions "by the coming of our Lord Jesus Christ" and "by our gathering together unto him" usually means "on behalf of" (ibid., p. 214 n. 1). According to Harald Riesenfeld, this meaning contains the "idea of protection" and thus carries the concept of "in defense of" (*"huper,"* in *Theological Dictionary of the New Testament,* 8:508). In line with this view, Morris claimed that in 2 Thessalonians 2:1 this preposition "signifies something like 'in the interests of the truth concerning'" (*The First and Second Epistles to the Thessalonians,* p. 214 n. 1).

Second, the Greek construction of verse one indicates that this coming of Christ and gathering together of the saints to Him "are two parts of one great event" (ibid., p. 214). Wolfgang Schrage claimed the same thing (*"episunagoge,"* in *Theological Dictionary of the New Testament,* 7:842). Thus, Paul was referring to the coming of Christ that would involve the gathering of saints to Him.

Third, regarding the phrase *unto him* in the expression "our gathering together unto him," Leon Morris wrote, "Notice the significance of 'unto him.' It is not simply that the saints meet one another: they meet their Lord and remain with Him for ever (cf. 1 Thess. 4:17)" (*The First and Second Epistles to the Thessalonians,* p. 214). Morris thereby signified that the gathering of saints to Christ in 2 Thessalonians 2:1 is the same event as that in 1 Thessalonians 4:17, namely, the Rapture. James Everett Frame (*A Critical and Exegetical Commentary on the Epistles of St. Paul to the Thessalonians,* p. 244), C. F. Hogg and W. E. Vine (*The Epistles to the Thessalonians,* p. 242), and Wolfgang Schrage all indicated the same point. Schrage stated, "it is to Him that the" gathering "of Christians will take place at the Lord's return. This is not active assembling; it is a being assembled and united (cf.

*harpagesometha,* 1 Thess. 4:17)" (*"episunagoge,"* in *Theological Dictionary of the New Testament,* 7:842). *Harpagesometha* is the Greek word translated "shall be caught up" in 1 Thessalonians 4:17. Thus, in 2 Thessalonians 2:1, Paul was referring to the coming of Christ that will involve the Rapture of the church from the earth to be with Him.

Taken together, these three observations indicate that Paul and his companions wrote their request to the Thessalonians for the purpose of defending or protecting the truth concerning the coming of Christ to rapture the church. This, then, was the significant relationship between their request and the coming of Christ and gathering together of church saints to Him. This fact indicates that the truth pertaining to that coming and gathering was being threatened by the false report that the Day of the Lord had already begun and that the church saints were already in it.

The combination of these three observations also implied that the report that the Day of the Lord had already begun and that the church saints were in it was contrary to the earlier teaching of Paul and his companions concerning two truths: the coming of Christ to rapture the church and the relationship of church saints to the broad Day of the Lord. The fact that the false report had caused the Thessalonians to fall into a constant state of alarm and nervous anxiety strongly implies that earlier Paul and his companions had taught the Thessalonians that Christ would come to rapture the church before the broad Day of the Lord would begin and that, therefore, the church saints would not enter the judgment phase of the Day of the Lord.

In light of what we have seen, we can conclude that the real issue at stake with the Thessalonians was not the *fact* of Christ's coming to rapture the church but the *time* of that coming and, therefore, the relationship of church saints to the judgment phase of the Day of the Lord.

To defend or protect the truth that he and his companions had already taught the Thessalonians, Paul gave them clear evidence that the Day of the Lord had not come. The apostle told them that the Day of the Lord "shall not come, except there come a falling away first, and that man of sin be revealed, the son of perdition" (2 Thess. 2:3). Obviously, neither of those events had happened yet, so how could the Day of the Lord have come already?

## The Apostasy and Revelation of the Man of Sin

### Pre-Wrath View

The Pre-Wrath view agrees that Christ will come and rapture the church before the Day of the Lord begins. However, it insists that the Day of the Lord will not start at the beginning of the seventieth week. Instead, it will not begin until part way through the second half of the seventieth week when the seventh seal is broken after the Great Tribulation. One support for this conclusion is the fact that in 2 Thessalonians 2:3 Paul taught that the Day of the Lord will not begin until *after* "a falling away" (literally, "the apostasy"; Rosenthal, *Pre-Wrath Rapture*, p. 197; Van Kampen, *The Sign*, p. 288).

The Pre-Wrath view identifies "the apostasy" of 2 Thessalonians 2:3 as the total abandonment by Jews of the God of Abraham, Isaac, and Jacob and of Israel's hope of the Messiah. This apostasy will begin with their entering into a covenant relationship with Antichrist at the beginning of the seventieth week of Daniel 9 and will continue through the first four seals of the first half of the seventieth week and the Great Tribulation of the fifth seal. The view supports this identification of "the apostasy" by claiming two things: first, that this future apostasy was foreshadowed by the apostasy of the Jews who forsook God's covenant and entered into a covenant relationship with Antiochus Epiphanes during the 170s and 160s B.C., and, second, that it is parallel with that past apostasy (Rosenthal, *Pre-Wrath Rapture*, pp. 197–202; Van Kampen, *The Sign*, pp. 136–42, 174–75, 199, 423). The view even goes so far as to imply that Paul told the Thessalonians that Israel would commit the apostasy of 2 Thessalonians 2:3, just as their ancestors did under

Antiochus (Van Kampen, *The Sign*, p. 138).

Thus, according to the Pre-Wrath view, because "the apostasy" of 2 Thessalonians 2:3 will start at the beginning of the seventieth week and will continue through the first five seals, it thereby will take place throughout the entire first half of the seventieth week and the Great Tribulation part of the second half. Thus, the apostasy will last for several years before the Day of the Lord will begin.

The Pre-Wrath view further supports for its conclusion that the Day of the Lord will not begin until part way through the second half of the seventieth week (when the seventh seal is broken after the Great Tribulation) with the fact that in 2 Thessalonians 2:3 Paul taught that the Day of the Lord will not begin until *after* the revelation of the man of sin (the Antichrist; Rosenthal, *Pre-Wrath Rapture*, p. 197; Van Kampen, *The Sign*, pp. 181, 288).

The Pre-Wrath view identifies the revelation of the Antichrist as that event when he will break his covenant with Israel by taking his seat in the future temple in Jerusalem and making the blasphemous claim that he is God (2 Thess. 2:4). Thus, it is Antichrist who will reveal himself through these actions (Van Kampen, *The Sign*, pp. 200, 423). This revelation will be the time that the Jews and the world will finally recognize the true identity and character of the Antichrist (Rosenthal, *Pre-Wrath Rapture*, pp. 207, 210). It will take place in the middle of the seventieth week and will begin the Great Tribulation (ibid., pp. 197, 207; Van Kampen, *The Sign*, pp. 192, 201, 417, 423, 437). The Pre-Wrath view asserts that, through Paul's reference to these actions of the Antichrist in 2 Thessalonians 2:4, he indicated the manner and time in which the revelation of the Antichrist will take place (Rosenthal, *Pre-Wrath Rapture*, p. 207).

In light of its two supports and identifications of "the apostasy" and the revelation of the Antichrist, the Pre-Wrath view develops the following argument. In 2 Thessalonians 2:3, Paul taught that the Day of the Lord will not begin until *after* the apostasy and revelation of the Antichrist. In light of this teaching, because the apostasy will take place throughout the entire first half of the seventieth week and the Great Tribulation part of the second half, and since the revelation of the Antichrist will take place in the middle of the seventieth week, then one must conclude that the Day of the Lord will not begin until sometime *after* the second half of the seventieth week has begun. The Day of the Lord cannot begin at the beginning of the seventieth week (as many pretribulation rapturists claim; Rosenthal, *Pre-Wrath Rapture,* p. 197; Van Kampen, *The Sign,* pp. 199, 288–89).

### Critique One

This conclusion of the Pre-Wrath view is based upon its identifications of the apostasy and revelation of the Antichrist. Its identification of the apostasy is questionable for three reasons.

First, because Paul did not identify the apostasy in his text of 2 Thessalonians 2, no modern reader can be certain of its identification. The most one can do is make an uncertain proposal concerning its identification. Thus, the Pre-Wrath view's identification is an uncertain proposal, and its implication that Paul specifically told the Thessalonians that Israel would commit the apostasy of 2 Thessalonians 2:3, just as their ancestors did under Antiochus Epiphanes, is an assumption that is not supported by what Paul wrote. In neither 2 Thessalonians 2 nor any other biblical writing did Paul state that the apostasy would be Jewish in nature or that it would begin with the establishment of a covenant relationship.

Second, we should note three facts concerning the expression "except there come the apostasy first" (literal translation).

First, the position of the verb translated "come" in the Greek text indicates that Paul emphasized the future point of time when the apostasy will begin, not how long it will continue after its beginning. Through this emphasis, Paul might have been indicating that it is only the beginning of the apostasy that will take place before the Day of the Lord will begin. This position would be contrary to the Pre-Wrath view that teaches that several years of the apostasy will take place before the Day of the Lord will begin.

Second, this emphasis upon the apostasy's beginning, together with the definite article *the* before the word *apostasy*, focuses attention on the following three aspects of this future apostasy.

1. In some respect, it will be distinct from apostasies of the past. It is not just *an* apostasy, but *the* apostasy that will begin. In line with this aspect, Robert L. Thomas suggests that the "special designation: '*the* apostasy'" indicates a worldwide, universal apostasy ("2 Thessalonians" in *The Expositor's Bible Commentary*, 11:322). An apostasy that is worldwide or universal in scope at its beginning would be distinct from the limited apostasies of the past (including the past apostasy of the Jews under Antiochus Epiphanes).

2. The apostasy's coming will be sudden (Frame, *A Critical and Exegetical Commentary on the Epistles of St. Paul to the Thessalonians*, p. 251). Its coming will not be a process over a period of time.

3. Several writers point out that 2 Thessalonians 2:3 is referring to apostasy in the absolute sense (Bauder, *"aphistemi,"* in *New International Dictionary of New Testament Theology*, 1:607; Schlier, *"apostasia,"* in *Theological Dictionary of the New Testament*, 1:513). When something is absolute, it is "complete," "free from mixture," and "free from external restraint or limitations" (*Webster's New International Dictionary*, 2d ed., unabridged, s.v. "absolute"). This point implies that when the apostasy of 2 Thessalonians 2:3 begins, three things will be true of it: it will be complete, it will not be diluted with a mixture that results from existence together with what is not apostasy, and it will be free from external restraint or limitations. The second and third of these items are supportive of the notion suggested earlier that the apostasy of 2 Thessalonians 2:3 will be worldwide or universal in scope.

Third, the Greek word rendered "apostasy" (literal translation) in 2 Thessalonians 2:3 means "rebellion, abandonment" (Arndt and Gingrich, *"apostasia,"* in *A Greek-English Lexicon of the New Testament,* p. 97). Arndt and Gingrich signified that in 2 Thessalonians 2:3 it refers to the rebellion of "the last days" (ibid.). Leon Morris defined it in that passage as rebellion against God's rule. Morris stated, "It is not so much forsaking one's first love and drifting into apathy that is meant, as setting oneself in opposition to God" (*The First and Second Epistles to the Thessalonians,* pp. 218–19).

In Romans 8:7, the apostle Paul clearly indicated that rebellion against God's rule is characteristic of the unsaved—"the carnal mind is enmity against God: for it is not subject to the law of God, neither indeed can be." By the carnal mind, Paul was referring to the unsaved person's man-centered or self-centered mind-set in contrast with the God-centered mind-set. That mind-set is hostile toward God. The evidence of that hostility is the fact that it refuses to submit to God's law and is incapable of submitting to God's law. Because God's law was an expression of God's rule, this was Paul's way of saying that the lawlessness of the unsaved is rebellion against God's rule.

The points that were noted concerning the expression "except there come the apostasy first" provide a list of characteristics that will be true of the apostasy of 2 Thessalonians 2:3:

- it will be distinct from past apostasies (perhaps worldwide or universal in scope, in contrast to the past limited apostasies);
- it will come suddenly;
- when it begins, it will be complete, it will not exist together with what is not apostasy, and it will be free from external restraint or limitations; and
- it will consist of rebellion by the unsaved against God's rule.

To be the apostasy of 2 Thessalonians 2:3, any proposed identification must conform with all of these characteristics.

The Pre-Wrath view's identification of the apostasy conflicts with three of these characteristics. First, the Pre-Wrath view claims that the apostasy of 2 Thessalonians 2:3 will be parallel with the past Jewish apostasy under Antiochus Epiphanes. By contrast, the apostasy of 2 Thessalonians 2:3 will be distinct from the apostasies of the past.

Second, the Pre-Wrath view teaches that the apostasy will start at the beginning of the seventieth week of Daniel 9 and will continue through the first four seals of the first half of the seventieth week and the Great Tribulation of the fifth seal. In addition, as we noted in an earlier chapter, it also teaches that church saints will go directly into the seventieth week at its beginning and will continue on the earth through the first half of the seventieth week, the Great Tribulation, and the sixth seal. In other words, according to the Pre-Wrath view, church saints (who will not be apostate) will exist on the earth together with the apostasy from its very beginning. In contrast, when the apostasy of 2 Thessalonians 2:3 will begin, it will not exist together with what is not apostasy.

This same characteristic of the apostasy of 2 Thessalonians 2:3 conflicts with the Pre-Wrath view's teaching that that future apostasy will parallel the past Jewish apostasy under Antiochus Epiphanes. From its beginning, the Jewish apostasy under Antiochus Epiphanes existed together with what is not apostasy. There were Jews of that time who did not take part in that past apostasy; rather, they resisted it and continued to obey God's covenant.

Third, the apostasy of 2 Thessalonians 2:3 will be free of external restraint or limitations at its beginning. By contrast, the Pre-Wrath view teaches that the apostasy will start at the beginning of the seventieth week but that the restrainer of lawlessness will not be removed until the middle of the seventieth week, namely, three and one-half years after the apostasy begins (Van Kampen, *The Sign*, pp. 199–200, 472–73).

Having noted these problems associated with the Pre-Wrath Rapture view's identification of the apostasy of 2 Thessalonians

2:3, an examination of how another proposed identification would conform to the list of characteristics that will be true of that apostasy would be helpful. Advocates of the pretribulation Rapture view could propose this other identification, which is as follows.

At its beginning, the apostasy of 2 Thessalonians 2:3 will be a worldwide or universal rebellion against God's rule. Before the beginning of the seventieth week, the Holy Spirit's work of restraining lawlessness will be taken away from the earth when the church is raptured to heaven. When the church is raptured, all saved people will be removed from the earth. Instantly, the total human population on the earth will change from a mixture of saved and unsaved coexisting to unsaved only. All of those who were not in rebellion against God's rule will be absent from the earth. All of those who were in rebellion against His rule will be left on the earth. Thus, as a result of the Rapture, a sudden worldwide or universal apostasy will occur.

The following characteristics will be evident at the beginning of this apostasy:

- it will be distinct from the past limited apostasies because it will be worldwide or universal in scope;
- it will come suddenly as the result of one event—the Rapture of all saved people from the earth;
- it will be complete because at the beginning of this apostasy, the saved people and the restraining work of the Holy Spirit will be gone, and the total population of the earth will consist of unsaved people who rebel against God's rule; and
- it will not exist together with what is not apostasy, and it will be free from external restraint and limitations.

Thus, this proposed identification of the apostasy of 2 Thessalonians 2:3 conforms to the list of characteristics that will be true of that apostasy.

The third reason why the Pre-Wrath view's identification of

the apostasy of 2 Thessalonians 2:3 is questionable is that it is based on the conclusion that Paul was saying that the apostasy and revelation of the Antichrist will occur *before* the Day of the Lord begins. Not all New Testament Greek scholars agree that that is what Paul was saying.

One matter that must be considered relative to this issue is the implication of the word *first* in the expression "except there come [the apostasy] first, and that man of sin be revealed" (v. 3). Did Paul mean that the apostasy will come "first" together with the revelation of the man of sin before the Day of the Lord begins? Or did he mean that the apostasy will come "first" before the revelation of the man of sin (the Antichrist)? On the basis of how other New Testament passages use the same combination of words translated "except . . . first" in 2 Thessalonians 2:3, Dr. Robert L. Thomas concluded that Paul meant the latter. In other words, Paul was saying that the apostasy will come first before the revelation of the man of sin, not before the Day of the Lord begins ("2 Thessalonians," 11:323).

In light of this fact, Dr. Thomas declared that the text of 2 Thessalonians 2:3 "does not explicitly say whether" the apostasy and revelation of the man of sin "will come before the day of the Lord or immediately after it begins" (ibid., p. 320).

Therefore, two ways exist of interpreting Paul's statement in verse three. One interpretation claims that Paul was saying that the apostasy and revelation of the man of sin must take place *before* the Day of the Lord will begin. This interpretation is advocated by the Pre-Wrath view. That this is what Paul meant is possible. However, even if that is what he meant, that interpretation by itself does not prove that the Pre-Wrath view teaching that the Day of the Lord will not begin until part way through the second half of the seventieth week is correct. In addition, that interpretation by itself does not disprove the pretribulation Rapture view. Some advocates of the pretribulation Rapture view believe that the apostasy and revelation of the man of sin could take place very quickly between the Rapture and the time that the Day of the Lord starts at the beginning of the seventieth week (even on the same day that the Rapture occurs and the Day of the Lord begins).

The other interpretation claims that Paul was saying that the apostasy and revelation of the man of sin will take place immediately *within* the beginning of the Day of the Lord. At the very beginning of the Day of the Lord, the apostasy will take place first, and immediately thereafter the man of sin will be revealed. On the basis of grammatical constructions, Robert Thomas indicates that the apostasy and revelation of the man of sin "are conceived of as within the day of the Lord, not prior to it" and that they "will dominate the day's opening phase" (ibid.). That this is what Paul meant is possible. This interpretation is contrary to the Pre-Wrath Rapture view, however, which insists that the apostasy and revelation of the man of sin must take place *before* the Day of the Lord begins. This interpretation does not, however, disprove the pretribulation Rapture view.

Both of these interpretations of verse three would have served Paul's purpose. His purpose was to prove that the Day of the Lord was not already present. According to the first interpretation, Paul gave the following proof: the Day of the Lord is not already present because the apostasy and revelation of the man of sin must occur before that day comes, and those two events have not happened yet.

According to the second interpretation, Paul gave the following proof: the Day of the Lord is not already present because at the very beginning of the Day of the Lord, the apostasy will take place first, and immediately thereafter the man of sin will be revealed, and those two events have not happened yet. The proof associated with this second interpretation would have served Paul's purpose as effectively as the proof associated with the first interpretation.

## Critique Two

There are three problems with the Pre-Wrath view's identification of the revelation of the man of sin (the Antichrist).

First, although Paul referred to the revelation of the Anti-

christ three times in 2 Thessalonians 2 (vv. 3, 6, 8), he did not
specifically state of what that revelation would consist or how
it would take place. For example, Paul did not specifically identify the revelation of the Antichrist as that event in the middle
of the seventieth week when he will break his covenant with
Israel by taking his seat in the future temple in Jerusalem and
making his blasphemous claim that he is God (2 Thess. 2:4).
Thus, the Pre-Wrath view's claim that that is how and when the
revelation of the Antichrist will take place is to be regarded as
an uncertain proposal.

Second, several New Testament Greek scholars point out that
the expression "except there come [the apostasy] first, and that
man of sin be revealed" could mean that the coming of the
apostasy will take place before the revelation of the man of sin,
or that both will occur at the same time. The Greek text will
allow either meaning (Frame, *A Critical and Exegetical Commentary on the Epistles of St. Paul to the Thessalonians,* p. 252; Morris,
*The First and Second Epistles to the Thessalonians,* p. 219 n. 14).
These scholars agree that either way, although the coming of
the apostasy and the revelation of the man of sin are not the
same thing, they are apparently associated both essentially and
chronologically.

The thought that either of these ways associates the coming
of the apostasy and the revelation of the man of sin chronologically implies that either the apostasy and the revelation of
the Antichrist will occur at the same point of time or that the
revelation of the Antichrist will occur immediately after the
coming of the apostasy. This implication conflicts with the Pre-
Wrath view teaching that the apostasy will come at the beginning of the seventieth week; but the revelation of the Antichrist
will not occur until the middle of the seventieth week, namely,
three and one-half years after the coming of the apostasy.

Third, all of the verb forms in 2 Thessalonians 2:4 that describe the Antichrist opposing and exalting himself above all
that is called God and taking his seat in the temple and show-
ing himself that he is God are in the active or middle voice.

This fact indicates that he is the one actively doing these things and that he is doing them for himself. No one else is doing these things to him or for him. Note that in line with this truth, because the Pre-Wrath view asserts that these actions of the Antichrist are what will constitute his revelation, it states that the Antichrist will reveal himself (Van Kampen, *The Sign*, pp. 200, 423).

In contrast, all of the verb forms that refer to Antichrist's revelation (vv. 3, 6, 8) are in the passive voice. This indicates that it is not the Antichrist who will reveal himself through actions that he performs. Instead, it is some other person or entity who will reveal him. In light of this fact, the question we must ask is, "Who or what will reveal the Antichrist?" To determine the answer, we must note three facts.

First, the Greek word translated "be revealed" in verses three, six, and eight means "to uncover, disclose" or "unveil" something "previously hidden" (Mundle, *"apokalupto,"* in *The New International Dictionary of New Testament Theology*, 3:310). To reveal is "to open up to view" (*Webster's New International Dictionary*, s.v. "reveal"). Thus, the purpose of revelation is to enable people to see what previously was hidden from their sight.

Second, in verse six, Paul stated that the Antichrist will be revealed "in his time." In this passage, the Greek word translated "time" refers to a "definite, fixed time" (Arndt and Gingrich, *"kairos,"* in *A Greek-English Lexicon of the New Testament*, p. 396). The word refers to "the specific and decisive point" and strongly emphasizes that God is the one who determined that definite, fixed, and decisive time (Delling, *"kairos,"* in *Theological Dictionary of the New Testament*, 3:460–61). Christ clearly indicated that the authority to determine such times belongs exclusively to God (Acts 1:7). Thus, Paul was indicating that the definite, fixed, and decisive time of Antichrist's revelation has been determined exclusively by God, not by Antichrist or Satan, and that Antichrist will not be revealed until that time. In line with this position, Leon Morris wrote that the Antichrist "will be revealed only as and when God permits. . . . Throughout this whole passage the thought of God's sovereignty is dominant" (*The First and Second Epistles to the Thessalonians,* p. 227).

Third, in an earlier chapter of this critique, we saw that God declared that He is the one who will "raise up" the Antichrist (Zech. 11:15–17). Concerning the meaning of the Hebrew verb translated "raise up" in verse sixteen, Francis Brown, S. R. Driver, and Charles A. Briggs stated the following: "Raise up = bring on the scene" (*"quwm,"* in *A Hebrew and English Lexicon of the Old Testament,* pp. 878–79). God thereby indicated that He will bring the Antichrist on the world scene.

In light of these three facts related to the issue of who or what will reveal the Antichrist, one can draw the following conclusion: God is the one who will reveal the Antichrist. At the definite, fixed, and decisive time sovereignly determined by God, He will bring the Antichrist onto the world scene, revealing him to be the next great world ruler. Before that time, the identity of that ruler will be hidden from the world. When God reveals him, the people of the world will be able to see who the next great world ruler is.

In conjunction with this, the Revelation 6:1–2 account of the first seal is most significant. The apostle John wrote, "And I saw when the Lamb opened one of the seals, and I heard, as it were the noise of thunder, one of the four beasts saying, Come and see. And I saw, and behold a white horse: and he that sat on him had a bow; and a crown was given unto him: and he went forth conquering, and to conquer."

Both the Pre-Wrath view (Rosenthal, *Pre-Wrath Rapture,* p. 142) and this critique identify the rider on this white horse as the Antichrist. The Pre-Wrath view (Van Kampen, *The Sign,* p. 177) and this critique agree that the first four seals are in the first half of the seventieth week. Because the first four seals are in the first half of the seventieth week, the first seal must be opened in the beginning stage of the seventieth week. This fact prompts the conclusion that the Antichrist will go forth in the beginning stage of the seventieth week.

In the New Testament, the stem of the Greek verb translated

"went forth" in the expression "and he went forth conquering, and to conquer" refers to a coming that "often has the sense of appearing, of coming forward publicly, of coming on the scene. It often is used of decisive events" (Schneider, *"erchomai,"* in *Theological Dictionary of the New Testament,* 2:667). The full verb translated "went forth" in Revelation 6:2, 4 "refers to the rise of mysterious and sinister figures" (*"exerchomai,"* ibid., 2:679).

These verbal references correspond significantly with the following items that we noted earlier: God is the one who will "raise up" the Antichrist or bring him "on the world scene." The definite, fixed, and decisive time of Antichrist's revelation has been determined exclusively by God, not by Antichrist or Satan. When God reveals Antichrist, the people of the world will be able to see who he is. In other words, his revelation will be public.

According to Revelation 6:2, the rider who went forth had a bow and a crown, "and he went forth conquering, and to conquer." All of these terms indicate that the rider is a victorious conqueror. The fact that a bow is mentioned without arrows might indicate his achievement of some victory through peaceful means (Thomas, *Revelation 1–7,* p. 423). Perhaps the Antichrist's establishment of the seven-year covenant with Israel at the beginning of the seventieth week (Dan. 9:27) will enable the world to escape the beginning of a major war in the Middle East. First Thessalonians 5:2–3 reveals that the Day of the Lord will begin when the world is convinced that it has peace and safety.

The crown that the rider wears is the conqueror's crown (Trench, *"stephanos,"* in *Synonyms of the New Testament,* p. 79). Note that the crown was given to the rider (Thomas, *Revelation 1–7,* p. 423). In light of the facts that God rules in the kingdom of men, appoints as rulers over it whomsoever He wants (Dan. 4:17; 5:21), and is the one who will bring the Antichrist onto the world scene, we must conclude that God is the one who, for His own sovereign purposes, will give the Antichrist the conqueror's crown.

The tense of the Greek verb form translated "conquering" in the expression "he went forth conquering, and to conquer" signifies a continuous string of victories (ibid., p. 424 and n. 40). It indicates that the rider of the first seal will be a great man of war. Daniel 11:38–44 reveals that this kind of conquering activity will be characteristic of the Antichrist at least during the first half of the seventieth week. The later words translated "to conquer" mean literally "in order that he might conquer." They indicate that Antichrist will carry on his extensive military conquests for the purpose of conquering the entire world and bringing it under his dominion.

These facts that have been observed from the Revelation 6:1–2 account of the first seal correspond significantly with the following concept established earlier concerning the revelation of the Antichrist: God will bring the Antichrist onto the world scene, revealing him to be the next great world ruler. God will do this through the breaking of the first seal by His Son, Jesus Christ. The fact that the rider will go forth through an act of Christ indicates that the revelation of the Antichrist will be instigated by divine action. The fact that from the very beginning of his going forth the rider's activity will be characterized by conquering (whether by peaceful or military means) with the goal of bringing the whole world under his dominion signifies that God will reveal the Antichrist to be the next great world ruler.

Three proposals are prompted by the facts that we have already seen. First, the revelation of the Antichrist referred to in 2 Thessalonians 2 is to be identified as God's sovereign act of bringing the Antichrist onto the world scene, revealing him to be the world's next great world ruler. Second, because God will do this through Christ's breaking of the first seal in the beginning stage of the seventieth week, the revelation of the Antichrist will occur in the beginning stage of the seventieth week, not in the middle of the seventieth week three and one-half years later, as the Pre-Wrath view claims. Third, because the revelation of the Antichrist will occur in the beginning stage of the seventieth week, and because, as we noted earlier, 2 Thessalonians 2:3 allows the interpretation that the revelation of the Antichrist will occur in the beginning stage of the Day of the Lord, then the Day of the Lord will begin at the beginning of the seventieth week. This position conflicts with the Pre-Wrath view teaching that the Day of the Lord will not begin until the seventh seal is broken part way through the second half of the seventieth week.

## The Restrainer

In 2 Thessalonians 2:6–8a, Paul wrote, "And now ye know what withholdeth that he might be revealed in his time. For the mystery of iniquity doth already work: only he who now letteth will let, until he be taken out of the way. And then shall that Wicked be revealed."

The words *withholdeth* and *letteth* are translations of participle forms of the same Greek verb. According to Arndt and Gingrich, in 2 Thessalonians 2:6–7, that verb means "restrain, check" (*"katecho,"* in *A Greek-English Lexicon of the New Testament,* p. 423). In light of this meaning, Paul was saying that some entity or person restrains or holds in check the revelation of the Antichrist until the definite, fixed, and decisive time determined by God for his revelation arrives. When that time arrives, the restrainer will be removed, and then the Antichrist will be revealed.

### Pre-Wrath View

The Pre-Wrath view teaches that the restrainer in 2 Thessalonians 2:6–7 is Michael the archangel. Proponents say that no biblical basis exists for identifying the restrainer as the Holy Spirit, the church, or human government. Daniel 10:13, 20–21 indicates that God assigned Michael to Israel as its angelic prince with the responsibility of restraining or standing firmly against enemy attacks against Israel. But Daniel 12:1 reveals that, in the middle of the seventieth week, Michael will "stand still" or stop God's restraint of enemy attacks against Israel. That action will free the Antichrist to reveal his wicked identity. He will break his covenant with Israel by taking his seat in the temple and making his blasphemous claim that he is God, and he will begin to desolate that nation severely. Michael's stopping of his restraining work on behalf of Israel will be God's way of punishing that nation for its rebellion against Him (Rosenthal, *Pre-Wrath Rapture*, p. 256; Van Kampen, *The Sign*, pp. 199–200, 435–36, 472–73).

## Critique

Two of the Pre-Wrath view claims are correct: the claim that Daniel 10:13, 20–21 indicates that God assigned Michael to Israel as its angelic prince with the responsibility of restraining or standing firmly against enemy attacks against Israel and the claim that Daniel 12:1 reveals something that will occur in the middle of the seventieth week. However, three of its other claims are questionable: its claim that the restrainer in 2 Thessalonians 2:6–7 is Michael the archangel; its claim that no biblical basis exists for identifying the restrainer as the Holy Spirit, the church, or human government; and its claim that Daniel 12:1 reveals that in the middle of the seventieth week Michael will "stand still" or stop God's restraint of enemy attacks against Israel. These claims are questionable for three reasons.

First, the King James Version of the Bible translates Daniel 12:1a as follows: "And at that time shall Michael stand up, the great prince which standeth for the children of thy people." It thereby translates the Hebrew verb *'amad* as "shall stand up." The New American Standard Bible translates it "will arise," and thereby assigns it the same meaning. The implication of these translations is that, in the middle of the seventieth week, Michael will stand up to exercise fully his restraining responsibility on behalf of Israel. Daniel 9:27, 12:1, Matthew 24:15–21, and Revelation 12 reveal why it will be necessary for Michael to do this. The middle of the seventieth week will begin the final and greatest attempt by Satan and his forces to totally annihilate Israel from the earth. Thus, at that time it will be necessary for Michael to go into full action to prevent that total annihilation.

The Pre-Wrath view rejects these translations and their

implication. It claims that the Hebrew verb 'amad should be translated "stand still," not "stand up" or "arise." It supports this other translation on the basis of the following items:

1. Rabbi Rashi, a noted scholar of Israel, claimed that 'amad means "stand still";
2. in light of Rashi's claim, the Jewish *Midrash,* in its comments on Daniel 12:1, accused Michael of being silent and not defending Israel;
3. the New American Standard Bible translates 'amad with similar meanings as "stand still" in some passages in other Old Testament books;
4. the context of the statement about Michael in Daniel 12:1 favors this translation; and
5. some Hebrew language reference works assign meanings to 'amad that support the translation "stand still." As an example of such a reference work, the Pre-Wrath view quotes the following meanings for 'amad from the authoritative *A Hebrew and English Lexicon of the Old Testament* by Francis Brown, S. R. Driver, and Charles A. Briggs: "stand still, stop, cease moving" and "stop flowing" (p. 764, 2a), "stop, cease doing" (p. 764, 2d; Van Kampen, *The Sign,* pp. 472–73).

We should note four facts concerning the supports that the Pre-Wrath view uses.

1. The verb 'amad does mean "stand still" in some Old Testament passages. But it also has other meanings in other passages, including the meanings "stand up" and "arise." Two items that determine the meaning are the form and context of the verb.

2. The reference work *A Hebrew and English Lexicon of the Old Testament* by Brown, Driver, and Briggs does present the meanings quoted by the Pre-Wrath view. But that same reference work does not assign any of those meanings to Daniel 12:1. Instead, it specifically assigns the following meanings to 'amad in Daniel 12:1: "arise, appear, come on the scene" (p. 764, 6a). In fact, it

indicates that these are especially its meanings in Daniel 12:1 (ibid.). It thereby contradicts the Pre-Wrath view translation and understanding of that passage.

3. The Jewish language scholars who produced the Septuagint (the Greek translation of the Hebrew Old Testament) during the 200s and 100s B.C. translated the Hebrew word *'amad* in Daniel 12:1 with the Greek word *anistemi* (*The Septuagint with Apocrypha: Greek and English,* p. 1069). They used the middle voice form of *anistemi* in their translation. All middle voice forms of that word mean "rise, stand up, get up" (Arndt and Gingrich, *"anistemi,"* in *A Greek-English Lexicon of the New Testament,* p. 69). The fact that these scholars used this form of the word that means "stand up" as the Greek translation of the Hebrew word *'amad* in Daniel 12:1 is significant. It indicates that they understood the Hebrew text of Daniel 12:1 to be saying that, in the middle of the seventieth week, Michael will "stand up" to protect Israel, not "stand still" or "stop" that protection, as the Pre-Wrath view claims.

4. The Pre-Wrath view assertion that the context of the Daniel 12:1 statement about Michael favors its translation is questionable. Immediately after the statement "And at that time shall Michael stand up," the text describes Michael as "the great prince which standeth for the children of thy people." Note that the Hebrew word translated "standeth" in this description is a form of the verb *'amad.* Here *'amad* has the sense of standing to protect the people of Israel (Keil, *Biblical Commentary on the Book of Daniel,* p. 474). It thereby emphasizes Michael's work of restraining enemy attacks against that nation. That the Scriptures would describe Michael as the being who stands to protect the people of Israel immediately after stating that in the middle of the seventieth week he will stop protecting them seems extremely unlikely. That description would contradict his action. More likely Michael is described this way at this point in the verse to emphasize why he will "arise" in the middle of the seventieth week—to protect Israel from total annihilation.

Second, the Pre-Wrath view's claim that the restrainer in

2 Thessalonians 2:6–7 is Michael the archangel has a problem. In at least three ways Michael does not fit the description of the restrainer in 2 Thessalonians 2.

1. Second Thessalonians 2:7 indicates that the restrainer restrains lawlessness, the lawlessness that works in the world before the revelation of the Antichrist (the Greek word translated "iniquity" in the expression "the mystery of iniquity" means "lawlessness" [Arndt and Gingrich, *"anomia,"* in *A Greek-English Lexicon of the New Testament,* p. 71]). In contrast, Michael's responsibility is to restrain enemy attacks against one nation, Israel. Thus, Michael and the restrainer in 2 Thessalonians 2 have two different objects of restraint.

2. The restrainer in 2 Thessalonians 2 is described by a neuter gender participle in verse six ("what withholdeth") and a masculine gender participle in verse seven ("he who now letteth"). By contrast, the Greek word translated "archangel" is only masculine in gender.

3. Second Thessalonians 2 has the restrainer's restraining work stopped by the restrainer's being "taken out of the way" (v. 7) and then the Antichrist's being revealed (v. 8). In contrast, in line with its translation and interpretation of Daniel 12:1, the Pre-Wrath view has Michael's restraining work stopped by Michael's "standing still" in the middle of the seventieth week, and then the Antichrist is revealed. Standing still is not the same thing as being taken out of the way. Thus, the Pre-Wrath view understanding of Daniel 12:1 and what Michael will do in the middle of the seventieth week does not fit the 2 Thessalonians 2 description of the restrainer.

Note that the other understanding of Daniel 12:1 and what Michael will do in the middle of the seventieth week (namely, that he will "stand up" or "arise" to protect Israel from total annihilation) does not fit the 2 Thessalonians 2 description of the restrainer, either.

The fact that neither of these understandings of Daniel 12:1 and what Michael will do in the middle of the seventieth week fits the 2 Thessalonians 2 description of the restrainer prompts the conclusion that Michael is not the restrainer of 2 Thessalonians 2. It also means that Daniel 12:1 and what Michael will do in the middle of the seventieth week cannot be used to support the Pre-Wrath view teaching that the removal of the restrainer and revelation of the Antichrist will occur in the middle of the seventieth week.

Third, the Pre-Wrath view claim that no biblical basis exists for identifying the restrainer as the Holy Spirit is invalid for at least two reasons.

1. The Bible signifies that the Holy Spirit functions as a restrainer of lawlessness. In Genesis 6:3, God said, "My Spirit shall not always strive with man." He thereby signified that His Spirit strove with lawless mankind in the days before the Noachic flood (vv. 5, 11–13). The Hebrew word translated "strive" means "to govern"; "it embodies the idea of government, in whatever realm" (Culver, *"din,"* in *Theological Wordbook of the Old Testament,* 1:188). God's statement indicated that the Holy Spirit has one of the same responsibilities or functions as government—the restraint of lawlessness in the world (Rom. 13:3–6; 1 Peter 2:13–14). Thus, the Holy Spirit's restraint of lawlessness has been a significant factor in the administration of God's rule over the world. Because this restraining work of the Spirit belongs to the administration of God's rule over the world, and because God is sovereign, only God has the authority to remove that restraint.

In Romans 8:2, Paul referred to "the law of the Spirit of life in Christ Jesus" that provides the believer with freedom "from the law of sin and death." Any kind of law—whether it be a natural, moral, spiritual, or governmental law—is established for the purpose of governing or controlling people or entities. In light of this fact, "the law of the Spirit" refers to the governing or controlling power of the Holy Spirit, and "the law of sin and death" refers to the governing or controlling power of the sin nature that causes people to be lawless and ultimately die (cf. Rom. 6:20–21, 23; 7:5, 7–13, 23). Paul was teaching that the governing or controlling power of the Holy Spirit provides the

Christian with freedom from the governing or controlling power of the sin nature, which causes people to be lawless. In other words, Paul indicated that the Holy Spirit has the function of restraining lawlessness in Christians. (For an in-depth study of this issue, see Showers, *The New Nature*.)

Second Thessalonians 2:3, 8 reveal that the Antichrist will be characterized by lawlessness. In verse three, the Greek word translated "sin" in the expression "that man of sin" means literally "lawlessness" (Arndt and Gingrich, *"anomia,"* in *A Greek-English Lexicon of the New Testament*, p. 71). In verse eight, the Greek word translated "wicked" in the expression "that Wicked" means literally "lawless one" (*"anomos,"* ibid.). Thus, both expressions reveal that the Antichrist will be the epitome or ultimate expression of human lawlessness.

In 2 Thessalonians 2:6–8, Paul indicated that the mystery of lawlessness was already working in his day. (As noted earlier, the Greek word translated "iniquity" in the expression "the mystery of iniquity" in verse 7 means literally "lawlessness.") But Paul also signified that some restraint of lawlessness was preventing the Antichrist, the ultimate expression of that lawlessness, from being revealed until the right time (v. 6). Paul further declared that the person causing that restraint would continue to do so until he, as the restrainer, would be "taken out of the way" (v. 7). Once the restrainer would be removed, the lawless one—the Antichrist—would be revealed (v. 8). As we noted earlier, the words *withholdeth* (v. 6) and *letteth* (v. 7) are translations of participle forms of the same Greek verb that means "restrain, check."

As noted earlier, because God's Holy Spirit has the function of restraining humanity's lawlessness, and because the Antichrist will be the ultimate expression of human lawlessness, Paul, in 2 Thessalonians 2:6–8, apparently was indicating that the restraining work of the Holy Spirit is the restraint that prevents the Antichrist from being revealed until the right time. The Holy Spirit will continue that restraining work until He, as the restrainer, is removed. Then the Antichrist will be revealed.

The Holy Spirit has other functions in addition to that of being a restrainer of lawlessness. For example, He also has functioned as a revealer (1 Cor. 2:10), a reprover or convicter (John 16:8), a regenerator (John 3:5–6; Titus 3:5), and a seal (Eph. 1:13–14). In light of this fact, we must note that when it is time for the Antichrist to be revealed, the Holy Spirit will be "taken out of the way" as a restrainer. He will not, for example, be "taken out of the way" as a regenerator. If He were removed as a regenerator, no people could get saved during the seventieth week, and yet the Scriptures clearly reveal that many people will get saved during that time (Rev. 7).

2. The second reason for the invalidity of the Pre-Wrath view claim that no biblical basis exists for identifying the restrainer as the Holy Spirit is as follows. Earlier, we noted that the restrainer in 2 Thessalonians 2 is described by a neuter gender participle in verse six ("what withholdeth") and a masculine gender participle in verse seven ("he who now letteth"). In line with this twofold description, the New Testament Greek word for the Spirit *(pneuma)* is neuter, and the New Testament also uses Greek masculine words (translated "he" and "him") to refer to the Spirit. For example, that combination is found in Christ's statements about the Spirit in John 14:26; 15:26, and 16:13–14.

Because the Bible signifies that the Holy Spirit functions as a restrainer of lawlessness, and because neuter and masculine words are used for the restrainer of 2 Thessalonians 2 and the Holy Spirit, we can conclude that a biblical basis does exist for identifying the Holy Spirit as the restrainer of 2 Thessalonians 2.

## Significant Questions

The fact that the Thessalonians were shaken and greatly disturbed by reports to the effect that the Day of the Lord was already present implies that at least some of them were beginning to believe those reports. How could they have been deceived into thinking that the Day of the Lord was already present when the great outpouring of God's Day-of-the-Lord wrath upon the world obviously had not yet begun? One cause for their deception could have been the persecution they were experiencing from the unbelievers of Thessalonica as a result of their profession of faith in Christ (Acts 17:5–9; 1 Thess. 1:6; 2:14; 3:3–4; 2 Thess. 1:4–7).

But why would the Thessalonians' persecution by the unbelievers prompt them to believe reports that the Day of the Lord was already present? The answer is that they understood that the time period covered by the Day of the Lord would be characterized by not only a great outpouring of God's wrath upon the world but also the persecution of professors of faith in Christ by unbelievers. The fact that Paul did not correct that understanding indicates that the time period covered by the Day of the Lord will indeed be characterized by the persecution of professors of faith in Christ by unbelievers.

From what source could the Thessalonian Christians have received this understanding? Because Paul had been their source of information about the Day of the Lord in the past (2 Thess. 2:2–5; cf. 1 Thess. 5:2), he apparently had taught them that the time period covered by the Day of the Lord would be characterized by not only a great outpouring of God's wrath but also the persecution of professors of faith in Christ by unbelievers.

This teaching of Paul is significant in light of the following three facts, which were exposited earlier in this critique:

- when Christ broke the fifth seal, John saw the souls of believers who had been martyred during the first four seals for their professions of faith in Christ;
- the first four seals are the beginning of birth pangs that Christ described in Matthew 24:5–8; and
- Christ placed the beginning of birth pangs in the first half of the seventieth week before the abomination of desolation.

The combination of these three facts indicates that the first half of the seventieth week will be characterized by the persecution of professors of faith in Christ by unbelievers.

Because the first half of the seventieth week will be characterized by the persecution of professors of faith in Christ by unbelievers, and because Paul apparently had taught the Thessalonians that the time period covered by the Day of the Lord would be characterized by the persecution of professors of faith in Christ by unbelievers, that Paul had also taught them that the Day of the Lord would include the first half of the seventieth week seems apparent.

## Conclusion

This chapter has presented reasons for concluding that the following teachings of the Pre-Wrath View are contrary to the Scriptures:

- Second Thessalonians 2:3 indicates that the Day of the Lord will not begin until after the apostasy;
- because the apostasy will exist from the beginning of the seventieth week through part of the second half of that time period, the Day of the Lord will not begin until part way through the second half of the seventieth week;
- the apostasy will be the total abandonment by Jews of the God of their ancestors and of Israel's hope of the Messiah;
- the revelation of the Antichrist will not take place until the middle of the seventieth week;
- the Day of the Lord will not begin until sometime after the middle of the seventieth week (after the revelation of the Antichrist); and
- the restrainer of 2 Thessalonians 2:6–7 is Michael the archangel, who will stop his restraint of enemy attacks against Israel in the middle of the seventieth week.

# CHAPTER TEN

# The Imminent
# Coming of Christ

## The Meaning of *Imminent*

To understand the concept of imminency, we must examine the meaning of the word *imminent*. The English word *imminent* comes from the Latin verb *immineo, imminere*, which means to "overhang" or "project" (Kidd, *Collins Latin Gem Dictionary*, s.v. *"immineo, imminere"*). In light of this fact, the English word *imminent* means "hanging over one's head, ready to befall or overtake one; close at hand in its incidence" (*The Oxford English Dictionary*, s.v. "imminent"). Thus, an imminent event is one that is always hanging overhead, is constantly ready to befall or overtake a person, or is always close at hand in the sense that it could happen at any moment. It "threatens to happen immediately" (*Webster's New International Dictionary*, s.v. "imminent").

Although an imminent event threatens to happen immediately, it does not have to happen immediately. "Imminence . . . refers to potential immediacy, not to necessary immediacy" (Payne, *The Imminent Appearing of Christ*, p. 98). Therefore, other things *may* happen before an imminent event, but nothing else *must* take place before it happens. The necessity of something else taking place first destroys the concept of imminency.

Because an imminent event threatens to happen immediately but does not have to happen immediately, a person cannot know when it will occur. In light of this uncertainty of time, three facts are true.

1. People cannot count on a certain amount of time transpiring before an imminent event occurs. Thus, they should constantly be prepared for it to happen at any moment.
2. People cannot legitimately set a date for an imminent event to occur. The setting of a date for an imminent event violates the concept of imminency. It signifies that a certain amount of time must elapse before that event can happen and thereby conflicts with the concept that the event could occur at any moment.
3. People cannot legitimately say that an imminent event will happen soon. The term *soon* implies that an event must take place "within a short time (after a particular point of time specified or implied)" (*The Oxford English Dictionary,* s.v. "soon"). In contrast, an imminent event may take place within a short time, but it does not have to take place soon to be imminent. Thus, *imminent* is not equal to *soon.* This truth is illustrated thus: the next coming of Christ was imminent in New Testament times, but because His coming has not occurred yet, it obviously was not soon then.

## The Concept of the Imminent Coming of Christ

In light of the meaning of the term *imminent* and the fact that the next coming of Christ has not occurred yet, the concept of the imminent coming of Christ is as follows. His next coming is always hanging over our heads, is constantly ready to befall or overtake us, and is always close at hand in the sense that it could happen at any moment. It could happen immediately, but it does not have to. Therefore, other events *may* happen before Christ's coming, but nothing else *must* take place before it occurs. The necessity of something else taking place first destroys the concept of the imminent coming of Christ.

Because Christ's coming could happen immediately but does not have to, we do not know when He will come. In light of this uncertainty of time, the following three facts are true.

1. We cannot count on a certain amount of time transpiring before Christ's coming; therefore, we should constantly be prepared for Him to come at any moment. "True uncertainty about the time of the Lord's appearing includes the possibility that He *could* come now, and this is the sum and substance of the classical doctrine of imminence" (Payne, *The Imminent Appearing of Christ*, p. 98).
2. We cannot legitimately set a date for Christ's coming.
3. We cannot legitimately say that Christ's coming will happen soon. It might happen soon, but it does not have to do so to be imminent.

## The Pre-Wrath Rapture View and the Imminent Coming of Christ

### Pre-Wrath View

The Pre-Wrath view rejects the imminency of Christ's coming. In conjunction with this rejection, it makes the following claims. The Bible does not teach imminency. What it does teach is expectancy—the concept that any generation since the first century could have been the one that would enter the seventieth week and, while enduring antagonistic persecution, would have the expectancy of Christ coming to rapture it out of the world before the beginning of the Day of the Lord with its outpouring of God's wrath. Thus, the Bible teaches an expectant rapture, not an imminent rapture (Rosenthal, *Pre-Wrath Rapture*, pp. 282–84).

The Pre-Wrath view claims that pretribulation rapturists have not given conclusive proof that the early church believed in an imminent coming of Christ and that the idea that the early church held to a doctrine of imminency has no valid support. It asserts that Bible scholar J. Barton Payne denied that the apostolic church held "an 'any moment' view of the Lord's coming" (quotation from Payne, *The Imminent Appearing of Christ,* p. 90; also see Rosenthal, *Pre-Wrath Rapture,* pp. 54, 55, 266).

## Critique One

The Pre-Wrath view distinction between imminency and expectancy does not rule out an imminent coming of Christ. The term *imminent* is an adjective used to describe the nature of an event. It depicts the kind of event that is always hanging overhead and could happen at any moment. In contrast, the term *expectant* is an adjective used to describe people's attitude toward an event (in other words, looking forward to, looking out for, or waiting for the happening of an event; *The Oxford English Dictionary,* s.v. "expectant" and "expectance"). People could have an expectant attitude toward either imminent or nonimminent events. *The Oxford English Dictionary* gives the following example of a person who had such an attitude toward an imminent event: "1877 Kinglake *Crimea* (ed. 6) V, i, 235, 'From moment to moment he was an expectant of death'" (ibid.). Thus, an expectant rapture could also be an imminent rapture.

Christians should have an expectant attitude toward Christ's coming. Because it is imminent and, therefore, could happen at any moment, believers should constantly look forward to, look out for, or wait for that event.

## Critique Two

The Pre-Wrath view appeal to J. Barton Payne as substantiation for its claim that no valid support exists for the idea that the early church held to a doctrine of imminency is of special interest to this author because he studied under Dr. Payne in graduate school. Dr. Payne was a post-tribulation rapturist by conviction. Note that he denied a belief in the imminency of Christ's coming only in "the early apostolic church," not in the latter part of the apostolic church. Immediately after stating that denial, Dr. Payne wrote,

> Even in those early days the end could have come about during the lifetime of those addressed. Indeed, the attitude that it should so come about is explicitly taught by inspiration: "*We* that are alive, that are left unto the coming of the Lord, shall in no wise precede them that are fallen asleep. . . . *We* all shall not sleep, but *we* shall all be changed. . . . then *we* that are alive, that are left, shall together with them be caught up in the clouds, to meet the Lord in the air: and so shall *we* ever be with the Lord." (1 Thess. 4:15, 17; 1 Cor. 15:51; *The Imminent Appearing of Christ,* p. 90)

Dr. Payne made comments to the effect that during the first half century of the church's existence it could not hold to an any-moment coming of Christ because of foretold events that had to transpire first. But after those foretold events of that first half century had been fulfilled, the church did hold to an imminent coming (ibid.). Dr. Payne asserted that in John 21:22–23, the apostle John indicated that the church in the latter part of the apostolic age believed that Christ would come before he (John) would die (ibid., p. 91).

In response to the argument that the New Testament passages that were written during the first half century, when Christ's coming could not be imminent, cannot now be regarded as teaching imminency, Dr. Payne declared that this argument does not "square with the Biblical evidence" (ibid.). In addition, he wrote, "The interpreter's primary task is therefore to discover, not what he feels the apostolic writers *could* have said about imminency, but what the text indicates that they did say" (ibid.). Then he asserted that as the interpreter seeks "a solution for the tension that may have existed between the apostles' statements on the imminence of the Lord's coming and their individual awareness of the events which for them lay antecedent to it," he does not have the liberty to deny the statements themselves (ibid.).

Later, contrary to the Pre-Wrath view claim, Dr. Payne stated, "Belief in the imminency of the return of Jesus was the uniform hope of the early church" (ibid., p. 102). He also declared that the early Christians "were waiting, eagerly awaiting, His imminent appearing" (ibid., p. 85).

Other scholars indicate that the early church believed in the imminent coming of Christ. For example, concerning the *parousia,* or coming of Christ, *The Oxford Dictionary of the Christian Church* states, "Primitive Christianity believed the event to be imminent and this belief has been revived from time to time in the history of the Church" (s.v. "parousia"). The word *parousia* is one of the terms in the Greek New Testament for the future coming of Christ.

In addition, Albrecht Oepke wrote, "Primitive Christianity waits for the Jesus who has come already as the One who is still to come. The hope of an imminent coming of the exalted Lord in messianic glory is, however, so much to the fore that in the NT the terms are never used for the coming of Christ in the flesh" (*"parousia,"* in *Theological Dictionary of the New Testament,* 5:865). In the latter part of this statement, Oepke was signifying that terms such as *parousia* are never used in the New Testament for Christ's First Coming (when He was incarnated in human flesh).

### Critique Three

Contrary to the Pre-Wrath view claim that the Bible does not teach imminency, numerous Bible scholars (including many who are not pretribulation rapturists) believe that it does teach the imminent coming of Christ. For example, J. G. Davies, the Edward Cadbury Professor of Theology at the University of Birmingham, stated that the expectation of Christ's "imminent coming" is "so vivid in the New Testament" (*The Early Christian Church,* p. 132).

J. Barton Payne, a post-tribulation rapturist, was convinced that eleven New Testament passages teach the imminent coming of Christ (Matt. 24:42–25:13; Luke 12:36–40; Rom. 8:19, 23, 25; 1 Cor. 1:7; Phil. 3:20; 4:5; 1 Thess. 1:9–10; Titus 2:12–13; James 5:7–8; Jude 21; Rev. 16:15; *The Imminent Appearing of Christ,* pp. 95–103). On the basis of the teaching of these passages, he wrote, "It must therefore be concluded that the denial of the imminence of the Lord's coming . . . is not legitimate" (ibid., p. 102). Concerning a view that denies the imminent coming of Christ, Dr. Payne asserted, "its inherited presuppositions against imminence have warped its exegesis of those Biblical passages that are relevant to it" (ibid., p. 103). Regarding the legitimacy of belief in the imminency of Christ's coming, he stated, "In fact, no natural reading of Scripture would produce any other conclusion" (ibid., p. 102).

Statements of a significant number of Bible scholars concerning the teaching of specific New Testament passages related to the coming of Christ will be quoted. This author wants to emphasize that his purpose for these quotations is to demonstrate that numerous Bible scholars from various church and theological backgrounds have come to the same conclusion, namely, that the New Testament teaches the imminent coming of Christ. The author's intention is not to give the impression that, because these scholars have come to that conclusion, they also believe that the New Testament teaches a pretribulation rapture of the church. To this author's knowledge, many of the scholars quoted do not advocate a pretribulation rapture. In addition to quotations, the author will in some instances present exegetical factors as evidences that some New Testament passages do teach the imminent coming of Christ.

### First Corinthians 1:7

**The Text.** "So that ye come behind in no gift; waiting for the coming of our Lord Jesus Christ."

**Comments.** The Greek word translated "waiting for" means "await eagerly" (Arndt and Gingrich, *"apekdechomai,"* in *A Greek-*

*English Lexicon of the New Testament,* p. 82). Friedrich Buchsel indicated that it referred to "the Christian attitude . . . of burning expectation" (*"apekdechomai,"* in *Theological Dictionary of the New Testament,* 2:56).

**Quotations.** J. Barton Payne stated that "the major stress of the passage rests upon the intensity of the saints' longing" for the Lord's coming, and "the lack of evidence for any postponement seems to suggest the 'perhaps today' possibility" (*The Imminent Appearing of Christ,* p. 99).

Concerning the latter part of 1 Corinthians 1:7, Gordon D. Fee stated that Paul had an "ever present" concern about Christ's "imminent return" (*The First Epistle to the Corinthians,* p. 42).

*First Corinthians 4:5*

**The Text.** "Therefore judge nothing before the time, until the Lord come, who both will bring to light the hidden things of darkness, and will make manifest the counsels of the hearts: and then shall every man have praise of God."

**Comment.** In this context (1 Cor. 3:8–4:5), Paul referred to the future time when all Christians will stand before the judgment seat of Christ in conjunction with His coming (cf. Rom. 14:10–12; 2 Cor. 5:10).

**Quotation.** On the basis of this passage, Johannes Schneider wrote, "Paul lives in expectation of the imminent coming again of Christ" (*"erchomai,"* in *Theological Dictionary of the New Testament,* 2:674).

*First Corinthians 15:51–52*

**The Text.** "Behold, I show you a mystery; We shall not all sleep, but we shall all be changed, in a moment, in the twinkling of an eye, at the last trump: for the trumpet shall sound, and the dead shall be raised incorruptible, and we shall be changed."

**Quotations.** In conjunction with these statements, Rudolf Bultmann said, "Believers are still subject, of course, to physical death, though in the early days of imminent expectation of the *parousia* it is seen that this fate will not overtake all Christians" (*"thanatos,"* in *Theological Dictionary of the New Testament,* 3:18).

Gaston Deluz declared, "Christ's return is always imminent; we must never cease to watch for it. The first Christians thought it so near that they faced the possibility of Jesus' return in their lifetime. Paul thinks he too may be alive when it happens" (*A Companion to 1 Corinthians,* p. 248).

A. L. Moore, in his book titled *The Parousia in the New Testament,* asserted the following view:

> Paul does not write as one who will certainly be dead at the Parousia, but as one who awaits the Parousia as an event which might occur at any moment and therefore he reckons with the possibility of his being alive at that time; but this does not mean that he included himself amongst those who would necessarily be alive at its coming. (p. 118)

R. C. H. Lenski stated, "The simple fact is that Paul did not know when Christ would return. He was in the exact position in which we are. All that he knew, and all that we know, is that Christ may come at any moment" (*The Interpretation of St. Paul's First and Second Epistle to the Corinthians,* p. 737).

### First Corinthians 16:22

**The Text.** "If any man love not the Lord Jesus Christ, let him be Anathema Maranatha."

**Comments.** The significant part of this statement in relationship to Christ's coming is the term Maranatha, which was one of several "eschatological statements concerning Christ's coming . . . within the framework of early Christian tradition" (Schneider, *"erchomai,"* in *Theological Dictionary of the New Testament,* 2:674). It was distinct among these statements because it was an Aramaic expression (ibid.). It had the form of a petition (ibid.). The *Didache* 10.6 (in *Documents of the Christian Church*), an ancient Christian manual of worship, used this petition in statements that were made at the end of the communion service. This usage helps to clarify the meaning of this expression, especially in light of Paul's reference to the future coming of Christ in conjunction with the observance of communion (1 Cor. 11:26).

Leon Morris said that the term Maranatha consists of three Aramaic words: *Mar* ("Lord"), *ana* ("our"), and *tha* ("come"); thus, the entire term meant "our Lord, come" (*The First Epistle of Paul to the Corinthians,* p. 248). In light of this meaning, Charles J. Ellicott declared that Maranatha was "practically equivalent to" the expression "The Lord is at hand" in Philippians 4:5 (*St. Paul's First Epistle to the Corinthians,* p. 344).

William Barclay explained the significance of Paul's use of this Aramaic term in a letter to a Greek church:

> It is strange to meet with an Aramaic phrase in a Greek letter to a Greek Church. The explanation is that this phrase had become a watchword and a password. It summed up the vital hope of the early Church, and Christians whispered it to each other, identified each other by it, in a language which the heathen could not understand. (*The Letters to the Corinthians,* p. 188)

In the same vein, K. G. Kuhn declared that "the untranslated Aram. term is meaningful only if it is a fixed formula" that began in the Palestinian Christian community and then was adopted untranslated by the Greek-speaking Christians (*"maranatha,"* in *Theological Dictionary of the New Testament,* 4:470). In light of this beginning and adoption of the term, Kuhn concluded that "maranatha is an important and authentic witness to the faith of the primitive Palestinian community" (ibid.).

Leon Morris asserted that the term *Maranatha* "must have expressed a sentiment that the early Church regarded as supremely important, else it would never have been taken over in this way by the Greek-speaking Christians" (*The First Epistle of Paul to the Corinthians,* p. 247).

Apparently, the fixed usage of the term *Maranatha* by the early Christians was a witness to their strong belief in the imminent return of Christ. If they knew that Christ could not return at any moment because of other events or a time period that had to transpire first, then why did they petition Him in a way that implied that He could come at any moment?

**Quotation.** Archibald T. Robertson and Alfred Plummer made the following statement concerning the significance of the term *Maranatha* in 1 Corinthians 16:22: "It warns them that at any moment they may have to answer for their shortcomings" (*A Critical and Exegetical Commentary on the First Epistle of St. Paul to the Corinthians,* p. 401).

*Philippians 3:20*

**The Text.** "For our conversation is in heaven; from whence also we look for the Saviour, the Lord Jesus Christ."

**Quotations.** The Greek word translated "look for" is a strong compound. The observations of several scholars concerning its emphasis and implications are significant. H. A. A. Kennedy wrote, "The compound emphasizes the intense yearning for the Parousia. . . . The dominant influence of this expectation in Paul's thinking and working is only beginning to be fully recognized" ("The Epistle to the Philippians," in *The Expositor's Greek Testament,* 3:463).

Alfred Plummer declared that the first part of the compound Greek word translated "look for" "implies disregard of other things and concentration on one object" (*A Commentary on St. Paul's Epistle to the Philippians,* p. 84).

F. F. Bruce said the following:

> But they did eagerly wait for their Savior, the Lord Jesus Christ, to come from heaven. This expectation was a constant element in the primitive apostolic preaching: the Thessalonian converts, for example, were taught to wait for the Son of God "to come from heaven—His Son

Jesus, . . . who rescues his people from the coming judgment" (1 Thess. 1:10). (*Philippians,* p. 108)

James Montgomery Boice stated that "the expectation of the Lord's personal and imminent return gave joy and power to the early Christians and to the Christian communities" (*Philippians,* p. 247).

**Comments.** We should note that Paul included himself among those who had this attitude toward Christ's coming. Thus, Philippians 3:20 indicates that the expectation of Christ's coming was so intense for Paul and the other Christians of New Testament times that it was the primary focus of their concentration. Would it have been so if no possibility existed of an any-moment coming?

### Philippians 4:5

**The Text.** "Let your moderation be known unto all men. The Lord is at hand."

**Quotations.** James Moffatt asserted that, in the context of Philippians 4:5, the expression "the Lord is at hand" "means the imminent arrival of the Lord rather than his spiritual presence within the Church" (*The First Epistle of Paul to the Corinthians,* p. 283).

William Hendriksen said that Paul's statement indicated that "it behooves every one to be ready, working, watching at all times" (*Exposition of Philippians,* p. 194)

Pat Edwin Harrell pointed out that, in Paul's declaration,

the imminence of the Lord's return is used as a motivation for Christian conduct. This does not mean that the apostle contemplated that return tomorrow. In another place in this letter he admits the possibility that he might die before this anticipated event transpires (cf. 1:23) and he reveals plans he has made (2:23). While the Lord's return may not be here, it is near and the Christians must conduct themselves accordingly. (*The Letter of Paul to the Philippians,* p. 137)

F. W. Beare declared, "The Apostle is not speaking of the nearness of the Lord in his abiding presence with us, but of the imminence of his coming" (*A Commentary on the Epistle to the Philippians,* p. 146).

Martyn Lloyd-Jones wrote, "In all we do we must always remember that the Lord may return at any time. His coming is always at hand, yes, but we do not know when, and so we must always live in the realisation that he is coming" (*Life of Peace,* p. 162).

Alfred Plummer stated that "at any moment they may have to answer for their conduct" (*A Commentary on St. Paul's Epistle to the Philippians,* p. 93).

### First Thessalonians 1:10

**The Text.** "And to wait for his Son from heaven, whom he raised from the dead, even Jesus, which delivered us from the wrath to come."

**Comments.** The Greek word translated "to wait for" consists of two parts. The first part means "up" (Vine, *"anameno,"* in *An Expository Dictionary of New Testament Words,* 4:194). The second part means "wait for, await" and is used of people who *"wait for* someone who is arriving" (Arndt and Gingrich, *"meno,"* in *A Greek-English Lexicon of the New Testament,* p. 505). Thus, the word refers literally to the activity of people who "wait up for" someone who is arriving. They do not go to bed at their normal time because they are expecting a guest to arrive at any moment. Their understanding is that no time period must elapse before that person can come. If they knew that he could not come for several more hours, they would not wait up. They would go to bed at their normal time and set their alarm to wake them at the known time of their guest's arrival.

W. E. Vine asserted that the Greek word that Paul used carries "the suggestion of waiting with patience and confident expectancy" (Vine, *"anameno,"* in *An Expository Dictionary of New Testament Words*, 4:194). Thus, the word referred to the activity of people who wait patiently for a guest to arrive because they are confident that he could arrive at any moment.

Paul used the present tense of the Greek word translated "to wait for." Archibald Thomas Robertson indicated that the present tense of this specific word gave it the sense of "to keep on waiting for" (*Word Pictures in the New Testament*, 4:14). It refers to the continuous action of waiting for someone.

The combination of the meaning and present tense of the Greek word translated "to wait for" in 1 Thessalonians 1:10 prompts the conclusion that Paul was indicating that the Thessalonian Christians were continuously and patiently expecting or waiting up for Christ to return from heaven because they were confident that He could come at any moment.

This continuous waiting up for the Lord to come prompts the following question. From whom or what did the Thessalonian believers derive this concept of the imminent return of Christ? Because Paul had been their teacher when he was with them before he wrote 1 Thessalonians (Acts 17; 1 Thess. 2:13; 2 Thess. 2:5), apparently he was the one who taught them to expect the Lord to return at any moment. This conclusion is supported by the fact that Paul did not tell the Thessalonians that they were wrong to have that expectancy. Instead, he referred approvingly to their expectant attitude.

**Quotations.** Concerning Paul's statement in 1 Thessalonians 1:10, D. Edmond Hiebert wrote,

> The infinitive rendered "to wait for" *(anamenein)* means "to await, expect, wait up for" and pictures them as people who are eagerly and expectantly looking forward to the coming of one whose arrival is anticipated at any time; the present tense gives this as their continuing attitude. Clearly the Thessalonians held the hope of the imminent return of Christ. (*The Thesssalonian Epistles*, p. 70)

I. Howard Marshall stated, "The hope (1:3) of the coming of Jesus was an integral part of the Thessalonians' religion; it was something that they anticipated as a real possibility in their own lifetimes (4:15, 17; 5:4). This hoped-for imminence of the *parousia* made it a vital part of their Christian belief" ("1 and 2 Thessalonians," in *The New Century Bible Commentary*, p. 58). J. Barton Payne asserted,

> The appreciation of the Thessalonians for the imminence of the coming of Christ that this passage describes was so marked that some of them seem to have given up their ordinary pursuits, the better "to wait for" His immediate return (II Thess. 3:10). Their excessive eagerness is felt to have been a major factor in Paul's writing II Thessalonians shortly after this (cf. 2:2), but its very presence witnesses to the vital contemporaneity of the apostolic preaching of the blessed hope. (*The Imminent Appearing of Christ*, p. 100)

John Lillie wrote,

> Observe that there was nothing in this attitude of the model church of Macedonia, that Paul thought it necessary to reprove or correct. So far from that, he mentions it as the legitimate and immediate fruit of conversion—as something that the brethren were everywhere talking of with joy, and to the honor of Thessalonica . . . Wherever the grace of God then appeared, it taught men, as one grand motive to all sober, and righteous, and godly living, to "look for that blessed hope, and the glorious appearing of our great God and Saviour Jesus Christ;" yea, to look for it as near—as a thing to be loved, and hastened, and waited for at all seasons, whether of sorrow or of joy. (*Lectures on the Epistles of Paul to the Thessalonians*, pp. 75–76)

Thomas L. Constable said, "The clear implication of this verse is that Paul hoped in the Lord's imminent return. Otherwise Paul would have told his readers to prepare for the Tribulation" ("1 Thessalonians," in *The Bible Knowledge Commentary, New Testament,* p. 693).

James Everett Frame declared, "The nearness of the thing expected is suggested by the very idea of waiting" (*A Critical and Exegetical Commentary on the Epistles of St. Paul to the Thessalonians,* p. 88).

D. Edmond Hiebert asserted,

> In 1 Thessalonians 1:10 the Thessalonian believers are pictured as waiting for the return of Christ. The clear implication is that they had a hope of His imminent return. If they had been taught that the Great Tribulation, in whole or in part, must first run its course, it is difficult to see how they would be described as expectantly awaiting Christ's return. Then they should rather have been described as bracing themselves for the Great Tribulation and the painful events connected with it. (*The Thessalonian Epistles,* p. 205)

**Comment.** To express it another way, the Thessalonian Christians were expectantly waiting for the coming of Christ, not for the coming of the Antichrist.

### Second Thessalonians 3:10–12

**The Text.** "For even when we were with you, this we commanded you, that if any would not work, neither should he eat. For we hear that there are some which walk among you disorderly, working not at all, but are busybodies. Now them that are such we command and exhort by our Lord Jesus Christ, that with quietness they work, and eat their own bread."

**Comments.** The Thessalonian church had a problem. Some of the believers had stopped working and were expecting their fellow believers to supply their daily needs. Paul's language indicated that these idlers had stopped earning their own livelihood, not because they were incapable of working, but because they had willfully determined not to work.

In addition to refusing to work, these people were "busybodies" (v. 11). Leon Morris explained this term as follows:

> These people were not simply idle, they were meddling in the affairs of others. We may conjecture that they were trying to do one or both of two incompatible things, namely, to get their living from others, and to persuade those others to share their point of view about the second advent, and so persuade them to stop working also. (*The First and Second Epistles to the Thessalonians,* p. 256)

What prompted such disorderly conduct? Morris is convinced that Paul gave a clue to the answer in his command and exhortation to these people to work "with quietness" (v. 12). "The root trouble was apparently their excitability. The thought of the nearness of the Parousia had thrown them into a flutter, and this had led to unwelcome consequences of which their idleness was the outstanding feature" (ibid.).

James Everett Frame agrees with this conclusion. He wrote that the expression "with quietness" "is to be understood as the opposite . . . of the feverish excitement of mind stimulated by the belief that the *Parousia* was at hand" (*A Critical and Exegetical Commentary on the Epistles of St. Paul to the Thessalonians,* p. 307).

Apparently, then, these idle Christians believed in the imminent coming of Christ; however, they concluded wrongly that "imminent" equals "soon." Thus, instead of believing that Christ *could* come soon, they were convinced that He definitely *would* come soon, and work was therefore no longer necessary for them.

Apparently Paul had taught these believers the imminent

coming of Christ. Paul's negative response to their actions, however, implies that their wrong conduct was the result of a perversion of his teaching (cf. vv. 6, 10). Contrary to them, Paul did not equate "imminent" with "soon" and think, therefore, that work was unnecessary.

## Titus 2:13

**The Text.** "Looking for that blessed hope, and the glorious appearing of the great God and our Saviour Jesus Christ."

**Comments.** The Greek word translated "looking" has the sense of "to await" and is "used of the subject of Christian expectation" (Grundmann, *"prosdechomai,"* in *Theological Dictionary of the New Testament,* 2:58).

Concerning the concept of hope, Donald Guthrie wrote, "In the New Testament *hope* does not indicate merely what is wished for but what is assured" (*The Pastoral Epistles,* p. 199).

Paul described this particular hope as "blessed." In the New Testament, this Greek word "refers overwhelmingly to the distinctive religious joy which accrues to a man from his share in the salvation of the kingdom of God" (Hauck, *"makarios,"* in *Theological Dictionary of the New Testament,* 4:367).

According to the Greek text, the expression "the glorious appearing" should be translated "appearing of the glory" (Vincent, *Word Studies in the New Testament,* 4:345). The full expression "the appearing of the glory of the great God and our Savior, Jesus Christ" does not refer to some event separate from the blessed hope. Instead, it describes the event that is that hope (ibid.). Thus, the Christians' hope is the appearing of the divine glory that belongs to God and Christ. Surely Christians will see that glory in Christ when He comes to rapture the church.

In light of these observations, we can conclude that, in the context of Titus 2, Paul was saying the following in verse 13: Grace is teaching Christians to live sober, righteous, and godly lives in this present age in conjunction with their expectant waiting for the appearing of the divine glory in Christ when

He comes to rapture the church. The assurance of that appearing is a source of great joy to Christians, for that appearing will bring incredibly happy changes for them, such as the loss of their sin nature and the reception of an immortal body.

**Quotations.** On the basis of Titus 2:13, Marvin R. Vincent wrote, "That which is *accepted* in faith, is *awaited* expectantly" (ibid., p. 344).

Newport J. D. White indicated that Paul "describes the glad expectancy which is the ruling and prevailing thought in the lives of men looking for their Lord's return" ("The Epistle to Titus," in *The Expositor's Greek Testament,* 4:195).

J. Barton Payne asserted, "In truth, the Titus context suggests that the blessed hope of Christ's appearing is as much an 'ever-present possibility' as is the life of sobriety, righteousness, and godliness" (*The Imminent Appearing of Christ,* p. 100).

William Barclay declared,

> The dynamic of this new life is the expectation of the coming of Jesus Christ. When a royal visit is expected, everything is cleansed and decorated, and made fit for the royal eye to see. The Christian is the man who is always prepared for the coming of the King of kings. (*The Letters to Timothy, Titus and Philemon,* p. 257)

**Comment.** Why should Christians always be prepared for Christ's coming, unless that coming could take place at any moment?

### James 5:7–9

**The Text.** "Be patient therefore, brethren, unto the coming of the Lord. . . . Be ye also patient; stablish your hearts: for the coming of the Lord draweth nigh. Grudge not one against another, brethren, lest ye be condemned: behold, the judge standeth before the door."

**Comments.** Note two important truths in conjunction with this passage. First, the epistle of James was written to Jewish

Christians, not to non-Christian Jews. Everett F. Harrison gave several evidences for this conclusion:

> It is clear that the Epistle of James would not have been received into the canon if the early church had understood it to be directed to Jews in general. It is equally clear that the epistle itself contains items that could hardly have been included in a document intended for non-Christians. Faith in the Lord Jesus Christ is presupposed (2:1). This in turn makes "the coming of the Lord" (5:7) a reference to Christ's coming rather than to some future intervention of the Lord God of Israel. The same is true of the description of the readers as born or brought forth by the word of truth (1:18). This is better understood as an allusion to regeneration than to creation. The good name that has been called upon the readers (2:7) is almost certainly that of Christ. Some interpreters see here an allusion to Christian baptism. (*Introduction to the New Testament*, p. 362)

In addition, James addressed his readers as "brethren" a total of fifteen times (just as he addressed Jewish Christian apostles and elders as "brethren" at the first church council; Acts 15:13), and "he bases his authority upon the fact that he is a 'servant of God and of the Lord Jesus Christ' (1:1)" (Hiebert, *An Introduction to the Non-Pauline Epistles*, p. 50).

Robert G. Gromacki further described James's readers as Christian Jews from the twelve tribes of Israel who were scattered throughout the Roman Empire (*New Testament Survey*, p. 338).

The identification of James's readers is important because the fact that it was written to Jewish Christians means that the coming of the Lord and the potential judgment to which James referred in 5:7–9 have implications for Christians and should concern them.

The second important truth to note about James 5:7–9 is the

fact that the Greek verbs translated "draweth nigh" (v. 8) and "standeth" (v. 9) are in the perfect tense and indicative mood. This fact means that each of these verbs refers to an action that was completed before James wrote his epistle and that continues on in that completed state (Dana and Mantey, *A Manual Grammar of the Greek New Testament,* p. 200). This fact implies that Christ's coming drew near before James wrote his epistle, and His coming continues to be near. In addition, Christ as judge began to stand before the door of heaven before James wrote his epistle, and Christ as judge continues to stand before the door of heaven. In other words, Christ's coming was imminent in New Testament times and continues to be imminent to the present day. James wanted to impress his readers with the fact that Christ could come through the door of heaven at any moment and cause them as Christians to stand before Him at the judgment seat of Christ. He could do so today.

In line with this view, Herbert Preisker stated that the Greek verb translated "draweth nigh" in the expression "the coming of the Lord draweth nigh" is used in James 5:8 "for a situation of tense eschatological expectation" (*"engus,"* in *Theological Dictionary of the New Testament,* 2:331). Preisker further declared that in the early days of Christianity the verb and its related adverb expressed "hope of the imminence of the coming world" (ibid., p. 332).

**Quotations.** On the basis of James 5:7–9, various scholars have made the following statements.

Robert G. Bratcher: *"the judge is standing at the doors:* this is another way of speaking of the imminent coming of the Lord" (*A Translator's Guide to the Letters from James, Peter, and Jude,* p. 55).

M. F. Sadler:

> The Lord had laid it upon His disciples that they should be ever looking for a coming which might be expected at any moment after His departure, and yet might be long delayed.

If the Apostles had believed that the Lord would come late in the ages, . . . there would have been no need for them to watch; but if they believed that the Lord might return in the "evening" that is, very shortly after His departure, it was very needful to watch, and so they did. (*The General Epistles of SS. James, Peter, John and Jude,* pp. 68–69)

James B. Adamson: "The imminence of the Parousia is another strong argument for the Epistle's early date" (*The Epistle of James,* p. 191), and "*At the door* is a picture of imminent judgment, and an incentive to patience" (ibid., p. 192).

Frank E. Gaebelein: James "does not treat the subject at length. He simply declares it as an inescapable fact, emphasizing, as he does so, its imminence" (*The Practical Epistle of James,* p. 112).

Vernon D. Doerksen: "The perfect 'is at hand,' literally meaning 'has drawn nigh,' denotes imminency" (*James,* p. 123), and "The picture of imminent judgment is as much an incentive to patience as is the coming of Christ to bring deliverance" (ibid.).

E. C. Blackman: "Endurance is necessary, but there is encouragement for those who have to face trials in the thought that the coming of the Lord is imminent" (*The Epistle of James,* p. 146).

J. A. Motyer:

His return is *at hand.* It has been so from the day of the apostles. James was not mistaken even though he lived over 1,000 years ago. The return of the Lord was then at hand; the return of the Lord is now at hand. We live in the last days, the day of the imminent return . . . the pressure upon us of that return is not to promote curiosity as to the date and circumstances, but to promote the life of holiness and fruitfulness, so that we may be ready to meet the Lord. (*The Tests of Faith,* p. 107)

C. Leslie Mitton: "James clearly believed, as others of his time did, that the coming of Christ was imminent" (*The Epistle of James,* p. 186).

Spiros Zodhiates: "When this verb is used of time, it speaks of imminence. James tells us that this blessed event of the second coming of the Lord will come at any time, is imminent. . . . Our hearts will be propped up if we live in the constant expectation of His coming" (*The Patience of Hope,* p. 90).

David P. Scaer: "The early church was caught up with the lively hope of the imminent return of Jesus" (*James the Apostle of Faith,* p. 126).

Douglas J. Moo:

> The accusation that James has erred on this matter rests on the supposition that James believed that the *parousia* must *necessarily* occur within a very brief period of time. But there is no reason to think that this was the case. The early Christians' conviction that the *parousia* was "near," or "imminent," meant that they fully believed that it *could* transpire within a very short period of time— not that it *had to.* (*The Letter of James,* p. 169)

Homer A. Kent Jr.: "James was referring to the return of Christ, which he thought might occur at any time" (*Faith That Works,* p. 176).

Harold T. Bryson: "He expected the Lord to return any day while he lived. . . . The idea in the New Testament is imminence. To lose sight of the nearness of the Lord's return is to depart from the New Testament as well as to doubt its certainty" (*How Faith Works,* pp. 116–17), and "The expression 'standing at the doors' implies the Lord's imminent entrance into history to make a distinction between what is good and what is bad" (ibid., p. 119).

Peter H. Davids: "That the judge, . . . who alone has the right to criticize the Christians (4:11–12) and who will judge the complaining Christian (e.g. 1 Cor. 3:10–17; 2 Cor. 5:10), stands before the door is an image, not of the place of judgment (i.e. the city gate, . . . ), but of its imminence" (*The Epistle of James,* p. 185).

Simon J. Kistemaker: "The reminder of the Lord's imminent return is necessary so that the readers will not lose heart in difficult circumstances" (*Exposition of the Epistle of James and the Epistles of John,* p. 165).

### First John 2:28

**The Text.** "And now, little children, abide in him; that, when he shall appear, we may have confidence, and not be ashamed before him at his coming."

**Comments.** John commanded believers to abide in Christ. The Greek verb translated "abide" is in the imperative, or command, mood (David Smith, "The Epistles of John," in *The Expositor's Greek Testament,* 5:181). This verb means to "remain, continue, abide" and is used "of someone who does not leave the realm or sphere in which he finds himself" (Arndt and Gingrich, *"meno,"* in *A Greek-English Lexicon of the New Testament,* p. 505). This meaning, together with the fact that John used the present tense, indicates that he was commanding Christians to abide continuously in right fellowship with Christ. John stated that Christians should continuously do this so that they can face Jesus with confidence and not be ashamed when He comes (*parousia*).

The Greek word translated "when" in the expression "when he shall appear" introduces an element of uncertainty relative to Christ's coming. John did not mean by this that the *fact* of Christ's coming was uncertain. Instead, the apostle meant that the *time* of Jesus' coming was uncertain, and "this is the reason for steadfast abiding in Him" (Smith, "The Epistles of John," 5:182). John's point was that Christ's coming "might be while they all still lived" (Westcott, *The Epistles of St. John,* p. 81).

In light of these observations, we can conclude that John's statements imply that Christ could come at any moment; therefore, Christians should continuously be ready for His coming by constantly having their lives in right relationship with Him.

**Quotations.** On the basis of 1 John 2:28, various scholars have made the following statements.

A. E. Brooke:

> The nearness of the day affords a new motive for the effort to which they are urged. The nearer the Parousia of their Lord the greater the need of constancy. . . . If that happens which, as circumstances have shown, may befall them now at any moment, they must be in a position not to be ashamed, when the object of their longing expectation is there. (*A Critical and Exegetical Commentary on the Johannine Epistles,* The International Critical Commentary, p. 65)

Charles H. Spurgeon:

> The date of that coming is concealed. When he shall come, no man can tell. Watch for him, and be always ready, that you may not be ashamed at his advent. Should a Christian man go into worldly assemblies and amusements? Would he not be ashamed should his Lord come and find him among the enemies of the cross? I dare not go where I should be ashamed to be found should my Lord come on a sudden. Should a Christian man ever be in a passion? Suppose his Lord should there and then come; would he not be ashamed at his coming? One here says of an offender, "I will never forgive her; she will never darken my doors again." Would you not be ashamed if the Lord Jesus came, and found you unforgiving? Oh, that we may abide in him, and never be in such a state that his coming would be unwelcome to us! Beloved, so live from day to day in duty and in devotion, that your Lord's coming would be timely. Go about your daily business and abide in him, and then his coming will be a glorious delight to you. (*Twelve Sermons on the Second Coming of Christ,* p. 134)

George G. Findlay:

Christ is to be manifested in His promised advent—*when* we know not, but it may be soon; and we must appear before Him, with shame or confidence. Abiding in Him, we shall be prepared whenever He may come. If the present should prove to be the world's last hour and the Lord should appear from heaven while we are yet on earth, how welcome His appearing to those who love Him and keep His word. (*Fellowship in the Life Eternal,* p. 232)

Christ stands waiting to return. At any moment the heavens may open and He "may be manifested." . . . The Christian man, susceptible to these impressions, will surely ask himself, "What if my Lord should now appear? how should I meet Him, if He came today: with joy or grief; with shame or rapture? This is a test that Christ's servants might often with advantage put to themselves. (Ibid., p. 233)

In this one instance St John writes of the *parousia,* as St Paul has done so frequently, and builds on the anticipation of a definitive return of the Lord Jesus. The fact that he does speak of it in this way, though but once, and that he lays a solemn stress on the expectation, proves his agreement with the prevalent eschatology of the Church. (Ibid.)

Robert S. Candlish:

Let me ever be asking myself, at every moment, If he were to appear now, would I have confidence? . . . Let us then be always abiding in him; every day, every hour, every instant; even as we would wish to be found abiding in him, were he to appear this very day, this very hour, this very instant. He is about to appear; to appear suddenly; to come quickly. (*The First Epistle of John*, p. 213)

*Revelation 3:11; 22:7, 12, 20*

**The Text.** "I come quickly."

**Quotations.** On the basis of these repeated assertions by Christ, scholars have made the following statements.

J. Barton Payne stated that the Greek word translated "quickly"

> means, not "soon," but "swiftly, all at once," that is before one can be aware and make preparations. . . . It should therefore be clear at the outset that imminency does not mean that Christ's coming *must* be soon. . . . His day *could* be soon, "close at hand in its incidence." Does this mean then that it could be so soon as to happen right away, at any time? This is the thought that is associated with imminency, "ready to befall or overtake one." (*The Imminent Appearing of Christ*, p. 86)

Archibald Thomas Robertson: "'I come' *(erchomai)*. Futuristic present middle indicative, 'I am coming' (imminent). . . . We do not know how soon 'quickly' is meant to be understood. But it is a real threat" (*Word Pictures in the New Testament*, 6:306).

Edward Schick: "Christ in this context repeats the announcement of his imminent advent" (*The Revelation of St. John*, p. 119).

W. Lincoln: "Also it is quite evident that He would have us to live in the constant expectation of His advent being imminent" (*Lectures on the Book of the Revelation*, p. 241).

Leon Morris: "The imminence of the coming is repeated" (*The Revelation of St. John*, p. 258).

J. B. Smith:

> This corresponds with the note of imminency in the latter part of Revelation 1:3, "for the time is at hand." (*A Revelation of Jesus Christ*, p. 301)

This is the second occurrence of the note of imminence in the concluding section (cf. verse 7). It occurs again in verse 20 in climactic and intensified form: "Surely I come quickly." (Ibid., p. 302)

Merrill C. Tenney: "Nowhere is a date set, nor was there any definite promise that the consummation would occur within the lifetime of the first century Christians. Nevertheless, the possibility of the Lord's advent was always present" (*Interpreting Revelation*, p. 150).

J. A. Seiss:

Nor is it here alone, but throughout the New Testament in general, that such expressions are used. Everywhere is the promised Apocalypse of the Lord Jesus represented as close at hand, liable to occur at any time. The impression thus made upon the early Christians was, that Christ might come at any day or hour, even in their own lifetime. Exactly when he would come, was nowhere told them. . . . Ever, as the Church moves on through time, and above all in the days in which we live, the next thing for every Christian to be looking for in this world is the coming of Christ to fulfill what is written in this Book. The Bible tells of nothing between us and that day. (*The Apocalypse*, p. 523)

**Comments.** In more than one of these passages Christ introduced His assertions "I come quickly" with the interjection "behold." The Greek word translated "behold" was used to arouse "the attention of hearers or readers" (Arndt and Gingrich, *"idou,"* in *A Greek-English Lexicon of the New Testament,* p. 371). In Jesus' last assertion (Rev. 22:20), He used the introductory expression "surely" to convey "solemn assurance" (*"nai,"* ibid., p. 535). Thus, through these assertions, Christ intended to do two things: arouse the attention of Christians to the fact that His coming could occur at any moment and give believers solemn assurance of the fulfillment of His promised imminent return.

*Revelation 22:17, 20*

**The Text.** "And the Spirit and the bride say, Come. And let
him that heareth say, Come. . . . Amen. Even so, come, Lord
Jesus."

**Comments.** In response to Christ's arousing attention to His
assertions, "I come quickly" (vv. 7, 12), the Holy Spirit (who
gave revelation concerning the coming of Christ through the
apostles and New Testament prophets) and the church (Christ's
bride, who, like the Jewish bride, waits eagerly for her betrothed
bridegroom to come for her after a period of separation) both
exclaimed, "Come" (v. 17). The Greek verb translated "come"
is in the imperative mood, indicating that the Spirit and the
church were so eager for Christ to come that they commanded
Him to fulfill His promise to come quickly.

In addition, individual Christians, who, through the public
reading of Revelation, heard Christ's promise to come quickly,
were commanded to demand Him to fulfill that promise (v. 17;
Swete, *The Apocalypse of St John,* p. 310).

In response to Christ's solemn assurance of the fulfillment
of His promised imminent return, John exclaimed, "Amen!
Come, Lord Jesus!" (v. 20, literal translation). "Amen" was John's
way of strongly expressing his conviction that Christ would indeed fulfill His promise to come quickly. Because John was so
convinced, he too commanded Christ to come.

**Quotations.** Concerning the church's response to Christ's
promise to come quickly, Archibald Thomas Robertson stated,
"There is intense longing (19:7) of God's people for the consummation of the marriage of the Lamb and the Bride" (*Word
Pictures in the New Testament,* 6:486). Johannes Schneider wrote,
"The Church of Christ lives in yearning expectation of His coming again (22:17, 20)" (*"erchomai,"* in *Theological Dictionary of the
New Testament,* 2:674).

Concerning John's response as the author of Revelation (v. 20), Schneider said, "The author expects the speedy return of Christ" (ibid.).

Leon Morris declared,

> *Amen* is the transliteration of a Hebrew or Aramaic participle with a meaning like "confirming." It indicates assent to what the previous speaker has said. This is reinforced with the prayer, *come, Lord Jesus.* . . . Charles points out that the Greek here is the equivalent of the Aramaic transliterated as *Maranatha* in 1 Corinthians 16:22. (*The Revelation of St. John,* pp. 262–63)

**Comment.** If the Holy Spirit, the church, and the apostle John knew that Christ could not return at any moment because of other events or a time period that had to transpire first, why did they command Him in a way that implied that He could come at any moment?

## Conclusions

This examination of New Testament passages related to the coming of Christ and the statements of scholars regarding the teaching of those passages prompts three conclusions.

First, the New Testament church, including the apostles, had the fervent expectancy that, although Christ's coming might not happen for a long time, it could occur at any moment.

Second, the New Testament not only indicates that this was the expectancy of the apostolic church, but also taught that the church should have that expectancy continuously and, therefore, should constantly be watching and prepared for Christ's coming at any moment.

Third, contrary to what the Pre-Wrath view claims, the New Testament does indeed teach the imminent coming of Christ.

In line with these conclusions, J. Barton Payne wrote, "If expectancy is present and the time, though perhaps long, *could* be short, then the doctrine of His imminent appearing must follow" (*The Imminent Appearing of Christ*, p. 88).

In addition, in his book *The Parousia in the New Testament*, A. L. Moore made the following statement in the chapter titled "The New Testament Insistence on the Imminence of the Parousia": "In this chapter we pass from the conclusion that Jesus and the early church appear to have awaited an actual Parousia of the Son of Man to the fact that this expectation appears to be coupled with an insistence on its imminence" (p. 80).

Moore also stated that imminency "accounts, too, for the otherwise irreconcilable juxtaposition of exhortations to watch expectantly beside warnings to patient endurance in face of the possibility of a delay" (ibid., p. 173). The concept that Christ's coming is imminent is the only notion that can harmonize and make sense of these two emphases of the New Testament, which would be contradictory apart from imminency.

**Additional Note**

Over the centuries since the time of the New Testament or apostolic church, numerous church leaders and other Christians have believed and taught the New Testament concept of the imminent coming of Christ. Some examples of those who have done so are as follows:

- between the time of the apostles and the Council of Nicea (325 A.D.)—Papias, Irenaeus, Justin Martyr, Tertullian, Hippolytus, Methodus, Commodianus, and Lactantius;
- during the 1500s—John Calvin and William Tyndale;
- during the 1600s—the Puritans, the Covenanters, and the Westminster Confession;
- during the 1700s—George Whitefield, John Wesley, and Thomas Coke; and
- during the 1800s—the Plymouth Brethren and Charles Haddon Spurgeon (see Showers, *Maranatha: Our Lord, Come!* pp. 143–47).

## Conclusion

Despite the biblical evidence and the opinion of many New Testament scholars, the Pre-Wrath view insists that the Bible does not teach that Christ's return is imminent. It has to insist on this point because the prophetic system that it has developed cannot work if Christ's coming to rapture the church is imminent. According to that system, Christ's coming to rapture the church cannot take place until after all of the events of the first six seals of Revelation have occurred. In other words, the entire first half of the seventieth week and a significant part of its second half (including the Great Tribulation) must transpire before Christ's coming. The belief that all of these other events must occur first requires the Pre-Wrath view to insist that Christ's coming cannot be imminent.

In light of this denial that Christ could come at any moment, the following statements by Charles Haddon Spurgeon, the outstanding English Baptist preacher and pastor of Metropolitan Tabernacle in London, are most appropriate:

> Brethren, I would be earnest on this point, for *the notion of the delay of Christ's Coming is always harmful,* however you arrive at it, whether it be by studying prophecy, or in any other way. . . . Do not, therefore, get the idea that the Lord delayeth his Coming, and that he will not or cannot come as yet. Far better would it be for you to stand on the tiptoe of expectation, and to be rather disappointed to think that he does not come. . . . He will come in his own time, and we are always to be looking for his appearing. (*Twelve Sermons on the Second Coming of Christ,* pp. 137–38)

> Oh, beloved, let us try every morning to get up as if that were the morning in which Christ would come; and when we go to bed at night, may we lie down with this thought, "Perhaps I shall be awakened by the ringing out of the silver trumpets heralding his Coming. Before

the sun arises, I may be startled from my dreams by the greatest of all cries, 'The Lord is come! The Lord is come!'" What a check, what an incentive, what a bridle, what a spur, such thoughts as these would be to us! Take this as the guide of your whole life. Act as if Jesus would come during the act in which you are engaged; and if you would not wish to be caught in that act by the Coming of the Lord, let it not be your act. (Ibid., p. 140)

People of the Tabernacle, you are set to watch tonight just as they did in the brave days of old! Whitefield and Wesley's men were watchers; and those before them, in the days of Luther and Calvin, and backward even to the days of our Lord. They kept the watches of the night, and you must do the same, until "Upstarting at the midnight cry, 'Behold your heavenly Bridegroom nigh,'" you go forth to welcome your returning Lord. (Ibid., p. 141)

# Conclusion

## Introduction

This critique has addressed primarily teachings of the Pre-Wrath Rapture view that have problems from a biblical perspective. But in the process it also has pointed out teachings of the view that are correct. The purpose of this conclusion is to summarize in survey fashion both the correct and problem teachings that were critiqued.

## Correct Teachings of the Pre-Wrath Rapture View

1. The beginning of birth pangs described in Matthew 24:4–8 are to be equated with the first four seals of Revelation 6:1–8.
2. The Great Tribulation will begin in the middle of the seventieth week of Daniel 9.
3. The beginning of birth pangs or first four seals will be present in the first half of the seventieth week.
4. The Great Tribulation is to be equated with the time of Jacob's trouble.
5. The rider on a white horse of the first seal is the Antichrist.
6. Once the church is raptured and taken to heaven by Christ, it will remain with Him forever.
7. The abomination of desolation spoken of in Daniel 9:27

will begin in the middle of the seventieth week when the Antichrist will take his seat in Israel's future temple, make his blasphemous claim that he is God, and demand that the world worship him as God.

8. God's wrathful Day-of-the-Lord judgment will come upon the wicked (the unsaved) on the earth.

9. In Matthew 24:37–41, two different Greek verbs are used for the Flood taking and the Second Coming taking, and these two verbs have different meanings.

10. The Greek word *eklektos,* which is translated "elect," is not used for the nation of Israel in the New Testament.

11. Daniel 10:13, 20–21 indicates that God assigned Michael to Israel as its angelic prince with the responsibility of restraining or standing firmly against enemy attacks against Israel.

12. Daniel 12:1 reveals something that will occur in the middle of the seventieth week.

## Problem Teachings of the Pre-Wrath Rapture View

1. To use the word *tribulation* for the entire seventieth week of Daniel 9 is wrong.

2. The Great Tribulation will be cut short to fewer than three and one-half years.

3. Antichrist will be "rendered useless," "helpless, idle, or paralyzed," or handcuffed shortly after the cosmic disturbances of the sixth seal part way through the second half of the seventieth week. He will not be destroyed, however, until thirty days after the end of the seventieth week.

4. No overlapping or involvement of the Great Tribulation with the Day of the Lord will occur. They will be completely distinct from each other. No wrath of God will be administered during the Great Tribulation. It will be characterized entirely by the wrath of man against man. The Day of the Lord will be characterized entirely by God's wrath against man.

5. God's wrath will not begin until the Day of the Lord begins with the opening of the seventh seal.

6. The first six seals of Revelation do not involve the wrath of God. Instead, they are God's commitment of eternal protection for His saints while they are under man's wrath.

7. No wrath of God occurs within the first six seals. The first five seals will consist of the wrath of man. The sixth seal will indicate that the wrath of God is about to come (when the seventh seal will be broken).

8. God would never turn the Antichrist loose on the world. If God were to do so, His house would be divided and opposing itself.

9. The warfare of the second seal, the famine of the third seal, and the death of one-fourth of the world's population of the fourth seal are totally the wrath of man and involve nothing of God's wrath.

10. The breaking of the fifth seal instigates and depicts the martyrdom of God's people by the Antichrist and his forces during the Great Tribulation. To say that the fifth seal is the wrath of God is to make God responsible for the killing of His own people.

11. God begins to intervene actively in the affairs of mankind when the sixth seal is broken, but the dramatic cosmic disturbances and the great earthquake of the sixth seal are not expressions of God's wrath.

12. During the sixth seal, the wrathful Day of the Lord is about to come, but it does not begin until the seventh seal is broken. Thus, the disturbances of the sixth seal will be a prelude or precursor to the beginning of the Day of the Lord with its divine wrath.

13. Nowhere does the Bible even imply two separate future comings of Christ. There will be only one Second Coming, but that one Second Coming will consist of a series of events, including Christ's coming four times.

14. The Second Coming will include Christ's continuous

presence for the rapture of the church and the administration of His Day-of-the-Lord judgments upon the unsaved.

15. Once the Antichrist begins his oppressive actions in the
middle of the seventieth week, he will be given 1,290 days
to continue before he is destroyed.

16. The battling of the armies of all nations against Jerusalem described in Zechariah 14:2 will take place just before the cosmic disturbances of the sixth seal.

17. The second future coming of Christ within the boundary
of the one Second Coming will take place immediately
after the end of the seventieth week and at the beginning
of a thirty-day reclamation period. The purpose of that
coming will be the spiritual salvation of Israel in fulfillment of Zechariah 12:10.

18. The disciples' question to Christ in Matthew 24:3 signified that two future signs will exist. The first sign, the sign
of the end of the age, will consist of the cosmic disturbances of the sixth seal. The second sign, the sign of
Christ's coming to which He referred in Matthew 24:30,
will immediately follow the cosmic disturbances of the
sixth seal.

19. The cosmic disturbances of the sixth seal are the same as
the cosmic disturbances to which Christ referred in Matthew 24:29.

20. The cosmic disturbances of the sixth seal will cut short
or end the Great Tribulation.

21. The Second Coming of Christ foretold in Matthew 24:30
will take place shortly after the cosmic disturbances of the
sixth seal.

22. The end of the age is the same episode as the Day of the
Lord. It will not be a onetime event. Instead, it will cover
an extended period of time and consist of a series of events
that will begin between the middle and the end of the
seventieth week and will continue through the thirty-day
period beyond the end of the seventieth week. It will include the seven trumpet and seven bowl judgments.

23. Christ's Matthew 24 coming and the end of the age are not to be equated with the coming of the Son of Man with the clouds of heaven that is foretold in Daniel 7:13–14.

24. Matthew 24:30–31 and 25:31 refer to two different comings of Christ.

25. In the parable of the tares (Matt. 13:24–43), the field into which the wheat and the tares are sown is the kingdom of heaven. Satan plants the tares in the kingdom of heaven.

26. In the parable of the tares, the gathering of the wheat into the barn refers to the rapturing of the church into heaven between the sixth and seventh seals before the Day-of-the-Lord wrath begins. The burning of the tares refers to God's wrathful Day-of-the-Lord judgment upon the wicked on the earth after the Matthew 24 Second Coming of Christ.

27. In the parable of the dragnet (Matt. 13:47–50), Christ taught that, at the time of His Matthew 24 Second Coming at the end of the age, the saved (the good fish) will be raptured to heaven before the unsaved (the bad fish) will enter God's wrathful Day-of-the-Lord judgment (i.e., are cast away).

28. In Matthew 24:37–41, Christ taught that the saved are the people who will be taken from the field and the mill at His Second Coming. They will be taken from the earth by rapture before the Day-of-the-Lord wrath begins. The unsaved are the people who will be left in the field and at the mill at His Second Coming. They will be left on the earth after the Rapture to be taken from the earth through the Day-of-the-Lord judgments.

29. Christ's Second Coming described in Matthew 24 and Luke 17 will begin with and on the same day as the Rapture.

30. Matthew 24:31 is a reference to the Rapture of the church.

31. Matthew 24:30–31 describes the same event as the 1 Thessalonians 4:15–17 Rapture passage.

32. The great multitude of Revelation 7:9–17 is God's elect (all of the Old Testament and church saints) who have

just been raptured to heaven out of the Great Tribulation between the breaking of the sixth and seventh seals.

33. The great multitude will not include the saints who will
be martyred during the Great Tribulation.

34. Revelation 7 seems to indicate that the people of the great
multitude will arrive in heaven suddenly as a complete
group, all at one point in time. They will not arrive there
progressively over a period of time through martyrdom.

35. Only one Day of the Lord is revealed in the Bible. All
passages that give information about the Day of the Lord
refer to the future time when God will pour out His wrath
upon the unrighteous on the earth and upon the
Antichrist's domain. The Old Testament prophets knew
nothing about more than one distinct Day of the Lord.

36. Of the various Hebrew words that refer to God's anger or
wrath, *ebrah* is by far the strongest. It is the only word used
specifically for God's Day-of-the-Lord wrath. In its context,
it is used for God's Day-of-the-Lord wrath against Gentile
nations, not against Israel.

37. The Day of the Lord will not include the Millennium. The
total nature of the Day of the Lord will be characterized
by the darkness of divine judgment upon all of the unsaved people of the earth. No part of the Day of the Lord
will be characterized by blessing. Those who claim that
the Day of the Lord will extend through the Millennium
have only one Bible verse upon which to base that view,
namely, 2 Peter 3:10. But 2 Peter 3:10 will be fulfilled before the Millennium through the Day-of-the-Lord trumpet and bowl judgments.

38. Because Malachi 4:5 indicates that Elijah will be sent before the beginning of the Day of the Lord, and because
the two witnesses (one of whom most likely will be Elijah)
will not be sent until the second half of the seventieth week
of Daniel 9, one can conclude that the Day of the Lord
will not begin until sometime during the second half of
the seventieth week. It will not begin at the beginning of

the seventieth week, as the pretribulation Rapture view claims.

39. Matthew 24 and Luke 17 teach that the Day of the Lord will begin on the same day as the Rapture and Christ's Second Coming.

40. In 2 Thessalonians 2:3, the apostle Paul taught that the Day of the Lord will not begin until *after* the apostasy. The apostasy will start at the beginning of the seventieth week and will continue throughout its entire first half and the Great Tribulation part of its second half. Thus, the Day of the Lord will not begin until part way through the second half of the seventieth week.

41. The apostasy of 2 Thessalonians 2:3 will be the total abandonment by Jews of the God of Abraham, Isaac, and Jacob and of Israel's hope of the Messiah. This apostasy will begin with their entering into a covenant relationship with Antichrist at the beginning of the seventieth week and will continue through the first half of the seventieth week and the Great Tribulation.

42. In 2 Thessalonians 2:3, the apostle Paul taught that the Day of the Lord will not begin until *after* the revelation of the man of sin (the Antichrist). Antichrist will not be revealed until the middle of the seventieth week, when he will break his covenant with Israel and make his blasphemous claim that he is God (2 Thessalonians 2:4). Thus, the Day of the Lord will not begin until sometime *after* the second half of the seventieth week has begun.

43. The restrainer in 2 Thessalonians 2:6–7 is Michael the archangel. No biblical basis exists for identifying the restrainer as the Holy Spirit, the church, or human government. Daniel 12:1 reveals that in the middle of the seventieth week Michael will "stand still" (not "stand up") or stop his restraint of enemy attacks against Israel, thereby freeing the Antichrist to reveal his wicked identity. This action will be God's way of punishing Israel for its rebellion against Him.

44. The Bible does not teach the imminency of Christ's return. What it does teach is expectancy—the concept that any generation since the first century could have been the one that would enter the seventieth week and, while enduring antagonistic persecution, would have the expectancy of Christ's coming to rapture it out of the world before the beginning of the Day of the Lord with its outpouring of God's wrath. Thus, the Bible teaches an expectant Rapture, not an imminent Rapture. The idea that the early church held to a doctrine of imminency has no valid support.

## Conclusion

The Pre-Wrath Rapture view has several teachings that are correct. But many of its teachings, including those that are foundational to the entire view, have problems from a biblical perspective. This fact prompts the conclusion that the Pre-Wrath Rapture view has a faulty foundation and is contrary to the Scriptures.

# Select Bibliography

## Books

Adamson, James B. *The Epistle of James.* Grand Rapids: Eerdmans, 1976.

Alden, Robert L. *"Hatak."* In *Theological Wordbook of the Old Testament.* Edited by R. Laird Harris, Gleason L. Archer Jr., and Bruce K. Waltke. 2 vols. Chicago: Moody, 1980.

Alexander, Ralph H. *"Yad."* In *Theological Wordbook of the Old Testament.* Edited by R. Laird Harris, Gleason L. Archer Jr., and Bruce K. Waltke. 2 vols. Chicago: Moody, 1980.

Alford, Henry. "The Second Epistle to the Thessalonians." Vol. 3 of *The Greek Testament.* Revised by Everett F. Harrison. Chicago: Moody, 1958.

*Apocalypse of Abraham.* Edited by G. H. Box. London: Society for Promoting Christian Knowledge, 1918. Written originally probably in Hebrew toward the end of the first century c.e. Quoted by Raphael Patai, *The Messiah Texts* (Detroit: Wayne State University Press, 1979). Also quoted by Gerhard Friedrich, *"salpigx,"* in *Theological Dictionary of the New Testament,* vols. 1–4 edited by Gerhard Kittel, vols. 5–9 edited by Gerhard Friedrich, translated and edited by Geoffrey W. Bromiley (Grand Rapids: Eerdmans, 1964–74).

Arndt, William F., and F. Wilbur Gingrich. *"Aetos."* In *A Greek-English Lexicon of the New Testament and Other Early Christian Literature.* 4th rev. and augmented ed. Chicago: University of Chicago Press, 1957.

———. *"Airo."* In *A Greek-English Lexicon of the New Testament and Other Early Christian Literature*. 4th rev. and augmented ed. Chicago: University of Chicago Press, 1957.

———. *"Ametameletos."* In *A Greek-English Lexicon of the New Testament and Other Early Christian Literature*. 4th rev. and augmented ed. Chicago: University of Chicago Press, 1957.

———. *"Anapsuxis."* In *A Greek-English Lexicon of the New Testament and Other Early Christian Literature*. 4th rev. and augmented ed. Chicago: University of Chicago Press, 1957.

———. *"Anemos."* In *A Greek-English Lexicon of the New Testament and Other Early Christian Literature*. 4th rev. and augmented ed. Chicago: University of Chicago Press, 1957.

———. *"Anistemi."* In *A Greek-English Lexicon of the New Testament and Other Early Christian Literature*. 4th rev. and augmented ed. Chicago: University of Chicago Press, 1957.

———. *"Anomia."* In *A Greek-English Lexicon of the New Testament and Other Early Christian Literature*. 4th rev. and augmented ed. Chicago: University of Chicago Press, 1957.

———. *"Anomos."* In *A Greek-English Lexicon of the New Testament and Other Early Christian Literature*. 4th rev. and augmented ed. Chicago: University of Chicago Press, 1957.

———. *"Apate."* In *A Greek-English Lexicon of the New Testament and Other Early Christian Literature*. 4th rev. and augmented ed. Chicago: University of Chicago Press, 1957.

———. *"Apekdechomai."* In *A Greek-English Lexicon of the New Testament and Other Early Christian Literature*. 4th rev. and augmented ed. Chicago: University of Chicago Press, 1957.

———. *"Aphoridzo."* In *A Greek-English Lexicon of the New Testament and Other Early Christian Literature*. 4th rev. and augmented ed. Chicago: University of Chicago Press, 1957.

———. *"Apostasia."* In *A Greek-English Lexicon of the New Testament and Other Early Christian Literature*. 4th rev. and augmented ed. Chicago: University of Chicago Press, 1957.

———. *"Archon."* In *A Greek-English Lexicon of the New Testament and Other Early Christian Literature*. 4th rev. and augmented ed. Chicago: University of Chicago Press, 1957.

———. *"Asphaleia."* In *A Greek-English Lexicon of the New Testament and Other Early Christian Literature*. 4th rev. and augmented ed. Chicago: University of Chicago Press, 1957.

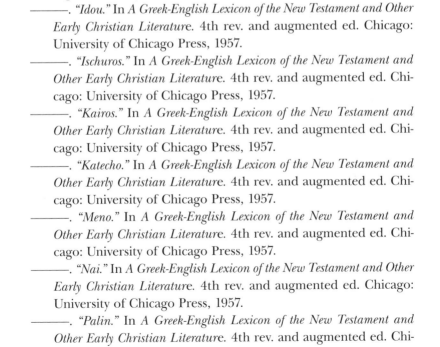

———. *"Chiliarchoi."* In *A Greek-English Lexicon of the New Testament and Other Early Christian Literature.* 4th rev. and augmented ed. Chicago: University of Chicago Press, 1957.

———. *"Ekloge."* In *A Greek-English Lexicon of the New Testament and Other Early Christian Literature.* 4th rev. and augmented ed. Chicago: University of Chicago Press, 1957.

———. *"Episunago."* In *A Greek-English Lexicon of the New Testament and Other Early Christian Literature.* 4th rev. and augmented ed. Chicago: University of Chicago Press, 1957.

———. *"Ethnos."* In *A Greek-English Lexicon of the New Testament and Other Early Christian Literature.* 4th rev. and augmented ed. Chicago: University of Chicago Press, 1957.

———. *"Genesis."* In *A Greek-English Lexicon of the New Testament and Other Early Christian Literature.* 4th rev. and augmented ed. Chicago: University of Chicago Press, 1957.

———. *"Hotan."* In *A Greek-English Lexicon of the New Testament and Other Early Christian Literature.* 4th rev. and augmented ed. Chicago: University of Chicago Press, 1957.

———. *"Idou."* In *A Greek-English Lexicon of the New Testament and Other Early Christian Literature.* 4th rev. and augmented ed. Chicago: University of Chicago Press, 1957.

———. *"Ischuros."* In *A Greek-English Lexicon of the New Testament and Other Early Christian Literature.* 4th rev. and augmented ed. Chicago: University of Chicago Press, 1957.

———. *"Kairos."* In *A Greek-English Lexicon of the New Testament and Other Early Christian Literature.* 4th rev. and augmented ed. Chicago: University of Chicago Press, 1957.

———. *"Katecho."* In *A Greek-English Lexicon of the New Testament and Other Early Christian Literature.* 4th rev. and augmented ed. Chicago: University of Chicago Press, 1957.

———. *"Meno."* In *A Greek-English Lexicon of the New Testament and Other Early Christian Literature.* 4th rev. and augmented ed. Chicago: University of Chicago Press, 1957.

———. *"Nai."* In *A Greek-English Lexicon of the New Testament and Other Early Christian Literature.* 4th rev. and augmented ed. Chicago: University of Chicago Press, 1957.

———. *"Palin."* In *A Greek-English Lexicon of the New Testament and Other Early Christian Literature.* 4th rev. and augmented ed. Chicago: University of Chicago Press, 1957.

————. *"Paralambano."* In *A Greek-English Lexicon of the New Testament and Other Early Christian Literature*. 4th rev. and augmented ed. Chicago: University of Chicago Press, 1957.

————. *"Prostasso."* In *A Greek-English Lexicon of the New Testament and Other Early Christian Literature*. 4th rev. and augmented ed. Chicago: University of Chicago Press, 1957.

————. *"Thanatos."* In *A Greek-English Lexicon of the New Testament and Other Early Christian Literature*. 4th rev. and augmented ed. Chicago: University of Chicago Press, 1957.

————. *"Thronos."* In *A Greek-English Lexicon of the New Testament and Other Early Christian Literature*. 4th rev. and augmented ed. Chicago: University of Chicago Press, 1957.

————. *"Tote."* In *A Greek-English Lexicon of the New Testament and Other Early Christian Literature*. 4th rev. and augmented ed. Chicago: University of Chicago Press, 1957.

Barclay, William. *The Letters to the Corinthians*. Philadelphia: Westminster, 1956.

————. *The Letters to Timothy, Titus and Philemon*. Rev. ed. Philadelphia: Westminster, 1975.

————. *The Revelation of John*. 2 vols. Philadelphia: Westminster, 1960.

Bauder, Wolfgang. *"Aphistemi."* In *The New International Dictionary of New Testament Theology*. Edited by Colin Brown. 4 vols. Grand Rapids: Zondervan, 1975-86.

Bauernfiend, Otto. *"Nikao."* In *Theological Dictionary of the New Testament*. Vols. 1-4 edited by Gerhard Kittel; vols. 5-9 edited by Gerhard Friedrich. Translated and edited by Geoffrey W. Bromiley. Grand Rapids: Eerdmans, 1964-74.

Beare, F. W. *A Commentary on the Epistle to the Philippians*. London: Adam and Charles Black, 1959.

Bertram, George. *"Odin."* In *Theological Dictionary of the New Testament*. Vols. 1-4 edited by Gerhard Kittel; vols. 5-9 edited by Gerhard Friedrich. Translated and edited by Geoffry W. Bromiley. Grand Rapids: Eerdmans, 1964-74.

Blackman, E. C. *The Epistle of James*. Naperville, Ill.: Allenson, 1957.

Boice, James Montgomery. *Philippians*. Grand Rapids: Zondervan, 1971.

Bratcher, Robert G. *A Translator's Guide to the Letters from James, Peter, and Jude*. New York: United Bible Societies, 1984.

Brooke, A. E. *A Critical and Exegetical Commentary on the Johannine*

*Epistles.* The International Critical Commentary. Edited by Charles Augustus Briggs, Samuel Rolles Driver, and Alfred Plummer. 48 vols. Edinburgh: T. and T. Clark, 1910.

Brown, Francis, Samuel Rolles Driver, and Charles Augustus Briggs. *"Quwm."* In *A Hebrew and English Lexicon of the Old Testament.* Oxford: Clarendon, 1972.

Bruce, F. F. *Commentary on the Book of the Acts.* The New International Commentary on the New Testament. Edited by Ned B. Stonehouse. 19 vols. Grand Rapids: Eerdmans, 1949.

————. *Philippians.* San Francisco: Harper and Row, 1983.

Bryson, Harold T. *How Faith Works.* Nashville: Broadman, 1985.

Buchsel, Friedrich. *"Apekdechomai."* In *Theological Dictionary of the New Testament.* Vols. 1–4 edited by Gerhard Kittel; vols. 5–9 edited by Gerhard Friedrich. Translated and edited by Geoffrey W. Bromiley. Grand Rapids: Eerdmans, 1964–74.

Bullinger, E. W. *The Apocalypse or "The Day of the Lord."* London: Eyre and Spottiswoode, 1935.

Bultmann, Rudolf. *"Thanatos."* In *Theological Dictionary of the New Testament.* Vols. 1–4 edited by Gerhard Kittel; vols. 5–9 edited by Gerhard Friedrich. Translated and edited by Geoffrey W. Bromiley. Grand Rapids: Eerdmans, 1964–74.

Burrows, Millar. "More Light on the Dead Sea Scrolls." In *Burrows on the Dead Sea Scrolls.* Grand Rapids: Baker, 1978.

Candlish, Robert S. *The First Epistle of John.* Grand Rapids: Zondervan, n.d.

Charles, R. H. *The Revelation of St. John.* The International Critical Commentary. Edited by Charles Augustus Briggs, Samuel Rolles Driver, and Alfred Plummer. 48 vols. Edinburgh: T. and T. Clark, 1910.

Constable, Thomas L. "1 Thessalonians." In *The Bible Knowledge Commentary, New Testament.* Edited by John F. Walvoord and Roy B. Zuck. Wheaton, Ill.: Victor Books, 1983.

Coppes, Leonard J. *"Haras."* In *Theological Wordbook of the Old Testament.* Edited by R. Laird Harris, Gleason L. Archer Jr., and Bruce K. Waltke. 2 vols. Chicago: Moody, 1980.

————. *"Nuah."* In *Theological Wordbook of the Old Testament.* Edited by R. Laird Harris, Gleason L. Archer Jr., and Bruce K. Waltke. 2 vols. Chicago: Moody, 1980.

Culver, Robert D. *"Din."* In *Theological Wordbook of the Old Testament.*

Edited by R. Laird Harris, Gleason L. Archer Jr., and Bruce K. Waltke. 2 vols. Chicago: Moody, 1980.

Dana, H. E. and Julius R. Mantey. *A Manual Grammar of the Greek New Testament.* New York: Macmillan, 1927.

Davids, Peter H. *The Epistle of James.* Grand Rapids: Eerdmans, 1982.

Davidson, A. B. *The Theology of the Old Testament.* International Theological Library. Edited by Charles A. Briggs and Stewart D. F. Salmond. 24 vols. New York: Charles Scribner's Sons, 1896.

Davies, J. G. *The Early Christian Church.* Garden City, N.Y.: Anchor Books, 1967.

Delitzsch, Franz. *Biblical Commentary on the Prophecies of Isaiah.* 2 vols. *Biblical Commentary on the Old Testament.* By Carl Friedrich Keil and Franz Delitzsch. Translated by James Martin. 25 vols. Grand Rapids: Eerdmans, 1949–50.

Delling, Gerhard. "*Kairos.*" In *Theological Dictionary of the New Testament.* Vols. 1–4 edited by Gerhard Kittel; vols. 5–9 edited by Gerhard Friedrich. Translated and edited by Geoffrey W. Bromiley. Grand Rapids: Eerdmans, 1964–74.

———. "*Koloboo.*" In *Theological Dictionary of the New Testament.* Vols. 1–4 edited by Gerhard Kittel; vols. 5–9 edited by Gerhard Friedrich. Translated and edited by Geoffrey W. Bromiley. Grand Rapids: Eerdmans, 1964–74.

Deluz, Gaston. *A Companion to 1 Corinthians.* Edited and translated by Grace E. Watt. London: Darton, Longman and Todd, 1963.

"*Didache.*" In *Documents of the Christian Church.* Selected and edited by Henry Bettenson. New York: Oxford University Press, 1956.

Doerksen, Vernon D. *James.* Chicago: Moody, 1983.

Durant, Will. *Caesar and Christ.* New York: Simon and Schuster, 1944.

Ellicott, Charles J. *St. Paul's First Epistle to the Corinthians.* London: Longmans, Green, and Co., 1887.

Fee, Gordon D. *The First Epistle to the Corinthians.* Grand Rapids: Eerdmans, 1987.

Fichtner, Johannes. "*Orge.*" In *Theological Dictionary of the New Testament.* Vols. 1–4 edited by Gerhard Kittel; vols. 5–9 edited by Gerhard Friedrich. Translated and edited by Geoffrey W. Bromiley. Grand Rapids: Eerdmans, 1964–74.

Findlay, George G. *Fellowship in the Life Eternal.* Grand Rapids: Eerdmans, 1955.

Fitzer, Gottfried. *"Sphragis."* In *Theological Dictionary of the New Testament.* Vols. 1–4 edited by Gerhard Kittel; vols. 5–9 edited by Gerhard Friedrich. Translated and edited by Geoffrey W. Bromiley. Grand Rapids: Eerdmans, 1964–74.

Foerster, Werner. *"Keras."* In *Theological Dictionary of the New Testament.* Vols. 1–4 edited by Gerhard Kittel; vols. 5–9 edited by Gerhard Friedrich. Translated and edited by Geoffrey W. Bromiley. Grand Rapids: Eerdmans, 1964–74.

Frame, James Everett. *A Critical and Exegetical Commentary on the Epistles of St. Paul to the Thessalonians.* The International Critical Commentary. Edited by Charles Augustus Briggs, Samuel Rolles Driver, and Alfred Plummer. 48 vols. Edinburgh: T. and T. Clark, 1910.

Friedrich, Gerhard. *"Salpigx."* In *Theological Dictionary of the New Testament.* Vols. 1–4 edited by Gerhard Kittel; vols. 5–9 edited by Gerhard Friedrich. Translated and edited by Geoffrey W. Bromiley. Grand Rapids: Eerdmans, 1964–74.

Gaebelein, Frank E. *The Practical Epistle of James.* Great Neck, N.Y.: Doniger and Raughley, 1955.

Glasson, T. Francis. *The Second Advent.* London: Epworth, 1963.

Goldberg, Louis. *"Ewil."* In *Theological Wordbook of the Old Testament.* Edited by R. Laird Harris, Gleason L. Archer Jr., and Bruce K. Waltke. 2 vols. Chicago: Moody, 1980.

Gould, Ezra P. *A Critical and Exegetical Commentary on the Gospel According to St. Mark.* The International Critical Commentary. Edited by Charles Augustus Briggs, Samuel Rolles Driver, and Alfred Plummer. 48 vols. Edinburgh: T. and T. Clark, 1910.

Grassmick, John D. "Mark." In *The Bible Knowledge Commentary, New Testament.* Edited by John F. Walvoord and Roy B. Zuck. Wheaton, Ill.: Victor Books, 1983.

Gromacki, Robert G. *New Testament Survey.* Grand Rapids: Baker, 1974.

Grundmann, Walter. *"Dei."* In *Theological Dictionary of the New Testament.* Vols. 1–4 edited by Gerhard Kittel; vols. 5–9 edited by Gerhard Friedrich. Translated and edited by Geoffrey W. Bromiley. Grand Rapids: Eerdmans, 1964–74.

———. *"Dunamis."* In *Theological Dictionary of the New Testament.* Vols. 1–4 edited by Gerhard Kittel; vols. 5–9 edited by Gerhard Friedrich. Translated and edited by Geoffrey W. Bromiley. Grand Rapids: Eerdmans, 1964–74.

———. *"Prosdechomai."* In *Theological Dictionary of the New Testament.* Vols. 1–4 edited by Gerhard Kittel; vols. 5–9 edited by Gerhard Friedrich. Translated and edited by Geoffrey W. Bromiley. Grand Rapids: Eerdmans, 1964–74.

Guthrie, Donald. *The Pastoral Epistles.* Grand Rapids: Eerdmans, 1957.

Harrell, Pat Edwin. *The Letter of Paul to the Philippians.* Austin, Tex.: R. B. Sweet Co., 1969.

Harrison, Everett F. "Romans." In *The Expositor's Bible Commentary.* Edited by Frank E. Gaebelein. 12 vols. Grand Rapids: Zondervan, 1976–92.

———. *Introduction to the New Testament.* Grand Rapids: Eerdmans, 1964.

Hauck, F. *"Makarios."* In *Theological Dictionary of the New Testament.* Vols. 1–4 edited by Gerhard Kittel; vols. 5–9 edited by Gerhard Friedrich. Translated and edited by Geoffrey W. Bromiley. Grand Rapids: Eerdmans, 1964–74.

Hendriksen, William. *Exposition of Philippians.* New Testament Commentary. Grand Rapids: Baker, 1962.

Hiebert, D. Edmond. *An Introduction to the Non-Pauline Epistles.* Chicago: Moody, 1962.

———. *The Thessalonian Epistles.* Chicago: Moody, 1971.

Hogg, C. F., and W. E. Vine. *The Epistles to the Thessalonians.* Fincastle, Va.: Bible Study Classics, 1914.

Irenaeus. *Against Heresies.* In *The Ante-Nicene Fathers.* Vol. 1. Edited by Alexander Roberts and James Donaldson. Buffalo: Christian Literature Publishing, 1885–97.

Jenour, Alfred. *Rationale Apocalypticum.* London: Thomas Hatchard, 1852.

Jeremias, Joachim. *"Arnion."* In *Theological Dictionary of the New Testament.* Vols. 1–4 edited by Gerhard Kittel; vols. 5–9 edited by Gerhard Friedrich. Translated and edited by Geoffrey W. Bromiley. Grand Rapids: Eerdmans, 1964–74.

———. *"Hades."* In *Theological Dictionary of the New Testament.* Vols. 1–4 edited by Gerhard Kittel; vols. 5–9 edited by Gerhard Friedrich. Translated and edited by Geoffrey W. Bromiley. Grand Rapids: Eerdmans, 1964–74.

Keil, C. F. *Biblical Commentary on the Book of Daniel.* 1 vol. *Biblical Commentary on the Old Testament.* By Carl Friedrich Keil and Franz Delitzsch. Translated by James Martin. 25 vols. Grand Rapids: Eerdmans, 1949–50.

————. *The Twelve Minor Prophets.* 2 vols. *Biblical Commentary on the Old Testament.* By Carl Friedrich Keil and Franz Delitzsch. Translated by James Martin. 25 vols. Grand Rapids: Eerdmans, 1949–50.

Kelly, James. *The Apocalypse Interpreted in the Light of "The Day of the Lord."* London: James Nisbet and Co., 1849.

Kennedy, H. A. A. "The Epistle to the Philippians." In *The Expositor's Greek Testament.* Edited by W. Robertson Nicoll. 5 vols. London: Hodder and Stoughton, n.d.

Kent, Homer A., Jr. *Faith That Works.* Grand Rapids: Baker, 1986.

Kiddle, Martin. *The Revelation of St. John.* New York: Harper and Brothers, n.d.

Kistemaker, Simon J. *Exposition of the Epistle of James and the Epistles of John.* Grand Rapids: Baker, 1986.

Kruger, Paul A. *"Pele."* In *New International Dictionary of Old Testament Theology and Exegesis.* Edited by Willem A. VanGemeren. 5 vols. Grand Rapids: Zondervan, 1997.

Kuhn, K. G. *"Maranatha."* In *Theological Dictionary of the New Testament.* Vols. 1–4 edited by Gerhard Kittel; vols. 5–9 edited by Gerhard Friedrich. Translated and edited by Geoffrey W. Bromiley. Grand Rapids: Eerdmans, 1964–74.

Lenski, R. C. H. *The Interpretation of St. Paul's First and Second Epistle to the Corinthians.* Columbus, Ohio: Wartburg, 1946.

Leupold, H. C. *Exposition of Daniel.* Grand Rapids: Baker, 1949.

Lillie, John. *Lectures on the Epistles of Paul to the Thessalonians.* New York: Robert Carter and Brothers, 1860.

Lincoln, W. *Lectures on the Book of the Revelation.* New York: Revell, n.d.

Lloyd-Jones, Martyn. *Life of Peace.* London: Hodder and Stoughton, 1990.

Marshall, I. Howard. "1 and 2 Thessalonians." In *The New Century Bible Commentary.* Edited by Ronald E. Clements and Matthew Black. Grand Rapids: Eerdmans, 1983.

Maurer, Christian. *"Rhiza."* In *Theological Dictionary of the New Testament.* Vols. 1–4 edited by Gerhard Kittel; vols. 5–9 edited by Gerhard Friedrich. Translated and edited by Geoffrey W. Bromiley. Grand Rapids: Eerdmans, 1964–74.

Michaelis, Wilhelm. *"Kratos."* In *Theological Dictionary of the New Testament.* Vols. 1–4 edited by Gerhard Kittel; vols. 5–9 edited by Gerhard Friedrich. Translated and edited by Geoffrey W. Bromiley. Grand Rapids: Eerdmans, 1964–74.

————. *"Romphaia."* In *Theological Dictionary of the New Testament*. Vols. 1–4 edited by Gerhard Kittel; vols. 5–9 edited by Gerhard Friedrich. Translated and edited by Geoffrey W. Bromiley. Grand Rapids: Eerdmans, 1964–74.

Milligan, George. *St. Paul's Epistles to the Thessalonians*. London: Macmillan, 1908.

Mitton, C. Leslie. T*he Epistle of James*. London: Marshall, Morgan, and Scott, 1966.

Moffatt, James. "The First and Second Epistles to the Thessalonians." In *The Expositor's Greek Testament*. Edited by W. Robertson Nicoll. 5 vols. London: Hodder and Stoughton, n.d.

————. *The First Epistle of Paul to the Corinthians*. New York: Harper and Brothers, n.d.

Moo, Douglas J. *The Letter of James*. Grand Rapids: Eerdmans, 1985.

Moore, A. L. *The Parousia in the New Testament*. Leiden: E. J. Brill, 1966.

Morris, Leon. *The First and Second Epistles to the Thessalonians*. The New International Commentary on the New Testament. Edited by Ned B. Stonehouse. 19 vols. Grand Rapids: Eerdmans, 1949.

————. *The First Epistle of Paul to the Corinthians*. Grand Rapids: Eerdmans, 1970.

————. *The Revelation of St. John*. Grand Rapids: Eerdmans, 1969.

Motyer, J. A. *The Tests of Faith*. London: InterVarsity, 1970.

Moulton, James Hope. *A Grammar of New Testament Greek*. Edinburgh: T. and T. Clark, 1906.

Mundle, Wilhelm. *"Apokalupto."* In *The New International Dictionary of New Testament Theology*. Edited by Colin Brown. 4 vols. Grand Rapids: Zondervan, 1975–86.

Murray, John. *The Epistle to the Romans*. The New International Commentary on the New Testament. Edited by Ned B. Stonehouse. 19 vols. Grand Rapids: Eerdmans, 1949.

Oepke, Albrecht. *"Apokatastasis."* In *Theological Dictionary of the New Testament*. Vols. 1–4 edited by Gerhard Kittel; vols. 5–9 edited by Gerhard Friedrich. Translated and edited by Geoffrey W. Bromiley. Grand Rapids: Eerdmans, 1964–74.

————. *"Enistemi."* In *Theological Dictionary of the New Testament*. Vols. 1–4 edited by Gerhard Kittel; vols. 5–9 edited by Gerhard Friedrich. Translated and edited by Geoffrey W. Bromiley. Grand Rapids: Eerdmans, 1964–74.

―――. *"Parousia."* In *Theological Dictionary of the New Testament.* Vols. 1–4 edited by Gerhard Kittel; vols. 5–9 edited by Gerhard Friedrich. Translated and edited by Geoffrey W. Bromiley. Grand Rapids: Eerdmans, 1964–74.

Oswalt, John N. *"Kala."* In *Theological Wordbook of the Old Testament.* Edited by R. Laird Harris, Gleason L. Archer Jr., and Bruce K. Waltke. 2 vols. Chicago: Moody, 1980.

Patai, Raphael. *The Messiah Texts.* Detroit: Wayne State University Press, 1979.

Patterson, Richard D. *"Seper."* In *Theological Wordbook of the Old Testament.* Edited by R. Laird Harris, Gleason L. Archer Jr., and Bruce K. Waltke. 2 vols. Chicago: Moody, 1980.

Payne, J. Barton. *The Imminent Appearing of Christ.* Grand Rapids: Eerdmans, 1962.

―――. *"Riah."* In *Theological Wordbook of the Old Testament.* Edited by R. Laird Harris, Gleason L. Archer Jr., and Bruce K. Waltke. 2 vols. Chicago: Moody, 1980.

―――. *The Theology of the Older Testament.* Grand Rapids: Zondervan, 1962.

Plummer, Alfred. *A Commentary on St. Paul's Epistle to the Philippians.* London: Robert Scott, 1919.

Preisker, Herbert. *"Engus."* In *Theological Dictionary of the New Testament.* Vols. 1–4 edited by Gerhard Kittel; vols. 5–9 edited by Gerhard Friedrich. Translated and edited by Geoffrey W. Bromiley. Grand Rapids: Eerdmans, 1964–74.

Quell, Gottfried. *"Eklegomai."* In *Theological Dictionary of the New Testament.* Vols. 1–4 edited by Gerhard Kittel; vols. 5–9 edited by Gerhard Friedrich. Translated and edited by Geoffrey W. Bromiley. Grand Rapids: Eerdmans, 1964–74.

Rengstorf, Karl Heinrich. *"Despotes."* In *Theological Dictionary of the New Testament.* Vols. 1–4 edited by Gerhard Kittel; vols. 5–9 edited by Gerhard Friedrich. Translated and edited by Geoffrey W. Bromiley. Grand Rapids: Eerdmans, 1964–74.

―――. *"Hepta."* In *Theological Dictionary of the New Testament.* Vols. 1–4 edited by Gerhard Kittel; vols. 5–9 edited by Gerhard Friedrich. Translated and edited by Geoffrey W. Bromiley. Grand Rapids: Eerdmans, 1964–74.

Riesenfeld, Harald. *"Huper."* In *Theological Dictionary of the New Testament.*

Vols. 1–4 edited by Gerhard Kittel; vols. 5–9 edited by Gerhard Friedrich. Translated and edited by Geoffrey W. Bromiley. Grand Rapids: Eerdmans, 1964–74.

Robertson, Archibald T. and Alfred Plummer. *A Critical and Exegetical Commentary on the First Epistle of St. Paul to the Corinthians.* The International Critical Commentary. Edited by Charles Augustus Briggs, Samuel Rolles Driver, and Alfred Plummer. 48 vols. Edinburgh: T. and T. Clark, 1910.

Robertson, Archibald Thomas. *Word Pictures in the New Testament.* 6 vols. New York: Richard R. Smith, 1931; also New York: Harper and Brothers, 1933.

———. *A Grammar of the Greek New Testament in the Light of Historical Research.* Nashville: Broadman, 1934.

Robinson, John A. T. *Jesus and His Coming.* Philadelphia: Westminster, 1979.

Rosenthal, Marvin J. *The Pre-Wrath Rapture of the Church.* Nashville: Nelson, 1990.

Rowley, H. H. "The Day of the Lord." In *The Faith of Israel.* Philadelphia: Westminster, 1957.

Sadler, M. F. *The General Epistles of SS. James, Peter, John and Jude.* 2d ed. London: George Bell and Sons, 1895.

*Sanhedrin.* In *The Babylonian Talmud.* Edited by Isidore Epstein. London: Soncino Press, 1935.

Scaer, David P. *James the Apostle of Faith.* St. Louis: Concordia, 1983.

Schick, Edward. *The Revelation of St. John.* New York: Herder and Herder, 1971.

Schlier, Heinrich. *"Apostasia."* In *Theological Dictionary of the New Testament.* Vols. 1–4 edited by Gerhard Kittel; vols. 5–9 edited by Gerhard Friedrich. Translated and edited by Geoffrey W. Bromiley. Grand Rapids: Eerdmans, 1964–74.

———. *"Thlibo, thlipsis."* In *Theological Dictionary of the New Testament.* Vols. 1–4 edited by Gerhard Kittel; vols. 5–9 edited by Gerhard Friedrich. Translated and edited by Geoffrey W. Bromiley. Grand Rapids: Eerdmans, 1964–74.

Schneider, Johannes. *"Erchomai."* In *Theological Dictionary of the New Testament.* Vols. 1–4 edited by Gerhard Kittel; vols. 5–9 edited by Gerhard Friedrich. Translated and edited by Geoffrey W. Bromiley. Grand Rapids: Eerdmans, 1964–74.

———. *"Exerchomai."* In *Theological Dictionary of the New Testament.* Vols.

1–4 edited by Gerhard Kittel; vols. 5–9 edited by Gerhard Friedrich. Translated and edited by Geoffrey W. Bromiley. Grand Rapids: Eerdmans, 1964–74.

Schrage, Wolfgang. *"Episunagoge."* In *Theological Dictionary of the New Testament.* Vols. 1–4 edited by Gerhard Kittel; vols. 5–9 edited by Gerhard Friedrich. Translated and edited by Geoffrey W. Bromiley. Grand Rapids: Eerdmans, 1964–74.

Schrenk, Gottlob. *"Biblion."* In *Theological Dictionary of the New Testament.* Vols. 1–4 edited by Gerhard Kittel; vols. 5–9 edited by Gerhard Friedrich. Translated and edited by Geoffrey W. Bromiley. Grand Rapids: Eerdmans, 1964–74.

———. *"Ekloge."* In *Theological Dictionary of the New Testament.* Vols. 1–4 edited by Gerhard Kittel; vols. 5–9 edited by Gerhard Friedrich. Translated and edited by Geoffrey W. Bromiley. Grand Rapids: Eerdmans, 1964–74.

Schweizer, Eduard. *"Anapsuxis."* In *Theological Dictionary of the New Testament.* Vols. 1–4 edited by Gerhard Kittel; vols. 5–9 edited by Gerhard Friedrich. Translated and edited by Geoffrey W. Bromiley. Grand Rapids: Eerdmans, 1964–74.

Scott, Jack B. *"Elil."* In *Theological Wordbook of the Old Testament.* Edited by R. Laird Harris, Gleason L. Archer Jr., and Bruce K. Waltke. 2 vols. Chicago: Moody, 1980.

Seiss, Joseph A. *The Apocalypse.* Grand Rapids: Zondervan, 1957.

*The Septuagint with Apocrypha: Greek and English.* Translated by Sir Lancelot Charles Lee Brenton. Peabody, Mass.: Hendrickson, 1986.

*Shabbath.* In *The Babylonian Talmud.* Edited by Isidore Epstein. London: Soncino Press, 1938.

Showers, Renald E. *Maranatha: Our Lord, Come!* Bellmawr, N.J.: Friends of Israel Gospel Ministry, 1995.

———. *The New Nature.* Willow Street, Pa.: Renald E. Showers' Publications, 1986.

Smith, David. "The Epistles of John." In *The Expositor's Greek Testament.* Edited by W. Robertson Nicoll. 5 vols. Grand Rapids: Eerdmans, n.d.

Smith, J. B. *A Revelation of Jesus Christ.* Scottdale, Pa.: Herald, 1961.

Smith, John Merlin Powis, William Hayes Ward, and Julius A. Bewer. *A Critical and Exegetical Commentary on Micah, Zephaniah, Nahum, Habakkuk, Obadiah and Joel.* The International Critical Commentary.

Edited by Charles Augustus Briggs, Samuel Rolles Driver, and Alfred Plummer. 48 vols. Edinburgh: T. and T. Clark, 1910.

Spurgeon, Charles H. *Twelve Sermons on the Second Coming of Christ*. Grand Rapids: Baker, 1976.

Stahlin, Gustav. *"Orge."* In *Theological Dictionary of the New Testament*. Vols. 1–4 edited by Gerhard Kittel; vols. 5–9 edited by Gerhard Friedrich. Translated and edited by Geoffrey W. Bromiley. Grand Rapids: Eerdmans, 1964–74.

Stifler, James M. *The Epistle to the Romans*. Chicago: Moody, 1960.

Swart, Ignatius, and Robin Wakely. *"Tsarar."* In *New International Dictionary of Old Testament Theology and Exegesis*. Edited by Willem A. VanGemeren. 5 vols. Grand Rapids: Zondervan, 1997.

Swete, Henry Barclay. *The Apocalypse of St John*. Grand Rapids: Eerdmans, n.d.

Tenney, Merrill C. *Interpreting Revelation*. Grand Rapids: Eerdmans, 1957.

Thayer, Joseph Henry. *"Horidzo."* In *A Greek-English Lexicon of the New Testament*. 4th ed. Edinburgh: T. and T. Clark, 1901.

———. *"Koloboo."* In *A Greek-English Lexicon of the New Testament*. 4th ed. Edinburgh: T. and T. Clark, 1901.

Thomas, Robert L. "2 Thessalonians." In *The Expositor's Bible Commentary*. Edited by Frank E. Gaebelein. 12 vols. Grand Rapids: Zondervan, 1976–92.

———. *Revelation 1–7: An Exegetical Commentary*. Chicago: Moody, 1992.

Trench, Richard Chenevix. *"Stephanos."* In *Synonyms of the New Testament*. Grand Rapids: Eerdmans, 1960.

Van Groningen, Gerard. *"Qesep."* In *Theological Wordbook of the Old Testament*. Edited by R. Laird Harris, Gleason L. Archer Jr., and Bruce K. Waltke. 2 vols. Chicago: Moody, 1980.

Van Kampen, Robert. *The Sign*. Wheaton, Ill.: Crossway, 1992.

Vincent, Marvin R. *Word Studies in the New Testament*. 4 vols. Grand Rapids: Eerdmans, 1946.

Vine, W. E. *"Anameno."* In *An Expository Dictionary of New Testament Words*. 4 vols. London: Oliphants, 1940; Grand Rapids: Zondervan, 1976.

———. *"Choinix."* In *An Expository Dictionary of New Testament Words*. 4 vols. London: Oliphants, 1940; Grand Rapids: Zondervan, 1976.

Von Rad, Gerhard. *"Hemera."* In *Theological Dictionary of the Old Testa-*

*ment*. Edited by G. Johannes Botterweck and Helmer Ringgren. Translated by John T. Willis. 10 vols. Grand Rapids: Eerdmans, 1974.

―――. *Old Testament Theology*. Translated by D. M. G. Stalker. 2 vols. New York: Harper and Row, 1965.

Westcott, Brooke Foss. *The Epistles of St. John*. Grand Rapids: Eerdmans, 1957.

White, Newport J. D. "The Epistle to Titus." In *The Expositor's Greek Testament*. Edited by W. Robertson Nicoll. 5 vols. Grand Rapids: Eerdmans, n.d.

Wood, Leon. *A Commentary on Daniel*. Grand Rapids: Zondervan, 1973.

Zodhiates, Spiros. *The Patience of Hope*. Grand Rapids: Eerdmans, 1960.

## Dictionaries

*The American College Dictionary*. Text ed. Edited·by Clarence L. Barnhart. New York: Harper and Brothers, 1948. S.v. "precursor."

Davidson, A. B. *A Dictionary of the Bible*. 5 vols. Edited by James Hastings. Peabody, Mass.: Hendrickson, 1988. S.v. "eschatology."

Kidd, D. A. *Collins Latin Gem Dictionary*. London: Collins, 1957. S.v. "immineo, imminere."

*The Oxford Dictionary of the Christian Church*. 2d ed. Edited by F. L. Cross and E. A. Livingstone. New York: Oxford University Press. 1988. S.v. "parousia."

*The Oxford English Dictionary*. Vol. 3. Oxford: Oxford University Press, 1897. S.v. "expectance" and "expectant."

*The Oxford English Dictionary*. Vol. 5. Oxford: Oxford University Press, 1901. S.v. "imminent."

*The Oxford English Dictionary*. Vol. 15. Oxford: Oxford University Press, 1989. S.v. "soon."

*Webster's New International Dictionary*. 2d ed. Unabridged. Springfield, Mass.: G. and C. Merriam Com., 1939. S.v. "absolute."

*Webster's New International Dictionary*. 2d ed. Unabridged. Springfield, Mass.: G. and C. Merriam Com., 1939. S.v. "imminent."

*Webster's New International Dictionary*. 2d ed. Unabridged. Springfield, Mass.: G. and C. Merriam Com. 1939. S.v. "reveal."

## Magazine Article

Rosenthal, Marvin J. "The Great Tribulation." *Zion's Fire* (May–June 1998): 9.